W9-BQW-097

SOTHEBY'S

ART AT AUCTION

The Art Market Review 1992–93

SOTHEBY'S
ART AT AUCTION
The Art Market Review 1992–93

RIZZOLI
NEW YORK

First published in 1993 by
Conran Octopus Limited
37 Shelton Street,
London WC2H 9HN

Copyright © Conran Octopus Limited 1993
Sotheby's illustrations (see p. 312) © Sotheby's
Sotheby's is a registered trade mark.

Trade distribution in the United States of America by
Rizzoli International Publications, Inc.
300 Park Avenue South, New York, NY 10010
ISBN 0-8478-5755-7

All rights reserved. No part of this book
may be reproduced, stored in a retrieval system, or
transmitted in any form or by any means,
electronic, electrostatic, magnetic tape, mechanical,
photocopying, recording or otherwise
without the prior permission
of the publisher.

British Library Cataloguing in Publication Data
A catalogue record for this book is available from
the British Library

ISBN 1-85029-538-7

Printed in Great Britain by
Jolly & Barber Ltd, Rugby, Warwickshire

ENDPAPERS: GIOVANNI DOMENICO TIEPOLO
Putti flying among clouds
SIGNED, PEN AND BROWN INK AND WASH,
18.9 x 25.6cm (7½ x 10⅛in)
London £4,620 ($7,250). 14.XII.92

PAGE 1: **An Attic lekythos fragment**
NEAR THE THANATOS PAINTER, *c.* 440BC, 18.1cm (7⅛in)
London £20,900 ($32,600). 10.XII.92

PAGE 2: HENRI MATISSE
L'Asie
SIGNED AND DATED *46*, OIL ON CANVAS,
116.2 x 81.3cm (45¾ x 32in)
New York $11,000,000 (£7,284,700). 10.XI.92

PAGES 4-5: A selection from The Uruguayan
Treasure of the River Plate
New York 24-25.III.93

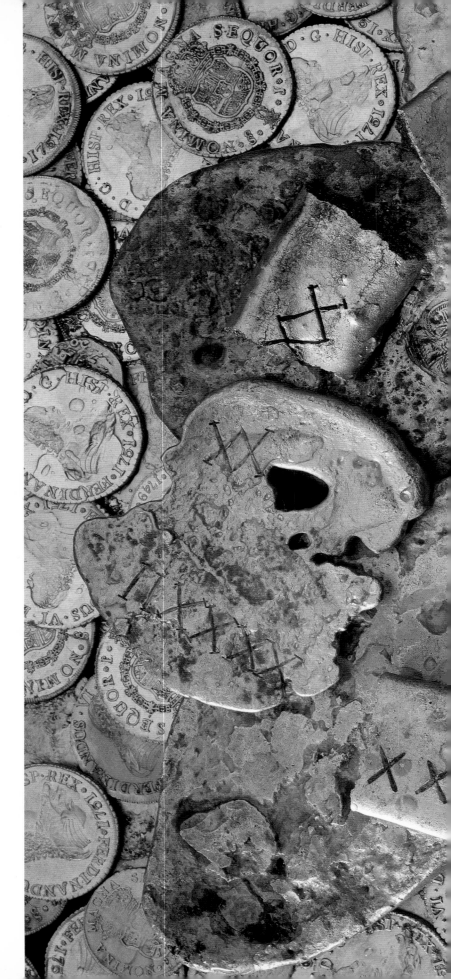

CONTENTS

CONTRIBUTORS

JOHN D. BLOCK is a Senior Vice President and member of the Board of Directors of Sotheby's North and South America. He is currently in charge of the Jewellery and Precious Objects Division in New York and has played a formative role in establishing the company's international pre-eminence in both these markets.

MELVYN BRAGG first started to work in television in 1961. In 1964 he helped launch BBC2, for which he edited several arts programmes. In 1978 he set up *The South Bank Show* for London Weekend Television, and he continues to edit and present that series. He is also currently Controller of Arts at London Weekend Television and Director of LWT Productions. He is the author of several books, screenplays and libretti, including that for the award-winning *The Hired Man*. He has also won the TRIC Award for Radio Programme of the Year (*Start the Week*, 1990) and a record three Prix Italia.

MABEL H. BRANDON has worked at Harvard University and the Metropolitan Museum of Art, and served on the John F. and Robert Kennedy presidential campaigns. In 1976 she founded Washington Corporate Arts Inc., which functioned as a liaison between the cultural and corporate communities in all aspects of corporate sponsorship. In 1980 she was asked by President Reagan to act as Social Secretary to the White House, during which time she also served as Special Liaison for the President's Committee on the Arts and Humanities. In 1989 she joined the Ford Motor Company where she is now Director of Corporate Planning.

DIANA D. BROOKS is President and Chief Executive Officer of Sotheby's Worldwide Auction Operations, a position that was created for her in 1993. She joined the company in 1979 and in 1990 was appointed President and Chief Executive Officer of Sotheby's North and South America. In both capacities she is closely involved with all major sales held by the company and has made a vital contribution to the co-ordination and integration of Sotheby's operations throughout the world.

EDWARD BULMER has been working in the conservation and restoration of historic buildings since 1986. Latterly with Alec Cobbe and now in independent practice, his work has included picture hanging and decorative work in privately-owned houses such as Harewood House in Yorkshire, and also in National Trust properties, including Petworth House, Sussex. In addition, he is a council member of the Ancient Monuments Society and a trustee of the Mappa Mundi Trust, Hereford.

MICHAEL CONFORTI is the Chief Curator and Curator of Decorative Arts and Sculpture at the Minneapolis Institute of Arts. He worked for Sotheby's in both London and New York between 1968 and 1971, before entering Harvard University's PhD programme in art history. Since the beginning of his museum career at the Fine Arts Museum in San Francisco he has written numerous articles and exhibition catalogues on nineteenth- and twentieth-century decorative arts, as well as on American institutional and private collecting practices over the past 150 years.

RICHARD CORK is the Art Critic of *The Times* and the Henry Moore Senior Research Fellow at the Courtauld Institute of Art. He has organized major exhibitions at the Hayward Gallery, the Royal Academy and the Tate. His books include *Vorticism* (1976) and *Art Beyond the Gallery* (1985), both prize-winning studies, and *David Bomberg* (1987), a monograph. From 1989-90 he was Slade Professor of Fine Art at Cambridge University. His latest book, *A Bitter Truth: Avant-Garde Art and the Great War*, will be published early in 1994.

PHILIPPE GARNER joined Sotheby's in 1970 and rapidly achieved a specialization in Photography and Twentieth-century Decorative Arts. He has remained one of the leading experts in both these fields and has published numerous books, including *The Contemporary Decorative Arts* (1980), *Eileen Gray: Architect and Designer* (1993) and a study of the work of Emile Gallé (1976).

THE RT HON. THE EARL OF GOWRIE is Chairman of Sotheby's Europe and a Director of Sotheby's Holdings Inc. He was Minister for the Arts from 1983 to 1985 as well as being responsible for the management of the Civil Service and a spokesman for HM Treasury in the House of Lords. His many books include *The Genius of British Painting: The Twentieth Century* (1975).

HILARY KAY joined Sotheby's in 1977. In 1978, aged 21, she became head of the Collectors' Department and one of Britain's first female auctioneers. In 1981 she set up the first-ever sale of Rock and Roll memorabilia, and in 1985 was made a Director of Sotheby's. She regularly appears on BBC Television's *Antiques Roadshow,* and is the author of *Rock 'n' Roll Collectables: An Illustrated History of Rock Memorabilia* (1992).

JOHN MARTIN ROBINSON is a partner in Historic Buildings Consultants, librarian to the Duke of Norfolk and Maltravers Herald of Arms. His books include *Country Houses of the North West* (1991), *Georgian Model Farms* (1984), and *Royal Residences* (1982). He is a Fellow of the Society of Antiquaries and a member of the Executive Committee of the Georgian Group.

PHILIP MOULD is a picture dealer specializing in paintings of the English face. He is well-known for his discoveries, including the lost half of Gainsborough's first portrait and major works by van Dyck, Dobson and Kneller. In 1987 he wrote and presented *Changing Faces,* a six-part history of British portraiture for Channel 4. He is Works of Art Advisor to the House of Commons and the House of Lords.

PAUL NEEDHAM is Director of the Books and Manuscripts Department for Sotheby's New York and a Senior Vice President. Before joining Sotheby's he served for eighteen years as the Astor Curator of Printed Books and Bindings at the Pierpont Morgan Library. A widely respected scholar, Dr Needham has published extensively on the histories of printing, binding and paper.

LYNN STOWELL PEARSON was an editor at the International Foundation for Art Research before joining Sotheby's New York in 1987, where she is an Assistant Vice President in the Publications Department and also editor of *Sotheby's Newsletter.* Other publications include a paper developed from her doctoral dissertation research, *Ancient Stones: Quarrying, Trade and Provenance,* published in 1992.

SIMON DE PURY is Deputy Chairman of Sotheby's Europe, Chairman of Sotheby's Switzerland and head of the European Fine Arts Division. He is based in Geneva and London but devotes a large amount of his time to travelling. He is an auctioneer, conducting major sales in London, Geneva, Monte Carlo, St Moritz and Zürich, and from 1979 to 1986, prior to joining Sotheby's, he was curator of the Thyssen-Bornemisza Collection, Lugano.

JOHN L. TANCOCK is Director of the Impressionist and Modern Paintings Department of Sotheby's New York and a Senior Vice President of the company. His publications include *The Sculpture of Auguste Rodin* (1976) and *Multiples: The First Decade* (1971).

RONALD VARNEY is a Vice President of the Marketing Department, Sotheby's New York. He has written extensively on the arts for *Esquire, Smithsonian* and *Connoisseur* magazines as well as for *The New York Times* and *The Wall Street Journal.*

GILES WATERFIELD trained at the Courtauld Institute of Art, London and subsequently worked at the Royal Pavilion, Brighton. Since 1979 he has been Director of the Dulwich Picture Gallery, London and from 1994 he will also serve as joint Director of the Attingham Summer School. During his time at Dulwich he has organized a number of exhibitions around the theme of architecture and collecting, including *Palaces of Art: Art Galleries in Britain 1790-1990.* He is currently working on a history of art museums in Britain.

INTRODUCTION *by Diana D. Brooks*

*I*n *this edition of* Sotheby's Art at Auction: The Art Market Review, *we continue to focus our editorial attention, as we did in last year's edition, on important developments and issues in the world art market. At the same time we again provide a comprehensive record of the past auction season at Sotheby's, a story vividly told in the many colour photographs we have presented here of the paintings, furniture, antiquities, jewellery and other works which highlighted the 1992-93 season.*

For our cover image we have chosen a work which perhaps best represents the successes of the 1992-93 season at Sotheby's – Paul Cézanne's monumental still life, Nature Morte: Les Grosses Pommes. *By way of historical footnote, Sotheby's offered this same painting in the famous Jakob Goldschmidt Collection sale in 1958 in London, where it achieved the then remarkable price of £90,000. On the evening of 11 May 1993 in New York, Sotheby's again offered this extraordinary work. With six active bidders it sold for $28,602,500, far outstripping the previous record for the artist. This was the first time since 1990 that any painting had broken the $20 million barrier.*

The overall success of this sale – which saw nine paintings in all sell for more than $1 million – was followed in June by a strong Impressionist sale at Sotheby's London featuring the distinguished Durand-Ruel Collection. Judging from comments by journalists, dealers and private collectors, all seemed to agree that the Impressionist and Modern art market had gained a healthy amount of confidence and momentum from the success of these sales, and they brought the 1992-93 season at Sotheby's to a most encouraging conclusion.

The international art market is complex and highly sophisticated, blending together very different cultural, aesthetic and professional viewpoints. As a company with a global presence, Sotheby's must understand these very different cultures and be responsive to the changes within them. On the following pages we provide our readers with timely, informative articles examining a range of issues to do with the international art market. Mabel H. Brandon

SIR LAWRENCE
ALMA-TADEMA
The Baths of
Caracalla (Thermae
Antoniniane)
(detail)
SIGNED, OIL ON CANVAS,
152.4 x 95.3cm (60 x 37½in)
New York $2,532,500
(£1,633,800). 26.V.93 (LEFT)

Jewelled gold
and hardstone
snuff box made for
Frederick II of
Prussia
AFTER A DESIGN BY JEAN
GUILLAUME GEORGE KRÜGER,
BERLIN, c.1770,
width 10cm (4in)
Geneva SF2,530,000
(£1,150,000:$1,805,500).
17.XI.92
From the Thurn und Taxis
Collection (BELOW)

discusses the growth of art collecting by commercial companies around the world, Melvyn Bragg reviews the history of television programmes on the visual arts, and Lord Gowrie examines different attitudes towards national heritage and the ownership of works of art.

The markets of Asia are the subject of John Tancock's article, and in it he discusses the implications of the growing economic strength of the nations of Asia. The process of 'discovering' works of art is a subject of abiding fascination, and Philip Mould delves into some recent notable stories. On another front Edward Bulmer reviews different philosophies in architectural restoration and conservation.

Complementing these articles are ones on American museum acquisitions, the popular collecting areas of Victorian paintings and photographs, and the major international exhibitions of the season. On a related theme, Giles Waterfield looks at the history of various styles of picture hanging and the reasons behind their use. And, in anticipation of our 250th anniversary next year, John Martin Robinson describes the various buildings Sotheby's has occupied since 1744.

Sotheby's performance in the saleroom in the 1992-93 season is vividly chronicled in these pages. Sotheby's conducts nearly 500 auctions a year in over 70 collecting areas, and the past season witnessed the sale of many exceptional works in such disparate fields as postage stamps and French furniture, medieval manuscripts and Chinese porcelain, Old Master paintings and Hollywood posters. Once again we have asked our senior specialists to provide summaries of the sale highlights and trends of individual specialist departments in Sotheby's worldwide offices during the past season. Each of these essays prefaces an extensive photographic selection of highlights that provides a rich, tapestry-like view of Sotheby's saleroom activity.

This view is further refined by Ronald Varney's article on many of the fine collections offered this season, which included those of Mrs Harry Winston (jewellery), Madame Hélène Beaumont (French furniture), Earl Mountbatten of Burma (paintings and works of art), Pierre Jourdan-Barry (silver), Norbert Schimmel (antiquities), Rudolf von Gutmann (books, drawings and prints), Otto Kallir (music manuscripts), Joseph M. Meraux (clocks) and Mollie Parnis Livingston (Impressionist and Modern paintings). The most glittering and publicized event of the auction

FRANÇOIS BOUCHER
L'Heureuse Fécondité
SIGNED AND DATED *1764*,
OIL ON CANVAS,
64.8 x 54cm (25½ x 21¼in)
New York $800,000
(£512,800). 20.V.93. (ABOVE)

Wucai Wine Jar
and Cover
JIAJING MARK AND PERIOD,
overall height 45.4cm (17⅞in)
New York $2,860,000
(£1,845,100). 1.XII.92
(BELOW)

season was our sale in November in Geneva of exquisite silver, jewellery and objects of vertu from the princely collections of Thurn und Taxis.

The story of the season is only partly told in the saleroom activity. There are also lectures, exhibitions, receptions, client dinners, symposiums, concerts, gallery walks, classes, free appraisals, wine tastings, benefit auctions and many other events involving our staff around the world. Sotheby's in London hosted an exhibition of mosaics from Jordan loaned by the Jordanian Government, as well as an exhibition of tapestries by London's leading tapestry studios. Sotheby's also sponsored a major exhibition in Prague of the work of the renowned Greek artist, Jannis Kounellis. In another vein Sotheby's sponsored the first ever 'stately home car boot sale' at Nostell Priory, West Yorkshire, with the proceeds benefiting the National Asthma Campaign. In New York, we hosted an array of benefit events, exhibitions and receptions, including a benefit auction and reception for the AIDS organization God's Love We Deliver. We also contributed to such causes as Art Against AIDS, the International Foundation for Art Research, the Neighorhood Coalition for Shelter and the New York City Partnership, as well as to many museums. These non-auction related activities are an integral part of the calendar at Sotheby's, and we are pleased to lend our support to these and other worthy causes.

As we prepare to celebrate our 250th anniversary in 1994, we are mindful of the great events in our long history that have helped shape and define Sotheby's. We are also mindful of the many individuals who have played leading roles throughout the firm's history. During this past year two such individuals – the Earl of Westmorland in London and Eunice (Sandy) Carroll in New York – passed on. David Westmorland, the former Chairman of Sotheby's, was associated with the firm for more than two decades and participated in the company's growth in the United States and Canada. He also served in Elizabeth II's household for more than 25 years. He was a wonderfully warm and generous person. Sandy Carroll served Sotheby's for over 40 years, and as the longtime director of Special Client Services was a legendary figure, and dear friend, to hundreds of her clients throughout the world. We honour the memory and contributions of both these colleagues.

Lord Gowrie, HRH Princess Sumaya El Hassan and Her Majesty Queen Noor Al Hussein of Jordan at the opening of the Mosaics of Jordan exhibition at Sotheby's London in January 1993. (LEFT)

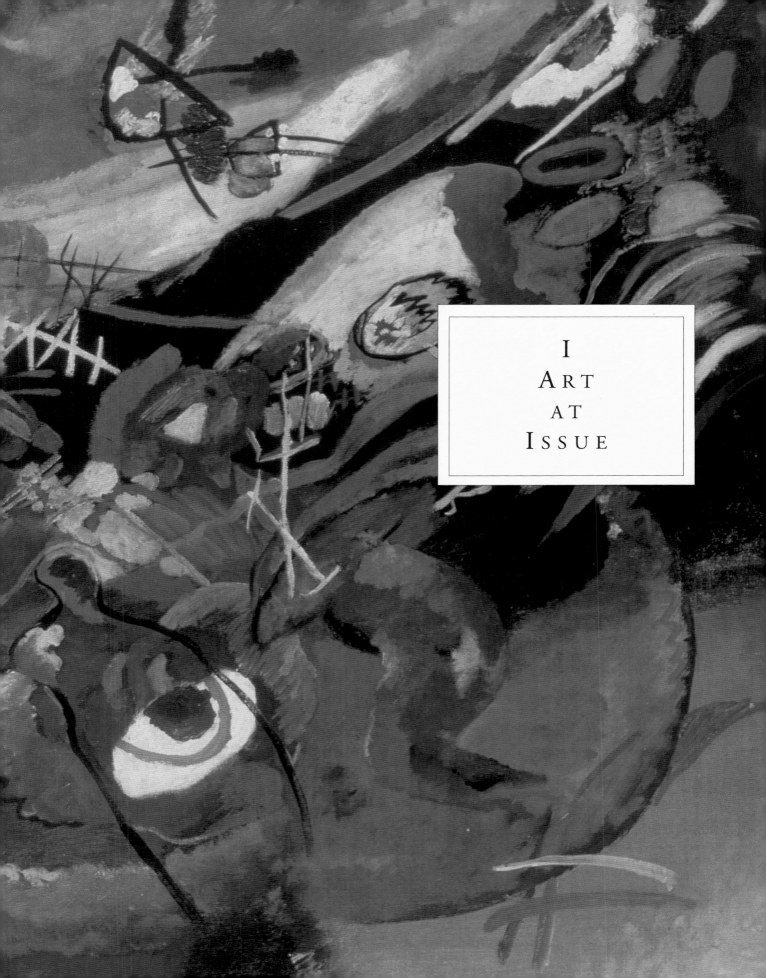

I
Art
at
Issue

GAMEKEEPERS V. POACHERS *by The Rt Hon. The Earl of Gowrie*

A VIEW OF THE NATIONAL HERITAGE

Gamekeepers who decide to become poachers are viewed with understandable suspicion, their opinions taken with a pinch of salt. For nearly three years, in the early 1980s, I was concerned with the measures taken by one country, Britain, to prevent the indiscriminate export of works of art considered important enough to be part of our national patrimony or heritage. For nearly seven years since, I have found myself arguing the case from another part of the wood and defending the interests of a free and open market in works of art, as in other goods. I have at least been consistent in my belief that protectionism is, after war, the worst threat to civilization and to our cultural as well as economic well-being. 'Grub first, then ethics', said Brecht. Protectionism is the enemy of both.

The tension between people's right to own property and the interest of the state or community in the products of its past is a very old one. Any right to own property should include the right to dispose of it freely; anything less is only partial or qualified ownership. There is also an extreme view which holds that cultural goods are unlike all other goods: they are products of the human spirit and in some undefined way should be held in common.

When Sotheby's held an auction of works by contemporary painters in Moscow in 1988, I tried to persuade officials and museum curators there how important it was to allow the works of young artists to be sold and exported if they were ever to become known in the West. 'But they are ours,' I was told, 'and you can of course borrow them for exhibitions.' This attitude conveniently overlooked the need for young artists to live, and ignored the fact that taste, in a culture, is built up in layers of individual activity. Museum shows and exhibitions reflect only what specific artists and their dealers or patrons have been getting up to: they are bulletins from the artistic front. Ideal-

istic supporters of a commonwealth of artistic goods are usually sentimental about other kinds of ownership, sentimentally opposed that is. You can argue that the 'modern' era that we inhabit is still only a product of that revolution in sensibility we call the Renaissance. At that time, the Church was losing its intellectual and cultural monopoly. The Empire or super-state was already fragmented. Conflict and competition raged: between states, classes, individuals and organizations. The modern world is a child of such circumstances, and does not make for a quiet life. It does, however, allow for great adventures in science and art. Like many merchant princes today, the Medici were neither model citizens nor model human beings. But more than committees they offered what artists want and need.

Our modern social democracies are seldom, of course, philosophically consistent. They listen to voters and voters often want contradictory things. In Britain, private property rights have eroded steadily throughout this century; this started long before the advent of Socialist governments. Indeed when Socialist governments have been in power they have often proved rather conservative in practice. In the same paradoxical way, highly conservative individuals fight for the right of owners of historic houses, for example, not to be allowed to alter them in any way. Most of the stately houses of England are (from one point of view) modest neo-classical phoenixes rising from the ashes of late-medieval, Tudor or Jacobean buildings. Some were destroyed by accident; some, in what today we would consider acts of vandalism, by design. Part of the fascination of Boughton House, for instance, the principal residence of the Dukes of Buccleuch, is that in the 1680s the family built a French-influenced château without altogether destroying the Tudor Boughton, so the house looks like a small village from the air. I see no reason why a contemporary

PABLO PICASSO
Weeping Woman
SIGNED AND DATED *37*,
OIL ON CANVAS,
60 x 49cm (23 x 19¼in)
Acquired by private treaty
through Sotheby's in October
1987. Now in the collection of
the Tate Gallery, London.
(LEFT)

Duke of Buccleuch should not be allowed to add a comfortable twentieth-century house, if he wished. I cannot see even a Conservative council or government giving him permission to do so.

Perhaps because the erosion of freedom has been slow, Britain at the end of our century does seem to have useful lessons to offer to other states worried by the balance between freedom to own or dispose of property and a nation's sense of its heritage. We should also add the interests of trade

in cultural artifacts to the equation. The art trade earns money and pays taxes and employs people. It is also an essential part of the culture itself, a disseminator. It is surely no coincidence that the decision of the French authorities, after the War, to maintain domestic restrictive practices in the art trade (the *commisseur priseur* system) saw the gradual erosion, against all environmental and historical odds, of Paris as the artistic capital of Europe. The action turned to London and New

ANTONIO CANOVA
The Three Graces
This version of this famous subject (which is similar to another version formerly at Woburn Abbey) is in the collection of the Duke of Rutland at Belvoir Castle. The Belvoir Estate does not have, nor has had, any plans to sell the Belvoir Castle Canova.
(ABOVE)

York, and later to German cities like Cologne. These centres were more open and international in respect of markets. The art market is not an evil imposed on a culture, or even a necessary evil for a culture to endure. It is part of that culture and tradition, part of the heritage; next year, for instance, Sotheby's will celebrate its two-hundred-and-fiftieth birthday. There are signs that Paris may be changing its view. If that is so, London must look to its laurels. The collecting hinterland of Britain is rather small for Britain to remain at the centre of the international trade for ever.

Since before the First World War, Britain has nevertheless balanced three important interests: the nation's concern for its heritage; the ownership of private property; the needs of legitimate commerce. The system gives a committee of expert advisors the chance to recommend to the Government that a work be denied an export licence for a sufficient period of time to allow a national institution (the system does not distort trade between individuals) to raise the funds needed to acquire it. There are also financial incentives for individuals to settle tax demands, usually estate duty, by deeding works of art to the nation. In exceptional circumstances these may be allowed to remain in the collections from which they came. Most of the works here illustrated entered national collections by the last method; it is the business of auction houses and dealers to negotiate the monetary values of any settlements made. Few people criticize the system; many are anxious whether sufficient funds are earmarked by governments to allow it to work effectively. My own view is that no great work of art of the unarguable first rank has left the country since Velasquez's *Portrait of Juan de Perrea* was sold to the Metropolitan Museum in New York in 1972. Canova's *The Three Graces* is to my mind a candidate but that is not a view shared by everyone in the art world.

Today, fifty years after the Second World War, Britain is trying, so far without much success, to edge its European partners towards a comparable balance of interests. Although trade in cultural goods is an immeasurably small part of the total European Community economy, it is also immeasurably sensitive. Issues such as value added tax on works of art, or the free movement of works of art, have created a log-jam of proposed directives. Most have failed to secure agreement and much polite blood has been spilled on official carpets.

Within the Community, there is something of a north-south divide. Italy has threatened to list thirty million works of art as being of national importance. Under this definition you can own such works, in the sense of keeping them on your walls; you may in some cases be able to sell them within the country; you will never be allowed to export them. As any fine art auctioneer knows, Italians are by nationality the most vigorous group of collectors in the world. Italian suspicion of the Italian fiscal system, however, and hostility to the immoderate restrictiveness of Italian heritage laws, have led to substantial holdings of works of art off-shore. A more liberal regime would ensure an influx of works of art for Italy, particularly if the system were guaranteed constitutionally. To a lesser extent, the same is true of Spain. The Spanish do not consider the export of works of art by Velasquez or Goya to Germany, say, as the free movement of goods envisaged by the Treaty of Rome. Nor, to be fair, did the Treaty of Rome. Article 36 of the Treaty allows members to protect their national patrimony. The difficulties arise when you try to define a national patrimony (can it possibly consist of thirty million works of art?) or suggest how member states can come to some kind of working agreement about it.

The northern states, as befits their protestant and nonconformist tradition, are more liberal. If Britain, or Germany, wish to prevent you from exporting a work of art they can do so. The instrument is delay only: they must in the end purchase the work at a fair market price. Before we get too sentimental about the northern states, it must be said that their fiscal arrangements, notably capital taxation, result in shooting themselves (or rather their taxpayers) in the foot. If conserving works of art is your aim, taxing capital is crazy. You want more capital, not less of it. Even held passively, in the form of works of art, capital generates interest, activity and employment. Most of the private treaty sales Sotheby's conducts between individuals and national institutions are dictated by the need to settle estate or capital taxes. The state ends up having to pay for something it had no need to acquire in the first place. A great majority of British private collections are open to the public on a regular basis; all but very few may be visited by appointment. Open market countries like Switzerland – at the heart of Europe though not of the Community – are much more sensible. Nor is there any evidence that the Swiss suffer cultural deprivation where works of art are concerned.

SIR ANTHONY VAN DYCK
Portrait of Lord John and Lord Bernard Stuart
OIL ON CANVAS,
237 x 121cm (93½ x 47½in)
Acquired by private treaty
through Sotheby's in April
1988. Now in the collection of
the National Gallery, London.
(ABOVE)

In some ways the pivot of the European Community, France may in the end determine how things turn out. It is understandably protective of an earlier part of its heritage, having lost so much as a consequence of the French Revolution, not least to Britain and thence, over time, to the United States and the wider world. Yet France has been generous to the point of profligacy in recent times, its astonishing dominance in the visual arts in the century to 1950 notwithstanding. Perhaps a self-confident culture is always outward looking. A lively artistic scene is to a

The Gospels of
Henry the Lion
LOWER SAXONY, C.1175-80
London £8,140,000
($11,314,600). 6.XII.83
Now in the Herzog-August-
Bibliothek, Wolfenbüttel,
Lower Saxony (ABOVE RIGHT)

A three-quarter suit
of armour made for
Henry of Valois,
DECORATED BY GIOVANNI
PAOLO NEGROLI, C.1540-45,
London £1,925,000
($3,080,000). 5.V.83 (ABOVE)

very great degree eclectic. It borrows. It exchanges ideas and objects and styles. It values the immigrant and approves of exile. You do a lot of harm by trying to restrict it. Henry Moore is the most famous modern British sculptor. He was for years better known, and more widely seen, in the United States than in Britain. With the inevitable shift in reputation following his death, he is perhaps most appreciated now in Italy and Japan. The only queues I have seen for the work of another modern British master, Francis Bacon, were in Paris and Moscow. Ebb and flow of reputation is a requisite of artistic freedom. The hope today must be for Paris to resume its place as one of the most outward-looking, cosmopolitan and culturally dynamic cities of the world.

It is odd that the European Community, in aggregate the richest group of nations in the world, is still so conditioned by the psychology of poverty. An obsession with heritage or export controls – with the feeling that your culture is up for grabs: raped by rich foreigners, ripped off by unscrupulous dealers – such is the embodiment of defeat: a folk-memory, almost, of tanks riding over your fields and trains carting off your paintings. Fifty years after the War, it is time we Europeans rid ourselves of such memories.

Britannia, as so often, is in some respects the odd woman out. Most other European countries consider their patrimony to be works of art owned by national collections or created by national artists. This applies very broadly and of course there are circumstances in which it would be extremely difficult to obtain an export licence for a Dutch painting from Italy, say, or an Italian painting from France. But in the case of Britain, about 80 per cent of our patrimony (including, in this instance, works in public collections), was once the patrimony of other people. That is the legacy of long periods of wealth and stability while others were less wealthy and less stable. It is also the legacy of imperialism. One nation's idea of heritage may be another nation's idea of loot. There are times, therefore, when the re-export of works of art is thoroughly desirable; how proud we were at Sotheby's to 're-patriate' the Gospels of Henry the Lion to Germany in 1983, or the Irish Bronze Age gold to Ireland in 1989. There are also times when it may be desirable to export a work by a national artist. When we sold John Constable's *The Lock* in 1990, an export licence was not issued for a considerable length of time as the Tate Gallery hoped to raise funds to acquire it. The Tate had every right to do so under our system, which does not confiscate but gives national institutions time to match the open market price. Nevertheless I myself believed we should have won the Queen's Award for Exports. Constable is not sufficiently seen in Europe, in spite of his substantial influence on the development of French painting. *The Lock's* arrival in a great European collection, the Thyssen-Bornemisza Collection in Madrid, should have been an occasion for rejoicing, and not only at Sotheby's. Were I a benevolent dictator, I would even consider selling one or two Turners or Constables from our national collections in order to purchase a great Goya, say, or a Georges de la Tour. The call is unlikely to come.

Of course death and taxes, money and trade are not the only threats to a nation's heritage. There is accident – this year in Britain we recall with great sympathy the dreadful fire at Windsor Castle – and theft. One of the greatest paintings in the long distinction of British portraiture is Lucian Freud's 1952 painting of Francis Bacon. It is at once a Memling-like masterpiece of the northern Renaissance and a thoroughly

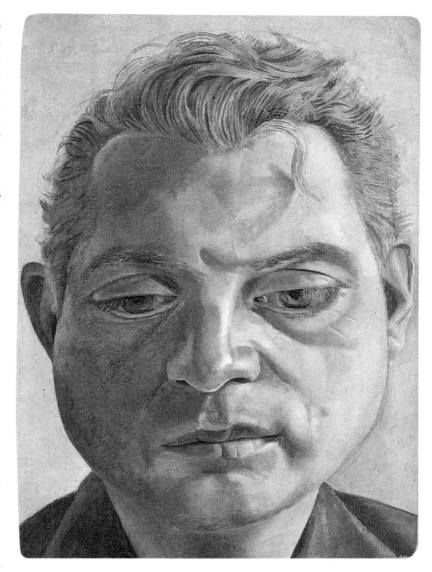

modern work; the critic Robert Hughes memorably described Bacon's face as looking like a hand-grenade about to go off. It is very small and painted on copper and belongs to the Tate Gallery. It was stolen off the wall at a loan exhibition in Berlin in 1988.

I suspect it was stolen by someone who liked it, not a commercially minded thief. It is a portrait of one great painter by another. It would be easy to return anonymously. Whoever you are, please give it back. It belongs to a national gallery. It is incontrovertibly ours.

LUCIAN FREUD
Portrait of Francis Bacon
OIL ON COPPER,
17.8 x 12.7cm (7 x 5in)
From the collection of the Tate Gallery (ABOVE)

THE NEW MEDICI *by Mabel H. Brandon*

The famous prices paid by Japanese organizations for Impressionist paintings during the late 1980s make it impossible to ignore the importance of corporate collectors in the art world. In the United States in recent years corporate buying has at times been responsible for over 30 per cent of all new art bought in the country, and while in Britain and other Western countries the figures are not quite as startling, the corporate collecting of works of art is both widespread and lively. The buying power of corporate collectors now exerts phenomenal muscle in many of the major art market centres in the world, and corporate collections of art now amount to an extraordinary resource, rivalling, in some cities, collections made by public institutions. Corporate support for the arts in the form of sponsorship also plays a mighty role in the international art world, and few great exhibitions of recent years have not relied upon such support to some degree or other.

Although the enormous influence of corporate patronage is largely a phenomenon of the last twenty years, corporate patronage is not a new invention, nor indeed solely a twentieth-century one. It could be argued that many of the great dynastic collectors of past centuries, such as the Medici, the Hapsburgs and the Bourbons, collected for reasons that were not entirely private, nor entirely altruistic. More direct ancestors of today's corporate collectors might be claimed amongst the guilds of late medieval Europe, who are renowned for having commissioned many precious and splendid works of art, chiefly as ceremonial objects.

The advent of the corporate collector in a wholly modern sense can be traced to the early eighteenth century, when a number of British merchant houses and banks commissioned prominent artists to paint portraits of leading members of staff. The Bank of England, Lloyds Bank and the Midland Bank still display collections of such portraits in their boardrooms and offices, and continue to add to them intermittently with new examples.

The level of commitment to the arts by these 'new Medici' was enhanced dramatically by the growing importance of advertising in corporate affairs. In the nineteenth century shops, hotels and other organizations employed graphic artists and illustrators to help promote business, but it was not until the first few decades of the new century that fine art came to be used regularly in advertising. One of the most famous examples in Britain of such a union is that originated by the oil company Shell. One of Shell's London employees in the 1920s, Jack Beddington, was offered responsibility for the company's advertising after having complained that existing efforts were too mundane. He it was who started a tradition of commissioning contemporary artists to design posters depicting places

PAUL NASH
The Rye Marshes
POSTER
One of a series of works commissioned by Shell for its 1930s' campaign 'Everywhere you go you can be sure of Shell'.
(BELOW)

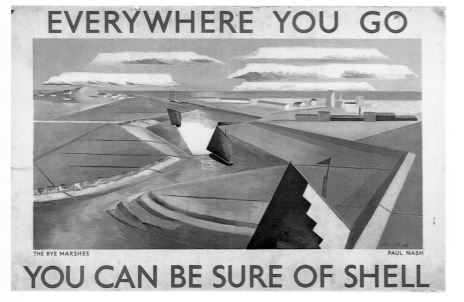

EVERYWHERE YOU GO

THE RYE MARSHES   PAUL NASH

YOU CAN BE SURE OF SHELL

Find Michelangelo at the V&A
Nearest station South Kensington

Find Michelangelo at the V&A by R B Kitaj RA
A new work of art commissioned by London Underground

R. B. KITAJ
**Find Michelangelo
at the V&A**
POSTER
One of a series of works
commissioned by London
Underground for its current
campaign 'Art on the
Underground'. (RIGHT)

to visit in the British Isles using Shell petrol. Although many of the artists who were asked to take part in the campaign were little known at the time, they are now considered as having been some of the greatest of those years: Ben Nicholson, Graham Sutherland, Rex Whistler, Vanessa Bell, Edward Bawden, Paul Nash, Edward Ardizzone and Tristram Hillier.

Beddington was not alone at that time in using such ideas. Stephen Tallents at the Post Office and Frank Pick at London Transport were also commissioning works from 'serious' artists to convey simple messages to the public. The early posters Pick commissioned were designed by commercial artists employed by the printers, but he soon moved beyond this limited source and made direct contact with established artists like Frank Brangwyn, also experimenting with new and untried names. His greatest 'discovery' was the American-born Edward McKnight Kauffer, who produced his first poster for the Underground in 1915 and went on to design over a

hundred more during the next twenty-five years. In the 1920s and 30s Pick commissioned posters from a huge variety of known and unknown artists, offering them the kind of massive exposure they could not hope to find through the usual gallery system. As well as having an unquestionably modern approach to the commercial application of art, Pick passionately believed that his posters should fulfil a loftier purpose: to enrich the quality of urban life in London, and it is certainly true that it was through the London Underground posters of the 1920s and 30s that many members of the public were first introduced to such concepts as Cubism, Futurism and Vorticism. London Transport has produced advertising campaigns using posters by contemporary artists ever since. There have been lean years, particularly in the 1950s and 60s, but the current campaign – 'Art on the Underground' – seems to have revived much of the success of those early years, using works by such established British artists as John Bellany, Ruskin Spear, Anthony Green, Frederick Gore and R. B. Kitaj.

In the United States, similar developments were underway in the 1920s and 30s. There, the first company to commission paintings specifically for advertising purposes was Steinway and Sons, which asked artists such as Harvey Dunn, N. C. Wyeth, Ernest L. Blumenschein and Rockwell Kent to create images in keeping with Steinway's musical interests. Other corporations soon began to appreciate the potential usefulness of such art, notably Hallmark Cards, which purchased works by Norman Rockwell, Charles Sheeler and Grandma Moses for use on its products. Before Steinway's involvement, the Atchison, Topeka and Santa Fe Railway Company had started to buy paintings representing the history of the American West by artists such as Walter Ufer, E. I. Course, Oscar Berninghaus and William Robinson Leigh. Many of the images were used for advertisements and dining-car menus, but it is particularly noteworthy that this was one of the first instances of an American corporation making a collection of art.

The idea of building a major 'museum-quality' corporate art collection was first taken seriously in the United States by International Business

Machines (IBM) which set out in 1939 to create two distinct collections. One was to be composed of international contemporary art, representing countries where IBM did business; the other was to gather together works by contemporary American artists. The IBM collections now include important paintings by Frederick Church, Alfred Bierstadt, Edward Hopper and Andrew Wyeth.

The post-War period popularized many different ways of involving art and artists in corporate affairs. Art was thought of as a good business investment, and a growing number of companies began to believe that it could add to their overall image of sophistication and prestige, while also helping to create a stimulating environment for employees and clients. Other facets of corporate patronage emerged in the United States, including the sponsorship of art competitions. Hallmark Cards, Pepsi-Cola, Metro-Goldwyn Mayer and Abbott Laboratories all initiated competitive events, and then purchased the winning entries to add to their permanent collections.

The 1960s saw a sharp increase in the numbers of American companies becoming involved in corporate collecting. The Chase Manhattan Bank started its extraordinary collection, which now comprises over 2,000 works including pieces by Francis Bacon, Francesco Clemente and Naim June Paik. Also in the 1960s, Time Inc. began its collection of commissioned works for use on the magazine's front cover. Among the artists commissioned for this task were such leading contemporary figures as George Segal, Alex Katz, Alice Neel, Irving Penn and Richard Avedon. Other American corporate collectors of this period included the Atlantic Richfield Company and Coca-Cola, which focused on major contemporary artists like Frank Stella, Andy Warhol and Picasso. At the same time Pepsico was creating an extraordinary sculpture garden designed by Russell Page in Purchase, New York, to show its outstanding collection of twentieth-century sculpture. During the last thirty years other companies in the United States have built indoor gallery spaces to display their collections. AT&T, IBM, the Prudential Insurance Company, General Mills, Paine-Webber, Bristol-Myers Squibb, the Equitable Life Assurance Company,

Security Pacific National Bank (now part of BankAmerica), and the Bank of Boston have all created their own galleries housed in large modern buildings. Two corporations have even built their own separate museums to house their collections: in Dearborn, Michigan, the Ford Motor Company built the Henry Ford Museum and Greenfield Village, and in Corning, New York, the Owens-Corning Fiberglass Corporation has set up the Corning Museum of Glass.

In Britain, the corporate collecting scene had been active since the 1930s. Baring Brothers, one of the oldest and most distinguished of London's private banks, had started its collection in the late 1920s when the late Lord Ashburton gathered together extraneous portraits and other pictures from Baring family collections. In this way Barings obtained, mostly on a loan basis, a fine collection of eighteenth- and nineteenth-century pictures including works by Lawrence, Reynolds, Gainsborough and Linnell. Further collecting at Barings was quiet until the 1970s, when a new generation of partners took over and the bank moved to new buildings. The nature of merchant banking was changing fast, creating the need for large numbers of rooms for meeting and entertaining clients, all of which had to be furnished to a high standard. Barings' response, like IBM's before it, was to build two distinct collections. One comprised eighteenth- and nineteenth-century British watercolours, complementing the existing collection of Baring family pictures; the other concentrated on works by modern British artists. These two collections, now firmly established, provide reflections of two sides of the essential character of the company: one modern and one traditional.

A number of different individuals had been involved in building the Barings collections, but in other cases in Britain the clear tastes of one person can easily be discerned. Robert Hiscox at Hiscox Holdings, Sir Nicholas Goodison at the Trustees Savings Bank and Alex Bernstein at Granada Television have all had strong influences on their companies' collections. All, significantly, in the area of modern British paintings.

There is no doubt that the 1980s provided the liveliest decade for corporate collecting, and it is not difficult to see why. Equally unsurprising is the more circumspect attitude that seems to be common in the 1990s. By 1988, some 80 per cent of the business support for the arts worldwide came from profits and revenues, compared to only 61 per cent in 1991. The recent economic recession, international mergers and acquisitions, and the decrease in corporate building construction have all contributed to a general climate of retrenchment. At BankAmerica the acquisition of Security Pacific Bank and Valley Bank doubled the size of the parent corporate art collection, requiring a completely new inventory and evaluation of the enlarged collection. Additional budget cuts have reduced the purchasing funds which are now restricted to acquisitions of art for new buildings. Similar budget reductions indicate profound changes in corporate patronage budgets around the world.

Corporate support for the arts in general, however, remains surprisingly healthy. A new relationship between business and the arts has developed that is now an integral part of corporate affairs, just as it is a vital part of the art world. In many Western nations government initiatives have encouraged such a union. In the United States encouragement for corporate support of the arts was generated in 1935 when the United States Internal Revenue Services permitted corporations to deduct up to 50 per cent of pre-tax income for gifts to qualified charities. Museums were amongst the early beneficiaries, but at the conclusion of the Second World War businesses were still contributing only a relatively small percentage. It was not until the mid-1960s, with the establishment of the National Endowment for the Arts, that corporations and the arts in the United States forged a partnership that was to have strong repercussions in museums and art markets around the world.

The first such organizations to be formed in Europe were the Association for Business Sponsorship of the Arts in Britain (founded in 1976) and ADMICAL in France (formed in 1979). These initiatives encouraged other countries to follow suit, producing the Stichting Sponsors voor Kunstin in the Netherlands, and similar organizations in Belgium, Greece, Ireland and

MICHAEL AYRTON
Night-Fall
SIGNED AND DATED *49*,
OIL ON BOARD,
69 x 51cm (27 x 20in)
London £8,250 ($17,100).
7.XI.90
Now in the collection of Baring Brothers & Co. Ltd. (LEFT)

JOHN DICKSON INNES
Cactus
SIGNED, OIL ON PANEL,
23 x 33cm (9 x 13in)
London £9,600 ($20,100).
7.XI.90
Now in the collection of Baring Brothers & Co. Ltd. (BELOW LEFT)

Outside the Toledo Museum of Art, during the 1989 touring exhibition *Impressionism; Selections from Five American Museums*, sponsored by the Ford Motor Company. (RIGHT)

PAUL SIGNAC
Place des Lices, Saint-Tropez
OIL ON CANVAS,
65.8 x 82cm (25¾ x 32⅛in)
This work from the Carnegie Museum of Art was included in the 1989 touring exhibition *Impressionism; Selections from Five American Museums*.
(ABOVE)

The main entrance of the Henry Ford Museum in Dearborn, Michigan, built by the Ford Motor Company.
(ABOVE RIGHT)

Austria. In Britain, business sponsorship of the arts increased significantly through the 1980s. 1984 saw the creation of the Business Sponsorship Incentive Scheme managed by the Association for Business Sponsorship of the Arts. The British Government offered to match funds, pledging one pound for every three pounds donated by new business sponsors. This brought a great number of new corporate patrons and sponsors into the arena, and increased financial support for the arts by some £27 million.

American corporations, despite the recent economic recession, continue to be the world leaders in arts support. According to a recent Business Committee for the Arts survey, 38 per cent of the businesses in the United States gave $518 million to the arts in 1991. This was a decrease from the $634 million given in 1988, but at that time only 35 per cent of businesses were involved. In comparison with such sums, Japanese businesses donated approximately $195 million in 1991-2, while British businesses gave the equivalent of around $129 million during the same year.

It is universally recognized by museum directors throughout the world that the era of the 'blockbuster' exhibition of the 1980s is drawing to a close. It is more than likely that such major American exhibitions as *Gauguin* and *The Age of Sultan Suleiman the Magnificent*, both sponsored by Phillip Morris, the *Post-Impressionism* show, sponsored by GTE, and *The New Impressionism*, sponsored by AT & T, will become less frequent in the future. The prohibitive costs of insurance have driven sponsorship requests too high for most major companies. A recent innovative experiment by a consortium of five American museums may, however, indicate a pattern for the future. Combining their permanent French Impressionist collections in 1989, museums in Kansas City, St Louis, Minneapolis, Toledo and Pittsburgh created a major travelling exhibition entitled *Impressionism: Selections from Five American Museums*. The event was sponsored by the

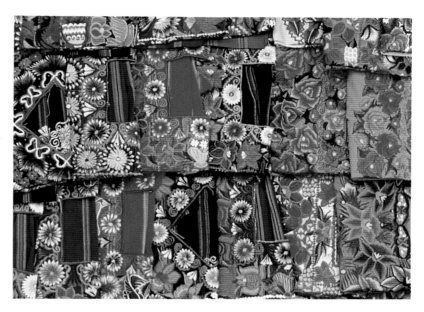

Ford Motor Company. An additional grant from the sponsor enabled the creation of strong educational and community outreach programmes, as well as strategic marketing and advertising campaigns. Each of the five cities became the beneficiary of these combined programmes, heightening the visibility of the corporate sponsor, as well as furnishing needed educational materials to teachers and pupils in local schools. By sharing their splendid collections and pooling staff resources, the museums were able to reduce greatly the cost of hosting such an exhibition.

Aware of current debates, the corporate community is increasingly turning its attention to critical social problems, which demand a more sophisticated involvement in the arts. In fragmented and diverse urban societies the corporate support of arts is now seen as being able to provide real benefits for common cultural education, as well as creating a possible bridge of understanding in ethnically polarized communities. In this new mode, the Ford Motor Company is sponsoring an innovative travelling exhibition of Latin American folk art, *Visiones del Pueblo: the Folk Art of Latin America*. Exhibition materials are bilingual and distributed widely throughout the educational system. Teacher-training workshops have been supported at each host museum to integrate the exhibition material into the arts and history curricula of local schools.

The roles that companies interested in the arts can play are many. The use of fine art in advertising can greatly help to give known and unknown artists a level of exposure unavailable elsewhere, while also introducing large sections of the public to works of art they might otherwise not see. The

building of art collections by corporations can also offer support to the artistic community, especially since the majority of corporate collectors seem to favour the work of contemporary artists. There has been a great deal of research compiled on the reasons why companies involve themselves in the arts. A survey taken in the United States in 1991 by the Business Committee for the Arts revealed that 91 per cent of companies involved in sponsorship were motivated by the desire to create an image of good corporate citizenship within the community. Some of the other motivations unearthed by the survey include the strengthening of employee relations, and the drive for higher visibility in the marketplace through the use of corporate advertising highlighting the arts.

The effect of corporate patronage on the art world is now substantial. Business sponsorship of museums, travelling exhibitions and other events is now a vital element in arts programming in many countries. Art markets, too, have come to rely heavily on corporate buyers. Clearly, the levels of cultural influence and responsibility gained by the 'new Medici', if not quite yet on a par with the achievements of the most glorious Renaissance princes, have earned the corporate sector a significant place in art historical study.

Exhibits from the 1993 travelling exhibition *Visiones del Pueblo: the Folk Art of Latin America*, sponsored by the Ford Motor Company. (ABOVE AND ABOVE LEFT)

ART ON TELEVISION *by Melvyn Bragg*

There are those who believe that the arts and television are mutually incompatible. There are others who claim that television itself is the arts centre of the second half of this century, a period impossible to understand or evaluate without giving television the fullest recognition. The former think that in the future television will be seen to have been a wart on the true values and civilization of the late twentieth century. The latter believe that, in a hundred years' time, those wishing to know about this extraordinary century will watch endless loops of videos. Somewhat aside from the larger debates which could be generated by the clash of such polarities, there are arts programmes.

Arts programmes flourish in British television. In one way this is surprising: they are not widely watched, they are often quite specialised, they

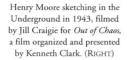

Henry Moore sketching in the Underground in 1943, filmed by Jill Craigie for *Out of Chaos*, a film organized and presented by Kenneth Clark. (RIGHT)

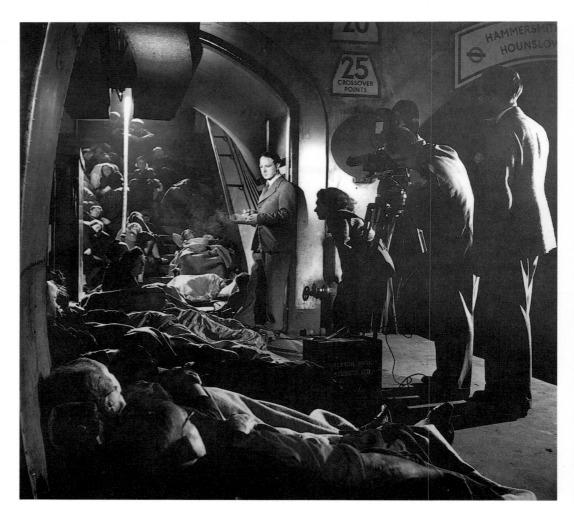

cater for one of the smaller segments of a richly segmented society, and they serve an audience which can have wider access to their core material elsewhere. Why watch the television programme, you might ask, when you could read the book, see the play, go to the gallery, go to the opera, watch the movie or hum the tune? But people do, in numbers that may be low by television's soap opera standards, but which are vast by, say, Covent Garden's opera attendance standards. A programme like *The South Bank Show* or *Omnibus*, provided it is transmitted at around 10.30 in the evening, can claim an average audience of two and a half to three million, and this sometimes for subjects which could be considered as way out of the mainstream, and not given much attention even by the sterner broadsheets.

It was a very much smaller audience that began watching television when the BBC first mounted regular transmissions in 1936. These were suspended in 1939, to restart in 1946. The pattern of arts programmes was set early, and owed much to the developments made by BBC Radio in the 1930s and 40s. Early in the field was John Read, son of Sir Herbert Read, who educated two generations in the Isms of twentieth-century art. His finely crafted documentary profiles on artists of the day encouraged the artist to reflect on his own work, and showed that work sympathetically to a public assumed to be interested but not especially learned. The first of Read's film profiles – on Henry Moore – was made for the BBC in 1951 and lasted twenty-six minutes.

The piece introduces Moore's art with views of his sculpture and film of him at work, accompanied by music composed for the film by William Alwyn. After a narration noting early career details, we are shown Primitive sculpture in the British Museum, with Moore speaking into camera on the immediacy of Primitive art. The artist then enthuses about the qualities of natural forms – stones, shells and bones – before we move to shots of Moore's life drawings, war drawings and maquettes, followed by four large stone and bronze works of the 1940s shown *in situ*. We cut to Moore drawing in his notebook, with voice-over quotations on

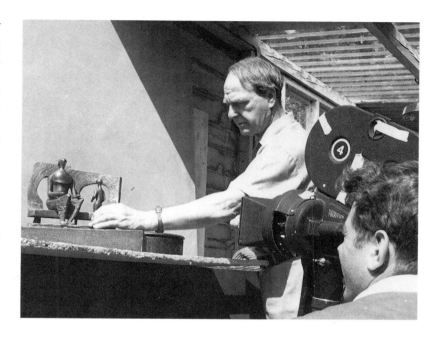

Henry Moore helps to arrange his sculpture for the camera during the filming of John Read's BBC documentary *A Sculptor's Landscape* in 1958. (ABOVE)

the creative process. The film finishes with our following a large-scale work from drawing and maquette through plaster and casting process to finished work and installation.

As a film study of the work of one artist it is a classic format, and one that Read was to explore and expand throughout the decade with films on Graham Sutherland, Stanley Spencer, John Piper, L.S. Lowry and others.

Read's films were a response to the age, and would not have been possible without an accompanying rise in the British public's interest in art. The post-War optimism of the 1950s generated an atmosphere that was as exciting for the arts as it was for television. The Festival of Britain awoke an enormous audience to new cultural adventures; John Osborne and Harold Pinter were electrifying the theatre; Pop Art was waiting in the art-school wings; a new age had begun and television was to play a leading role.

In 1958, all of Read's profiles were re-run as part of the opening of a new arts magazine programme that, for many years, was to set the pace – *Monitor*. *Monitor* was edited by Huw Wheldon, who had an infectious enthusiasm for the arts, and whose background had been in children's programmes. He was a fierce editor, holding to clarity, teasing the best out of directors and gravely tackling artists about their work. It was the combination of good film-making, accessibility and the unconcealed view of art as a celebration which caught a mood. Although much of Wheldon's work has been mocked and knocked since that time, both the mood and the approach were true enough to give the programme lasting fame. Marcel Duchamp, Ezra Pound, Paul Tortelier, Ben Shan, Orson Welles – *Monitor's* roll call of those who were persuaded to give insights into their own work is very impressive indeed.

Not all of *Monitor's* investigations into art were in the manner of a John Read profile. Apart from head-to-head interviews, there was also a number of dramatized biographies by Ken Russell, providing an extra dimension to the programme and a new format for the exploration of art on television. Russell's openly poetic films, notably those on the lives of Elgar, Debussy and Delius, have some claim to being works of art themselves, and were to set off a confidence in film for film's sake which was to ignite talent throughout 1960s' television.

Although *Monitor* set many of the standards for arts magazine programmes for years to come, it was by no means the only television programme covering the arts at that time that was to have a lasting influence. *Panorama* and *Tonight* – both current affairs programmes – included interviews with authors in the 1950s, and established the idea of dealing in a topical way with living artists, something which continues today, most abundantly on *The Late Show*. Kenneth Tynan's ITV programme *Tempo*, which first came on the air in 1961, attempted to cast a cooler eye on the arts world – an approach now finely honed in the *Without Walls* series.

In the 1960s, although ITV produced arts programmes (some, as today, regional magazines which outclassed the BBC) it was the BBC which began the build-up to the present heavy representation of the arts on the screen. BBC2 came along a little like an afterthought, and the younger end in television were given precious air time, small budgets and *carte blanche*. Many new

programme ideas reached the screen, including such pieces as *New Release*, a topical arts programme which aimed to do what *Monitor* did but for a younger or different audience. *New Release* included films on Salvador Dali in New York, David Jones in his bedsit in Harrow, and Jean Renoir in his house in Paris. On BBC1, *Omnibus* took over from *Monitor*, which, in an exhilarating roller-coaster run with Jonathan Miller as editor, had introduced a shocked British public to the seriously questing world of Susan Sontag, Robert Lowell and others of the New York Intelligentsia.

The 1960s also saw the rise of a new phenomenon in arts programming, a format that was to gain enormous popularity and command huge budgets: the blockbuster series. The first of these, broadcast in 1968, was *Civilisation – A Personal View*. The 'person' was the art critic and former Director of the National Gallery, Kenneth Clark. His chosen task, to summarize the artistic achievements of man. Clark had already had some involvement in television and film, and as early as 1937 had chaired a quiz programme that he later claimed to have been the first arts programme on British television. In 1943 he organized and presented *Out of Chaos*, a documentary on artists in wartime involving Moore, Sutherland, Paul Nash and Spencer. The format of *Civilisation*, with the presenter as lecturer, was an idea born in the academic world, but one which transferred to television with remarkable success. Clark's superbly confident manner was the key to that success. Twenty-five years on, his manner seems almost ludicrously grandiose. As Isaiah Berlin is said to have commented, 'It was all very well, but Clark did rather give the impression that civilisation wouldn't have happened without him.'

A small sample will serve to remind us of the style of the programme. Clark, dressed in a tweed suit with head held high, is walking towards the camera past an Adam fireplace in an ordered eighteenth-century drawing room. He is talking. 'An enclosed world becomes a prison of the spirit, one longs to get out, one longs to move, one realises that uniformity and consistency, whatever their merits, are

Kenneth Clark on the Isle of Iona in western Scotland during the filming of his BBC series *Civilisation – A Personal View* in 1968. (LEFT)

enemies of movement.' A chord is struck on the soundtrack. 'And what is that I hear? That note of urgency, of indignation, of spiritual hunger. Yes, it's Beethoven, it's the sound of European man, once more reaching for something beyond his grasp. We must leave this trim, finite room and go to confront the infinite.' At which point Clark flings open a pair of doors at the end of the drawing room to reveal the sea crashing on some rocks below. 'We've a long, rough voyage ahead of us.' Whether this was good history or not, it was certainly a wonderful piece of television.

This kind of 'personal view' lecture series became a frequently used format in the 1970s and on into the 80s. Some of the more memorable include Professor Bronowski's *The Ascent of Man*, John Berger's *Ways of Seeing*, Ronald Harwood's *All the World's a Stage*, Margot Fonteyn's *The Magic of Dance*, Jonathan Miller's *The Body in Question* and Robert Hughes' *The Shock of the New*. All of these offered us a personal view, although in the majority of cases, it was easy to mistake that personal view for some concept of established truth. Berger's *Ways of Seeing* stands out as one of the few of such programmes to

Leon Golub in his studio from
Sandy Nairne's 1987 Channel 4
series *State of the Art*. (ABOVE)

question seriously the validity of having only one
point of view about a subject. This was something that was tackled head on in Sandy Nairne's
series *State of the Art*, which looked at contemporary art in the 1980s. Instead of having a single,
visible presenter on screen to take us through the
subject, Nairne provided a collage of disembod-
ied voices reading, commenting and reminiscing.

State of the Art was made for Channel 4, which
was introduced in 1982 as the fourth British television broadcast service, with an obligation to
service minority audiences, and to 'encourage
innovation and experiment in the form and
content of programmes'. With its arrival,
the stream of arts programmes became a flood.
Channel 4 was, and remains, frequently bolder
than the other channels, and the current vigour
of its arts programme is exemplary.

ITV now puts out about thirty hours a month
of arts programming nationally, and many more
in its regions. The BBC has recently beefed up
its commitment to *Omnibus* on BBC1, where
the number of hours had fallen sadly, although
surprisingly the numbers still fall short of
its mirror image on ITV. Channel 4 darts
around the territory and also keeps a regular
presence. BBC2 relays opera – as does Channel 4
– and sets itself big targets, especially in its
current preoccupation with film, while *The*

Late Show fulfils an arts news and review role
too long neglected by television.

We have come a long way since John Read
first filmed Henry Moore. The arts are now a
wider brief. The choice is not, for example, Dylan
or Keats, but both, with a current leaning
towards the former. It is taken for granted by
editors of all the television programmes that
Rembrandt can be included in the same season as
John Lee Hooker; that a series by John Berger
can be commissioned by the same editor who
wants to bring in the Blues. Television drama-
tists, film directors and screen writers are as much
on the agenda as poets and painters. The 'low' art
of television has gobbled up its inheritance and
redelivered it in a variety of forms, including
cannibalizing and redelivering its own self.

One of the main pulses is still the educative –
even evangelical – notion that art can be discussed, be explained, to some extent be taught,
and that this will do the viewer good. This is now
challenged far more than it used to be, but the
tendency is still very strong. The observation that
television programmes lack a critical edge is justi-
fied, both in the general failure to challenge the
strong current thinking that art is good for
you, and in a particular failure to take on artists
with the sort of oppositional vigour found in
so many newspapers and magazines. What is
not argued so much is that there are other ways
of doing, other ways of meeting and embracing
artists, different places to stand.

Unpredictability must be allowed to play
its part. It could not have been planned, for
example, that Francis Bacon would join in
his own *South Bank Show* self-portrait in 1985
with such a vengeance, and with such compelling
results. It must surely always be exciting
and enlightening to attempt, with an artist as
collaborator, the journey towards uncovering
what that artist had in mind. If the producer and
the researcher have genuine respect and admiration for the artist, it is a quest which, though it
can never fully succeed, can, on the road to
failure, bring some valuable revelations.

One thing that is not in doubt is the calibre of
those involved. That Kenneth Clark took the
necessary time and trouble, not merely to top and

Carlo Maria Mariani in his studio from the 1987 Channel 4 series *State of the Art*. (ABOVE)

tail a series or do a short voice-over, but to write and help construct what was, for so many, a defining arts experience, is testimony to the attractions that British television has held and still holds for all those connected with the arts. Building on the Reithian experience of BBC Radio in the 1930s and 40s, with its determined alliances with the best creative talents of the day, British television was from very early on considered a place where composers, authors and artists of all kinds saw that they could do good work, have it produced with care, and reach an audience of millions. They were willing to come into the arena with television and join forces with a medium which in other countries artists despised. Thanks to the basic trust that grew up in radio days, British television in the second half of the twentieth century now has an archive of artists creating, performing, discussing and dissecting their own and others' work which will be of unparalleled value in the future.

Nor is there any doubt, as Clark said towards the end of his series, that 'the informed audience for art is much bigger and more thoroughly informed than ever before'. Television has played some part in this. Its failures have often occurred when it has tried to ape the newspapers and the magazines, and simply deliver review columns in hardback chairs. Its successes have been when it has gone back to its own medium, to documentary, the eclectic collage which may indeed make television itself an art form. It is a mongrel beast, but it seems that in the area of the arts, it is also a commendably energetic and frisky beast.

THE GROWING MARKETS OF ASIA *by John L. Tancock*

During the period since the Gulf War, when recessions of varying degrees of severity have affected the fortunes of developed countries around the world, the ability of the economies of the Asian nations to weather international trends and local traumas has been remarkable. At a time when the annual economic growth rate of the developed member countries of the Organization of Economic Cooperation and Development amounts to only 1½ per cent, the nations of Asia (the newly industrialized economies, the members of the Association of Southeast Asian Nations and China) have been achieving rates of 7 per cent and more. The 'New World Order' has yet to materialize, but in Asia far-reaching political changes, together with industrial might, have led to a situation in which the Asian nations are much more likely to show strong economic growth in the next decade than the countries of Europe or America.

On the political front, events such as the lifting of martial law in Taiwan in 1987 and the removal of restrictions on travel to China have had major repercussions. In August 1992 China established diplomatic relations with South Korea and, at the fourteenth Congress of the Communist Party of China, reaffirmed the country's market-oriented 'reform and opening' policy. Against this background of major political change the Asian nations have been able to create a multilateral trade structure. As a result of rising labour costs in their own countries, Japan and the newly industrialized economies have vastly increased their investments in Indonesia, Malaysia and Thailand. It is a fluid situation, but without doubt Asia is the area of the world where most wealth is currently being created. With such a shift in the balance of economic power taking place, the implications for the international art market are clear: henceforth, the nations of Asia will assume an increasingly important role.

Of all the Asian nations, Japan has the most developed and diversified art market, and the longest history of collecting Western art. The Japanese enthusiasm for Western art, particularly French Impressionism and the École de Paris, was certainly one of the main factors contributing to the extraordinary rise in prices during the second half of the 1980s. Equally, the abrupt withdrawal of these newly affluent buyers was one of the main causes of the steep decline of this market in 1990-1. Long before this episode, however, there was a tradition of collecting that was the opposite in all respects to this very public display of wealth. Discreet and intensely private, Japanese collectors demanded similar characteristics of the dealers who handled their affairs.

ZHANG DAQUIAN
Grand View of the Blue Mountains (detail)
SIGNED AND DATED *REN YIN* [1962], SET OF FOUR HANGING SCROLLS, INK AND COLOUR ON PAPER, 195 x 555.4cm (76¾ x 218⅜in)
Hong Kong HK$7,480,000 (£613,100:$971,400). 29.X.92
(RIGHT)

Long-established relationships based on trust characterized an art market that was essentially closed. Goods changed hands at private auctions organized with great frequency by the *bijutsu-kai* (association of dealers), but this was never headline news. As a result of an increasing knowledge of the generally more open practices of the West, a much more competitive and ultimately public approach was grafted onto this traditional way of doing business. Today, in the pages of *Nikkei Art*, graphs chart the rise and fall of the fortunes of Renoir and Utrillo, as well as the masters of *yoga* (Japanese Western-style oil painting) and *nihonga* (traditional Japanese-style painting), formerly traded only with the utmost discretion. Now, as the result of a severe recession, the art market in Japan is in a state of shock as it adjusts to the dramatic changes of the last three years. There is still a large amount of collecting, however, albeit at a lower level and in diverse fields, and this is surely an encouraging sign for the future.

In Hong Kong, Taiwan and South Korea the emergence of a developed art market is of more recent origin. There were, of course, sophisticated collectors of Chinese art in Hong Kong when Sotheby's held its first auction there twenty years ago, but it could not have been predicted that this small British colony, until then not known for its cultural sophistication, would shortly become one of the world's leading markets for Chinese art, rivalling London and New York. Many factors account for this startling transformation, not least the colony's economic prowess and its proximity to the other major centres for collecting Chinese art: Japan and Taiwan. Hong Kong did not have the long history of fascination with European culture that characterizes Japan and as a result, when newly affluent businessmen reached a stage when they could begin collecting, pride in the achievements of their own culture prevailed. The Min-Chiu Society, founded in 1960, gathered together a group of fifteen collectors and connoisseurs who would hold fortnightly meetings to discuss new acquisitions of Chinese art. In recent years, essentially private activities of this nature have become the basis for private museums. In 1981 Dr K. S. Lo made his initial donation of Yixing ware, which is now housed in Hong Kong's Flagstaff House Museum of Teaware. More recently, in September 1992, the new facilities of the T. T. Tsui Museum opened in the Old Bank of China building in Central District. The taste of today's Hong Kong collectors is not limited to the traditional areas of Chinese collecting or to the scholarly pursuits of the Min-Chiu Society. Jewellery and Modern Chinese painting are both important areas of collecting activity, with a younger generation responding as much to Western-influenced oil painting as to work in more traditional media. Zhang Daquian's 1962 *Grand View of the Blue Mountains* sold for HK$7,480,000 on 21 October 1992 to a Taipei gallery. On 29 April 1993 a cabochon jadeite ring sold for $684,783 to an Asian collector, giving some idea of the potential of the jewellery market in this part of the world.

The development of the jewellery market by Sotheby's over the last twenty years is paradigmatic of the way other areas of the art market may be expected to develop in the next decade. Through travelling exhibitions, local interest is cultivated and collectors are eventually brought into the international market. At first, a wide range of jewellery was sold in Hong Kong, but recently the emphasis has been on jadeite,

PARK SOO-KEUN
Two Seated Men
OIL ON BOARD,
21.5 x 27.5cm (8½ x 10¾in)
Sold privately through
Sotheby's New York. (BELOW)

PAUL CÉZANNE
Esquisse de
Baigneurs
OIL ON CANVAS,
20.3 x 33cm (8 x 13in)
New York $1,102,500
(£715,900). 11.V.93 (ABOVE)

the stone for which there has been most local enthusiasm, and for which record prices have been achieved. Such exhibitions have led to an increase in the activities of Asian buyers in New York and Geneva, and at the Thurn und Taxis sale on 17 November 1992, 11 per cent of the buyers were Asian. A mutually beneficial dialogue between East and West has been established.

In Taiwan and South Korea the development of active markets is of even more recent origin. In Taipei and Seoul the handful of well-established galleries has been joined by many newcomers representing a broad range of specialities. Although there is a growing familiarity with the art of the West, it is the taste of the older generation that characterizes the first forays of new collectors who can afford to start buying art. The National Palace Museum in Taipei and the National Museum in Seoul are symbols of national pride, setting standards to which private collectors cannot hope to aspire, but the

repatriation of national treasures and the support of more contemporary artists is more possible. Recent Sotheby's auctions in Taipei and auctions of Korean art in New York give clear examples of these trends. Since Taiwanese law forbids the export of works of art more than 100 years' old, Sotheby's devoted its first auction in Taipei (27 March 1992) to Modern and Contemporary Chinese Paintings. Taiwanese collectors had already been an important factor in the success of the Chinese painting sales in Hong Kong and at the first auction *Turtle Mountain Island* by Lia Chi-Chun was bought for $290,820, a world record for a Chinese oil. Taiwanese collectors favour the works of the first generation of modern Taiwanese artists (born just before 1900), and in buying their works feel they are buying part of the history of their newly powerful country.

In South Korea, too, there is an extremely active market for Korean art. In its troubled history of invasions and domination by foreign powers, much has been destroyed or is now in the hands of foreign collectors. Korean celadons, early Buddhist paintings, eighteenth- and nine-teenth-century blue and white wares, and works by twentieth-century Korean masters are all eagerly sought after by Korean collectors. On 22 October 1991 a rare silk hanging scroll of the late fourteenth-century Koryo dynasty, the *Water-Moon Avalokitesvara*, was sold at Sotheby's for $1.76 million. Very few scrolls of this type remained in Korea itself, and the possibility of returning this historic work to that country was the cause of enormous pride and excitement.

The art market in such growing economies tends initially to focus on the achievements of indigenous culture, both ancient and modern. Although Japan, with its long engagement with the West, has seen the establishment of an art market in which Western art forms a significant component, elsewhere in Asia this is not yet the case. There are, however, numerous signs that the internationalization of the local art markets will occur with surprising speed. Perhaps the most important factor is the establishment of museums which can provide standards of comparison and criteria for new collectors. In Japan, the building of numerous local and prefectural museums has not always had the desired effect since the build-ing itself often seems to have had priority over the forming of a collection, but the most important of the new museums, including the recently opened Aichi Prefectural Museum in Nagoya, the Tokyo Metropolitan Art Museum and the Osaka Municipal Museum of Art (the last two sche-duled to open in 1995 and 1997 respectively), should do much to remedy the currently rather deficient presentation of Modern and Contem-porary art in Japan. Other privately founded museums, such as the Idemitsu Museum in Tokyo, and the Kawamura Memorial Museum of Art in Sakura (the collection of the Dai Nippon Ink Company), are models of their kind. Mention has already been made of the new private museums in Hong Kong, but the newly reopened and expanded Hong Kong Museum of Art has provided a much needed forum for the display of its permanent collections and special exhibitions. In South Korea, in addition to the

Imperial *Famille-Rose* 'Nine Peach' vase
QIANLONG SEAL MARK AND PERIOD, height 51.4cm (20¼in)
New York $374,000
(£241,200). 1.XII.92 (LEFT)

massive National Museum of Contemporary Art and the privately funded Seoul Arts Centre, there are numerous corporate museums, including the distinguished Hoam Museum set up by Lee Byung-Chull, the founder of the Samsung Electronics Corporation, and the Sonje Museum of Contemporary Art in Kyongju. In Singapore in 1992 plans were announced to create a museum precinct, to include a Singapore Art Museum scheduled to open by the end of 1994, and an Asian Civilizations Museum. In order to facilitate the rapid building of collections, favourable tax incentives have been announced.

During the past decade the number of inter-national art fairs has increased tremendously in the West, but only recently has the viability of this method of displaying and selling works of art been tested in Asia. The Nihon International Contemporary Art Fair (NICAF) in Yokohama in March 1992 and the first Art Asia Hong Kong held in October 1992 both benefited from extensive international participation as well as generating considerable local interest. The intro-duction of public auctions in Asia has also begun to change the internal dynamics of the localized art markets, since the public nature of the process and the provision of verifiable information regarding prices is having a strong regulatory

PEPON OSORIO
The Scene of
the Crime
(Whose Crime?)
MIXED MEDIA
As installed for the 1993
Biennial Exhibition at the
Whitney Museum of American
Art, which was then transferred
to the National Museum of
Contemporary Art in Seoul,
South Korea. (ABOVE)

effect. There is no doubt that the introduction of regular, properly catalogued auctions in Hong Kong twenty years ago has done much to stabilize and strengthen the market for Chinese art worldwide. In Japan, the process has been less straightforward, since a highly stratified network of dealers and private auctions already existed. The example provided by Sotheby's with its first auction in Tokyo in October 1989 was shortly followed not only by a newly established auction company Shinwa, but also by the Tokyo Bijutsu Club itself. Unfortunately the timing was bad; the sudden proliferation of auctions coincided with the downturn in the economy.

In China, recent developments have provided a clear indication of the role that that vast country will almost inevitably play in the next century. For the first time since 1949, the authorities in Beijing permitted an auction to take place in which foreigners were officially allowed to purchase works dating back to the earliest periods of Chinese civilization. The Beijing International Auction, held in October 1992, suffered from organizational problems and appears not to have been a success. As a clear signal of the Chinese government's intention to suppress smuggling and establish a regulated art market, however, it was an encouraging step. At a more recent event, the first auction of Duo Yua Xuan Chinese paintings held in Shanghai in June 1993, there was a much higher rate of success, with collectors from Hong Kong, Taiwan and South Korea buying many of the top lots.

In spite of a number of unresolved political problems, the general outline of the art market in Asia seems to be reasonably clear. Not only

Li Meishu
Scenery of Sanxia
Signed, oil on canvas,
61 x 73cm (24 x 28¾in)
Taipei NT$5,000,000
(£124,100:$196,700). 18.IV.93
(Above left)

will there be a growth in buying power, but ultimately a vast increase in the geographic spread of potential collectors. For classic Chinese, Japanese and Korean art there is both a local and worldwide demand that is destined only to grow. As China becomes increasingly integrated into the capitalist world, more works of art may come into circulation and the Chinese diaspora will compete to own them. For the Modern and Contemporary art of these nations the international demand is more limited, although local markets will remain strong. As knowledge of Western art increases through exhibitions, art fairs, magazines and auctions, collectors may start to diversify and look more seriously at European or American art although, for historical reasons, this enthusiasm is unlikely to rival the Japanese passion for the culture of the West.

In August and September 1993, part of the controversial, politically and sexually oriented Whitney Biennial was transferred from New York to be exhibited at the National Museum of Contemporary Art in Seoul: an event that is more likely to have influenced the work of young artists than the taste of collectors. Earlier this year, however, a major exhibition of sculptures by Auguste Rodin, including the monumental *Thinker*, travelled from Paris to Beijing, Shanghai and Taipei. This was followed shortly after by an exhibition of recent pieces by the London artists Gilbert and George at the National Gallery in Beijing and the Arts Museum in Shanghai. If the Chinese can move from Rodin to Gilbert and George in a matter of a few months, the prospects for the future development of the art market in Asia look favourable indeed.

HANGING AND REHANGING *by Giles Waterfield*

'Enjoyment of the beauty of works of art is exquisite and sensitive, easily marred, easily dissipated. A picture, like a scented flower, has a charm and an essence peculiarly its own. Every effort should be made to preserve its individuality unspoiled and undisturbed.' This comment by an Aesthetic critic in *The Studio* in 1893 reflects a very particular attitude to the display of paintings, typical of its period. Ways of showing paintings have always reflected evolving attitudes to the social and historical role of works of art, and it is enlightening to explore some of the approaches to what superficially might appear a simple matter.

Some of the earliest picture collections, made in the sixteenth century, were intended to present dynastic statements of the importance of individuals and their social groupings. This was usually done through sets of portraits, hung in straight lines or in massed formations in galleries or cabinets. On the evidence of contemporary depictions of galleries in the Netherlands, it appears to have been the practice of leading collectors such as the Archduke Leopold William to hang their fine pictures as densely as possible, often leaving no space at all between the frames.

During the eighteenth century princely and noble owners began to organize their collections differently. One of the prime examples of this new style was the Electoral Gallery at Düsseldorf, where the collection of the Elector Palatine with its outstanding Rubenses (now in Munich) was arranged in a special picture gallery. Although this was an assertively private collection, with a statue of the Elector in front of the building, the paintings were more than personal possessions. As is made clear in the impressive catalogue of 1778, *La Galerie Electorale de Düsseldorf*, the collection played a particular political role in reinforcing the status of the prince. The placing of the paintings in the rooms of the Gallery combined symmetry with systematic grouping. They were shown in three galleries and two cabinets, with the Northern and the Italian works (these being regarded as the two major schools) segregated. The hang is recorded in the catalogue in prints delineating each wall's arrangement. A large important painting was placed in the centre of each principal wall. On each side hung paintings of similar, preferably identical, size, arranged in symmetrical patterns. These might be double or even triple hung. Underneath this set piece, a continuous row of small cabinet paintings was often placed in a line, about a yard from the floor.

This style of symmetrical courtly hang shaped the character of princely galleries in many European countries during the eighteenth century. In Italy, surviving examples can be seen in such ensembles as the Pitti Palace. In England, largely intact schemes of symmetrically hung saloons survive in such houses as Kedleston Hall in Derbyshire and Holkham Hall in Norfolk. In such arrangements of paintings, much thought was given to a pleasing overall visual appearance. In fact it was common practice to cut down, or add to, paintings in order to accommodate them within a decorative scheme – a practice which poses an interesting ethical problem for the modern restorer. In some cases, frames were adapted to suit the character of the collection: thus the Elector of Saxony decreed in the 1760s that all his paintings should be displayed in identical frames. Early catalogues generally identified the size of figures within a painting, whether life size, half size, or smaller, even though very little other information might be given about the work. It was important for such schemes that the proportions of figures within the whole arrangement should be properly related, and that the figures in the paintings on the upper tiers should not be on a smaller scale to those below.

The principle of the symmetrical hang depended on a generally accepted canon of major artists. The supremacy of artists was much discussed in the eighteenth century, with Raphael, Michelangelo and the Carracci variously hailed as the predominant masters. Conventional taste regarded Italian art of the sixteenth and seventeenth centuries as of particular importance, with Flemish and Dutch artists playing an important but subsidiary role.

In the later eighteenth century enlightened monarchs increasingly made their collections available to a limited public, often organizing their pictures and classical sculpture to be shown at stated times in special galleries. These galleries were generally adapted stables or palaces rather than purpose-built structures. The experts who arranged the works investigated the possibilities of placing them in chronological order, with the schools separated. One of the most important examples of this approach was the Imperial Gallery at Vienna, shown in the Upper Belvedere Palace from 1781. The Gallery was organized by the scholar Christian von Mechel. In the introduction to his catalogue of 1781, von Mechel commented that the collection was important not only for its intrinsic quality but for the light it shed on the development of art from the earliest days, and claimed that, as a work of reference and instruction, it was comparable to a library.

WILLIAM KENT
One of two designs for the elevations of the north and south walls of the Saloon, Houghton Hall, Norfolk
SIGNED AND DATED *1725*, PEN AND BLACK INK WITH GREY AND BROWN WASHES, 25.7 x 25.7cm (10⅛ x 10⅛in) London £57,200 ($87,500). 19.XI.92 (LEFT)

The visitor to this temple of art, as it was described, would find the Italian paintings subdivided by region, and all the schools shown in chronological order.

The ideas of von Mechel and a small number of contemporary experts dominated the development of museums of art in the nineteenth century. However, they did not represent the only approach. Academies of art, when in control of collections, tended to arrange pictures in a much more visually dominated way, with comparisons between the composition of works of art underlying their position on the walls. A good example of this from the later eighteenth century was the hang at the Luxembourg Palace in Paris, which showed selected works from the royal collection in a way which specified the visual connections between the works.

In the best organized museums, notably those of Germany, which led the world in art historical studies, a chronological display was applied throughout the nineteenth century, though there was much discussion over the relative values of chronology and geography as guiding principles. Such debates were inspired by a new attitude to the display of paintings: instead of the accepted range of sixteenth-, seventeenth- and some eighteenth-century works, museums were expected to show pictures of all periods, notably of the early Italian and Northern schools. Though these were often regarded as barbarous and of no intrinsic merit, they demonstrated the development of art, and indeed the progress made by mankind. In the Altes Museum in Berlin, which opened in Schinkel's building in 1830, and in the Alte Pinakothek in Munich of the same period, early paintings acquired for their archaeological interest were shown by school and period. In the National Gallery in London, which opened in its new building in Trafalgar Square in 1838, the efforts of the staff to organize a display on historical principles were frustrated by the hopeless inadequacies of space. It was a problem not solved until the 1880s.

The problems experienced at the National Gallery were reflected by numerous museums in the nineteenth century. In France, regional museums were afflicted by the *envoi* system, by which

Interior of one of the exhibition rooms at the Altes Museum, Berlin, in 1910. (ABOVE)

large numbers of paintings were despatched by central government to local museums, the latter having no say in what they received. The result tended to be ill-organized and incongruous collections on a massive scale. In Britain, the municipal museums which flourished from the 1860s often showed their paintings in highly crowded settings, while in the United States some museums which were ostensibly public centred on commemorative displays of the possessions of wealthy families. Views of mid- and late nineteenth-century galleries frequently show rooms hung much like a chaotic academy exhibition, with pictures piled up the walls with little thought for clarity of presentation or the total effect.

The arrangement of paintings, both in public galleries and in private houses, was closely related to changing ideas about interior decoration. As taste moved in the last quarter of the nineteenth century away from richly decorated rooms towards more spare and discriminating interiors, so the style of showing works of art altered. Under the influence of such figures as the painter J. M. Whistler and the writer Edith Wharton, artists and their friends began to decorate their houses in a new manner, with paintings and other works of art carefully related to one another and to the whole room. Olana, the house of Frederick Church on the Hudson River, is a notable surviving example of this approach. The change in attitude was partly encouraged by a new style of painting practised by many artists. Instead of painting on the traditional dark ground and applying forcefully coloured layers of paint, painters such as the Pre-Raphaelites used paler grounds and lighter colours. They found that the dark wall colours of nineteenth-century rooms provided an unsympathetic background to their works, and preferred less intense shades, in particular maroon, sage green or in some cases grey. White was generally considered suitable only for showing prints. At the same time, they wanted their paintings to be hung with a greater degree of independence from their surroundings. Double hanging was to be avoided, and a reasonable space was to be provided between each work. The new approach to hanging (though not to wall colours) was pioneered in Britain at the Grosvenor Gallery, which opened in Bond Street in 1876 for temporary exhibitions by living artists. At much the same time, Whistler organized a number of influential exhibitions, beginning with his one-man show at the Flemish Gallery in 1874. Influenced by the Japanese cult of light-coloured pure interiors which encouraged the contemplation of a small number of exquisitely chosen objects, Whistler showed his own works in a way that carried the ideas of his contemporaries much further. In particular, his presentation of prints and watercolours, in broad mounts with narrow dark frames, overturned the traditional attempt to make works on paper resemble oil paintings.

The idea of showing paintings in pale settings, and of allowing space around them so that they do not fight with the surrounding images, has become so unfashionable in some circles in recent years that it is helpful to recall the origins of this approach. By the end of the nineteenth century it was usual for museums and for advanced private collectors to show their works of art in this new sparse manner. Throughout Europe, it became customary to seek qualities of harmony and

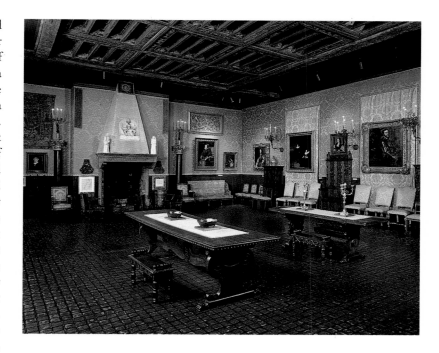

repose while arranging galleries, qualities in sympathy with the interiors created by the proponents of Art Nouveau and Jugendstil. Much attention was devoted to the introduction of carefully selected pieces of furniture and ceramics, as well as to suitable wall hangings.

At the end of the nineteenth century an alternative style was explored in Berlin. This was the period room, developed by the great director of the Berlin museums, Wilhelm von Bode. In a typical Bode installation, paintings in contemporary frames, sculpture and furniture, all of the same period, were shown together in an architecturally sympathetic setting, underlining the importance of the historical context of a work of art, as well as the relevance of the contemporary decorative arts. The paintings were not usually densely arranged in such a scheme, playing only one part in the total performance. Bode's ideas were extremely influential, shaping the character of many interiors, especially those belonging to great American collectors around the turn of the century. The Isabella Stewart Gardner Museum in Boston and the Pierpont Morgan Library in New York remain fine examples of the style. It was symptomatic of the importance

The Dutch Room at the Isabella Stewart Gardner Museum, Boston. (ABOVE)

Interior view through five galleries at the Dulwich Picture Gallery, London. (ABOVE)

Interior view of one of the newly refurbished rooms at the National Gallery of Scotland, Edinburgh. (ABOVE RIGHT)

attached to the effect of historic interiors that Isabella Stewart Gardner stipulated that none of the interior arrangements in her museum should be altered.

This period should be distinguished from the 1930s and later, when the impact of Modernism inspired a quite different approach. 'Meaningless' decoration came under increasing criticism, and a belief in the neutral interior became established under the impact of such innovatory institutions as the Museum of Modern Art in New York, which opened its first exhibition in 1929. Under the influence of the Bauhaus, the Museum of Modern Art presented paintings and sculpture in small, unintimidating, quasi-domestic white rooms, in which paintings were placed in a single line with considerable spaces between them, often with a deliberately irregular aesthetic in their hang. While such museums benefited from purpose-built rooms, older institutions were faced with apparently out-of-date interiors. From the 1930s until at least the 1970s, efforts were made in museums throughout the world to introduce false partitions and walls, and to conceal roof lights and dadoes in pursuit of the neutral setting. For contemporary art such an approach was doubtless appropriate; the problem was that

this bare style was applied to paintings of every period. Curators neglected the Victorian principle that paintings should be shown on a background darker than the light tones in a painting, but lighter than the dark tones. Instead, they tended to use light backgrounds which turned traditional oils, painted on a dark ground and possibly covered with old discoloured varnish, into looming masses of blackness.

By the late 1970s the white wall and the single hang were under fire, especially in Britain, where the work of the National Trust and the Victoria and Albert Museum was of pioneering importance in the restoration of historic interiors. In the early 1980s the Manchester City Art Gallery, London's Dulwich Picture Gallery and the National Galleries of Scotland all underwent major restorations, intended to emphasize the architectural character of the building and to return, not to nineteenth-century museum practice, but to the symmetrical, aristocratic aesthetic of an earlier period. In Britain, at least, the restoration of country house interiors has often shown a similar tendency: at Holkham the principal rooms have recently been reinstalled, with paintings which had been removed to the attics being returned to the positions they occupied in the eighteenth century. Petworth House, rehung after the Second World War by Anthony Blunt according to school and period, has recently been restored, allowing the extraordinary collection of early nineteenth-century British paintings to throng the rooms.

The hanging of paintings has recently been much discussed. The 'historic' style has not met with universal approval. Though generally considered suitable for historic houses, it has often been thought inappropriate for major Old Masters. At the Walters Art Gallery in Baltimore, for example, the upstairs picture galleries have recently been sumptuously refurbished with strongly coloured brocades, but this approach has not been supported by the hang: the paintings continue to be hung in a single line, creating for some spectators the uncomfortable effect of great areas of empty red and green fabric above the pictures. The present Director of the London National Gallery has made it clear that his galleries will not be double hung. The paintings are too important to be sacrificed for decorative effect. The Gallery has, on the other hand, cautiously questioned the traditional rigid division of paintings by school, by introducing Northern works into the new galleries of the Sainsbury Wing.

In very recent years, experiments have continued. One positive development has been the display of drawings along with paintings, a practice explored at the Art Institute of Chicago and in the French galleries at the Louvre in Paris. In other museums the recent interest in examining paintings as the products of social and political developments has produced a radically new approach. In one installation at the Laing Art Gallery in Newcastle, the paintings are primarily used to illustrate the history of the city, and in the Kelvingrove Museum and Art Gallery in Glasgow, many of the paintings are arranged by theme, rather than by school or period. The only point generally accepted among all this experimentation is that the arrangement of a painting within a space radically affects the impact it makes on the spectator. For better or worse, the creation of a neutral setting for paintings is a virtually impossible target.

The North Gallery at Petworth House, Sussex, showing a recent programme of rehanging nearing completion. (ABOVE)

Rooms in the Sainsbury Wing of the National Gallery, London, opened in 1991. (TOP)

EXHIBITIONS OF THE SEASON *by Richard Cork*

ERIC GILL
Mother and Child
BATH STONE,
height 58.8cm (23in),
London £61,600 ($96,000).
4.XI.92
This work was featured in the
exhibition of the artist's work
held at the Barbican Art
Gallery, London, from
November 1992 to February
1993. (RIGHT)

HENRI MATISSE
La Plage Rouge
SIGNED, OIL ON CANVAS,
33 x 40.6cm (13 x 16in)
From the collection of
Wright S. Ludington
This work was included in the
exhibition *Matisse: A
Retrospective*, held at the
Museum of Modern Art, New
York, from September 1992
to January 1993, as well as in
the exhibition *Henri Matisse
1904-1917*, held at the Musée
National d'Art Moderne,
Paris, from February to June
1993. (BELOW)

In a year when the most outstanding exhibition failed to reach Britain at all, questions were inevitably raised about London's continuing ability to mount the shows which everyone wants to see. The great Matisse survey, commencing with enormous success at New York's Museum of Modern Art before travelling in a much-altered form to the Pompidou Centre in Paris, carried everything before it. In New York, two entire floors of the Museum of Modern Art building were devoted to John Elderfield's immense, magisterial round-up of Matisse's long and prolific career. Despite the waning intensity noticeable in his inter-war years, the event as a whole was a triumph. Even visitors who are normally averse to exhausting blockbusters found themselves energized by Matisse's exuberance and inventiveness.

The Paris version, concentrating on the heroic years between 1904 and 1917, filled only a single floor of the Pompidou Centre. But it was just as enthralling. Matisse was at his finest in the decade after he gained widespread notoriety as a Fauve, and virtually all his most impressive works of the period were assembled in a superb, all-white installation. Even though the grand *Music* canvas was too frail to travel from St Petersburg, its companion *Dance* provided the exhibition with a joyful climax. A profusion of other Russian loans, combined with key pictures from Europe and the United States, made for an exhilarating experience. The powerful *Interior with Aubergines*, unavailable for the New York show, made the journey to Paris from Grenoble to prove that Matisse in 1911 was already on the brink of exploring the pictorial possibilities which would give his final phase of painted paper cut-outs their audacity and zest after the Second World War.

Patrick Heron, who had tried so hard to procure the Russian Matisses for a London show during his time as a Tate Gallery trustee, was not alone in deploring Britain's inability to stage this

sumptuous survey. Many commentators shared his dismay, and asked whether London was now in danger of missing the most impressive shows touring the international circuit. The answer, in Matisse's case, was that Paris and New York held the trump cards in their ability to negotiate. Between them, the Museum of Modern Art and the Pompidou own many of his masterpieces, and so were far more likely to achieve deals with their Russian counterparts. The Tate, by contrast, has meagre Matisse holdings.

But what of the Royal Academy, equipped with the gallery space and resources needed to mount surveys on the grand scale? Its principal achievements this year have centred on home-grown artists. *The Great Age of British Water-colours* achieved great popularity, but included only a sparing sample of the visionary images of Blake and Palmer, whose formidably original contributions revolutionized the British water-colour tradition in the early nineteenth century. Cotman was one of the show's heroes, exploring the advent of blast furnaces in the English

landscape with the same passion for order and lucidity that he bestowed on pastoral subjects. Girtin's work was displayed with equal gener-osity. His capacity to invest *The White House at Chelsea* with a beacon-like luminosity was one of the high points of the exhibition – notwith-standing the presence of well-selected Turners representing many phases of his protean career. If Girtin had lived longer, he might have equalled Turner's achievement as a watercolourist. But his untimely death at the age of twenty-seven meant that Turner went on without him, tirelessly opening up new expressive directions for a medium where he often seems more at home than in his surprisingly uneven oil paintings.

Sickert, whose work was summarized in a well-balanced Royal Academy retrospective, likewise benefited from longevity. A slow starter, who spent some time as a professional actor before committing himself to art, he was over-shadowed as a young painter by older mentors. The shades of Whistler, and more particularly Degas, dominated the first room of the show.

THOMAS GIRTIN
The White House at Chelsea
DATED *1800*, WATERCOLOUR, 29.8 x 51.4cm (11⅗ x 20in)
From the collection of the Tate Gallery, London
This work was included in *The Great Age of British Watercolours* exhibition held at the Royal Academy, London, from January to April 1993. (ABOVE)

WALTER SICKERT
Baccarat
SIGNED AND DATED *1920*,
OIL ON CANVAS,
61 x 44.5cm (24 x 18in)
London £95,000 ($143,400).
30.VI.93
This work was included in the
Walter Sickert exhibition held at
the Royal Academy, London,
from November 1992 to
February 1993. (ABOVE)

Sickert shared Degas' love of popular urban entertainment, but his early music-hall paintings reveal signs of an independent vision. Fascinated by the encrusted architecture of the Old Bedford Theatre's interior, Sickert showed as much interest in the audience as he did in performers like Little Dot Hetherington, spotlit on the stage.

If he had died in mid-career, Sickert would be remembered best today as an artist who applied the lessons of Impressionism to exploring the dingy streets of north London. His paintings of dilapidated, claustrophobic interiors in Mornington Crescent are often as sombre as the murderous subjects he favoured. Having fathered

a whole school of young painters, who shared his devotion to Camden Town, Sickert might easily have rested content with such an achievement. After the First World War, though, he underwent an extraordinary transformation. The latter-day Impressionist cast aside his former reliance on empirical observation. Photographs, often of the most blurred and ephemeral kind, became his starting-point. Many of his earlier admirers were affronted, and Sickert's late work suffered from widespread critical disfavour long after his death. Now, however, the paintings of the 1930s can be seen as an unpredictable final flowering. The octogenarian artist took the whole of society as his subject, from monarchs to miners. His handling of paint became astonishingly broad and summary, adept at disclosing the vulnerability of the newly-crowned Edward VIII as well as the self-confident vigour of Lord Beaverbrook. For the first time, the Royal Academy disclosed the full scope and underlying unity of Sickert's work in exhibition terms. It was well received, and the market duly responded to the enhanced reputation of this hitherto under-valued artist. His *Baccarat*, a work of 1920 which had been included in the exhibition, fetched a surprising £95,000 at Sotheby's in June.

Munch, whose multi-part *Frieze of Life* was brought together in a powerful survey at the National Gallery in London, is in no need of a boost to his reputation. His paintings, though, are scarcely visible in British public collections, and the loan of his finest early canvases from Norwegian museums added up to an unnerving experience. Although some of the paintings from the *Frieze of Life* were dispersed during his lifetime, he always regarded them as an ensemble. The National Gallery's exhibition, therefore, did Munch a particular service by reuniting all these haunted testaments to the artist's obsessive reactions to life, love and death.

Basing most of the paintings on the water's edge enabled Munch to confront his figures with a sense of immensity. Apart from reinforcing the work's dreamlike character, these deserted settings accentuate the pervasive sense of isolation. Even when seen in groups, talking or dancing, Munch's people always appear marooned within their own introspection. At its quietest, this alienation results in the melancholy of the young man seated on a rock, brooding over his unrequited infatuation with the woman glimpsed in the distance. At its most disturbing, the outcome centres on trauma. The celebrated image of *The Scream*, accompanied here by a fascinating wall of preliminary studies and related versions, reduces the protagonist to a shuddering, bald-headed victim of indeterminate gender stranded on a bridge. While the sunset fills the sky with an almost blood-red vehemence, the sufferer's mouth parts in a cry loud and primal enough to echo round the world.

If we knew more about the mysterious rituals of ancient Mexico, its sculpture might well take on a similarly ominous character. The carvings assembled at the Hayward Gallery, London, in October 1992 were frequently associated with ceremonial purposes, servicing religions which insisted on the need for sacrificial victims. Seen in this light, the monumental deities standing on tall plinths throughout the dramatically sloping first room assume an implacable identity. They seem ready to preside over the most merciless proceedings imaginable, and their fixed, staring expressions add to their air of stony detachment. It is a wonder that Henry Moore, who made no secret of his indebtedness to the Chac Mool carvings, transformed them into embodiments of beneficence. While retaining the monumentality of Chac Mool prototypes, Moore's recumbent women enjoy a reassuring identity. They are as fertile as the earth itself, whereas the Chac Mool figures have a more sentinel-like character, vigilant and even defensive as they twist their heads to scan the surrounding space.

Although the Hayward show was splendidly installed, it did raise the question of cultural misrepresentation. By uprooting these artifacts from their original context, and displaying them in the spotless, sanitized environment of a modern gallery, the exhibition was bound to show its contents in a distorting light. Credit, then, to the organizers for concluding the survey with a spectacular audio-visual presentation of the principal surviving sites. Ruined and awesome, they provided a salutary reminder of how

these carvings often originated in a close alliance with architecture of monumental proportions.

Of all the twentieth-century artists who owe a debt to Mexican culture, Georgia O'Keeffe acknowledged it most freely. She spent the last decades of her long career living in Abiquiu, sustained by the isolation and serenity of a location at the furthest possible remove from the Manhattan gallery world where her reputation was made. Legendary in her own country, and in recent years revered as an icon by feminist art historians with whom she had little in common, O'Keeffe has been neglected in Britain. The retrospective at the Hayward Gallery offered London an opportunity to become acquainted with her paintings, watercolours and drawings.

EDVARD MUNCH
The Scream
TEMPERA AND PASTEL
ON BOARD,
91 x 73.5cm (35¾ x 29in)
From the collection of
The National Gallery, Oslo
This work was included in the
*Edvard Munch: The Frieze of
Life* exhibition held at the
National Gallery, London, from
November 1992 to February
1993. (ABOVE)

The first room of
The Art of Mexico exhibition,
held at the Hayward Gallery,
London, from September to
December 1992. (ABOVE)

Were enough of them on display, however? O'Keeffe, a prolific artist, can be properly assessed only if a substantial cross-section of her output is available. The selection here bordered on the frugal. New York, where she spent some of her most energetic years alongside Alfred Stieglitz, inspired a group of memorable paintings. They were barely represented here, in an exhibition bent on establishing O'Keeffe as a ruralist at the expense of her urban scenes. To that end, it offered a whole roomful of her flower paintings, where sexual symbolism is overplayed to a cloying, repetitive extent. Her prowess as a landscape painter seemed strangely limited, too. The Mexican subjects often bordered on the merely picturesque, so it was a relief to go upstairs where James Turrell had prepared a rigorous series of installations.

This visionary Californian transformed his allotted rooms into a sequence of breathtaking spaces. Turrell is a master-manipulator of light, but to approach *Wedgework IV* visitors groped their way through corridors as dark as midnight. Then blackness gave way to a vast and airy chamber, filled with misty red light. In the distance, beyond public access, a large rectangular opening led to a distant room. Partially visible and veiled with a softer radiance than before, its effect was intensified by an aura of unattainability. Spare yet overwhelmingly sensuous, *Wedgework IV* seduced at once. The neighbouring exhibit, though, worked far more stealthily. A dark corridor led, this time, into a far cooler chamber. The main illumination was provided by pools of light on the left and right walls, flanking an opening as wide as a cinema screen. As you approached, the opening gave out onto an infinitely mysterious emptiness beyond. It seemed to be swimming with fog; under Turrell's deft manipulation light almost becomes palpable.

His wizardry was at its most captivating in the final installation, a room specially built on the gallery forecourt. Seen from Waterloo Bridge, this bunker-like structure looked as unprepossessing as the Hayward's own architecture. Inside, though, it was a thing of wonder. A tunnel-like entrance guided us through to a startlingly bright space, lined on all four walls with plain wooden benches. Their high backs sloped away, inviting you to lean against them and look upwards without neck-strain. They terminated in a hidden strip of light, running round the room and brilliantly illuminating the walls extending about twenty feet in the air to a plain ceiling. Here, a square aperture had been cut out, giving directly onto the sky. Heavy clouds, combined with the encroaching dusk, should have ensured a dull spectacle beyond the roof. But by contrasting it with the brightness of the room below, Turrell intensified the sky's colours with extraordinary potency. By the time darkness settled in, the square opening had been turned into an irresistible expanse of deep, rich blue. It was as if a swathe of velvet had been attached to the ceiling, and the effect was mesmeric.

During the 1960s, when Turrell was only beginning to define his singular vision, London witnessed the burgeoning of far more frenetic art forms. Many of them were reassessed in a large, crowded and multi-faceted survey at London's Barbican Art Gallery in 1993. Its organizer, David Mellor, tried to challenge the stereotyped notion that Pop Art dominated everything else in the city. He resurrected the forgotten William Green, a young action painter who enjoyed brief notoriety for attacking his canvases and setting fire to them. Such activities culminated in the Auto-Destructive art devised by Gustav Metzger, who systematically assailed his work in public demonstrations on the South Bank.

The Barbican show made clear that a widespread interest in abstraction also characterized avant-garde painting in the early 1960s. Stimulated by recent developments in American art, young painters experimented with a remarkably simplified, hard-edged language. They could hardly have been more divorced from the concerns of Pop-orientated artists like the

One of the exhibition spaces at *The Sixties Art Scene in London* show, held at the Barbican Art Gallery, London, from March to June 1993, showing works by Bridget Riley and Anthony Caro.(ABOVE)

young David Hockney, whose precocious early work was underplayed to a falsifying extent in this show. Mellor called attention to the short-lived Pauline Boty, a proto-feminist artist preoccupied with gender and sexuality. He also celebrated the single-minded optical attack of another woman artist still active today: Bridget Riley, whose eye-battering images looked at home in the same room as a sprightly aluminium sculpture by Anthony Caro.

Although some of the work on show turned out to have fared badly, bearing the hallmark of the 60s at their most superficial, the leanest and most energetic of these abstractionists forged a language which served them long after the decade had ended. They, rather than the much-hyped practitioners of Pop, emerged with credit from an event which, like all worthwhile exhibitions, changed our perception of the subject it set out to explore.

II
Art
at
Auction

THE FINE ARTS

The past season saw the gradual reappearance on the market of top quality paintings in the Impressionist and Modern field. The boom period in the late 1980s attracted an unprecedented number of major paintings that were being consigned by discretionary vendors. The severe readjustment to that market which followed was not so much due to the withdrawal of Japanese buyers, but to a dramatic drop in the volume of paintings coming onto the market, an absence of first quality works and a near standstill in discretionary selling. Before the beginning of this season, observers were questioning if there was 'any life' above the $10 million mark.

The appearance of two major Matisses in the November series of sales answered the question impressively. The sales coincided with the milestone exhibition dedicated to the artist held at the Museum of Modern Art in New York. On 10 November Matisse's L'Asie, a seminal late work of 1946 from the collection of the late Mollie Parnis Livingston, sold for $11 million. The next day the artist's Harmonie Jaune of 1927-28 sold for $14,520,000.

While the market above $10 million is quite different from that below this watershed, and even more different from the market below $1 million, what happens at the top end sets the tone for the overall market. This was evident during the sales that followed, starting with Sketch 1 for Composition VII painted in 1913 by Wassily Kandinsky, which was consigned by the Klee family to our December auction in London where it sold for £5,500,000.

What happened in the autumn gave sufficient confidence to discretionary vendors for them to consign outstanding works to the May sales in New York. Cézanne's Nature Morte: Les Grosses Pommes had been in the same hands since 1958 when it was sold at Sotheby's as part of the collection of Jakob Goldschmidt for £90,000. This time its estimate was $12-15 million. Its superb quality, freshness to the market and realistic estimate caused fierce competition amongst bidders, and the price rose rapidly to $28,602,500 – a figure that even at the height of the market would have been hard to match.

SIR EDWARD COLEY
BURNE-JONES
**The Godhead Fires,
from the
Pygmalion series**
SIGNED AND DATED 1870,
66 x 51cm (26 x 20in)
London £661,500 ($992,200)
for the series of four. 8.VI.93.
(ABOVE)

MARY CASSATT
**Young Lady in
a Loge, gazing
to the right**
SIGNED, PASTEL AND
GOUACHE ON PAPER,
64.8 x 54.6cm (25½ x 21½in)
New York $2,530,000
(£1,675,400). (LEFT)

The scarcity of great works on the market means that when something of major quality and rarity does turn up, it causes greater competition amongst potential purchasers. In the same sale as the Cézanne, we offered a rare Matisse entitled La Mulâtresse Fatma. Painted in 1912, it was bought around 1916 by one of the great collectors of this century, Josef Müller. Again, brisk bidding by several contenders drove the price to $14,302,500, nearly matching the record for Matisse set six months before.

These results further strengthened the confidence of collectors. The June sales in London not only achieved the highest total for a sale of Impressionist and Modern art held there since 1989, but also had the lowest percentage of unsold works since then. Several records were achieved, notably for Le Fardeau (La Blanchisseuse) by Honoré Daumier (£1,651,500) and La Joie de Vivre by Paul Delvaux (£1,013,500).

Unlike last season, when works by Rembrandt and Bellotto were sold in London, this season saw fewer works of the finest quality appear on the Old Master paintings market. This fact, coupled with the somewhat more discreet participation of the Italian buyers (who traditionally are key players in this area), produced a season that was a little subdued. There were, however, notable exceptions such as Goya's Bullfight. Suerte de Varas, the last late bullfighting scene by Goya left in private hands, which sold in London in December for £4,950,000. Other highlights were a School of Bruges Portrait of Jacob Obrecht which sold for $2,422,500 in New York in January and a group of seven paintings by various Italian artists depicting the history of the Medici family, from the collection of Lord Elgin, that brought £1,651,000 in London in April.

The Latin American art market continued to be highly active this season, with fourteen new records established. The November sale in New York saw strong competition for nineteen works by Joaquín Torres-García from the Estate of Royal S. Mark which made $1,856,250. During the same sale artists' records were set for Fernando Botero (La Casa de las Gemelas Arias, $1,540,000) and Rufino Tamayo (Mujer en éxtasis, $1,485,000).

Sotheby's American paintings sale in New York in May was exceptionally strong, achieving the highest result in this category since 1989. An important Childe Hassam, The Room of Flowers, was sold for $5,502,500 (a record for an American Impressionist painting) and a William Merritt Chase, entitled Peonies, fetched $3,962,500 (a record price for the artist).

ROBERT RAUSCHENBERG
Press
SIGNED AND DATED *1964*,
OIL AND SILKSCREEN INK
ON CANVAS,
213.4 x 152.4cm (84 x 60in)
New York $1,100,000
(£728,400). 17.XI.92. (ABOVE)

HONORÉ DAUMIER
**Le Fardeau
(La Blanchisseuse)**
SIGNED, OIL ON CANVAS,
116.3 x 89.2cm (44¾ x 35⅛in)
London £1,651,500
($2,510,200). 22.VI.93
(ABOVE)

This season has been the best ever in the Victorian paintings area. Strong prices were fetched in both London and New York, including two major works by Sir Lawrence Alma-Tadema. The first, The Baths of Caracalla, was sold in New York for a record price of $2,532,500, and the second, Caracalla and Geta, was sold in London for £1,431,500. Academic French ninteenth-century painters also fared well, with good prices being achieved for works by Jean-Léon Gérôme and William Adolphe Bouguereau.

The renewed confidence that has brought back works of great quality to the Impressionist and Modern paintings department has been less evident in the Contemporary art market. Nevertheless, there were some fine results such as Andy Warhol's Marilyn x 100 which sold for $3,740,000 in New York in November and Bruce Nauman's One Hundred Live and Die which achieved a record $1,925,000. The total for the Contemporary art sale in London in June, £4,979,963, was the highest since June 1991. The sale included two portraits by Francis Bacon. The first, Study for a Portrait, made £562,500, the second, a Portrait of Lucian Freud, £221,500. Strong prices were also obtained for works by Gerhard Richter, Anselm Kiefer and Eduardo Chillida. These results suggest that with the return of top quality works the market for Contemporary art might show a similar resilience to that for Impressionist and Modern paintings.

Lastly, Prints and Photographs are both areas which continue to win more collectors. Solid sales for the Print department this season included the Dr Otto Schäfer collection of etchings by Rembrandt, which made $3,871,925 in May in New York, while the Photography department established a new world record for a single photograph at auction when Glass Tears by Man Ray sold for £122,500 in London in May.

JAMES AND JOHN BARD
The Steam Engine Paddle Wheeler Thomas Powell: A Ship's Portrait
SIGNED AND DATED 1846, OIL ON CANVAS, 78.7 x 139.7cm (31 x 55in)
New York $96,000 (£65,300). 24.VI.93. (ABOVE)

OLD MASTER PAINTINGS

SCHOOL OF BRUGES
Portrait of Jacob Obrecht
OIL ON PANEL, 43.8 x 27.9cm (17¼ x 11in)
New York $2,422,500 (£1,583,333). 15.I.93

The sitter for this late fifteenth-century portrait has been identified as Jacob Obrecht, a renowned Flemish composer who died in 1505. At the time it was painted Obrecht was living in Antwerp, and the picture may be by an artist from that city. However, no Antwerp painter is known who would have been capable of producing a work of this quality, and Dirk de Vos of the Bruges Stedelijke Museum has suggested that it is by the Bruges artist Hans Memling. Obrecht had strong enough links with Bruges for this to be possible, and a very similar treatment of the facial features can be found in major works by Memling.

It is difficult, though, to substantiate such a hypothesis given the absence of any comparable portraits by Memling from this late period in his career. The panel is probably the left-hand wing of a diptych or triptych, as there are hinge marks on the frame. (LEFT)

JACOB CORNELISZ. VAN
OOSTSANEN
The Crucifixion
DATED 1507, OIL ON PANEL,
99.1 x 78.7cm (39 x 31in)
New York $607,500 (£397,059).
15.I.93

The Crucifixion is an
important, previously
unpublished addition to
the corpus of Jacob van
Oostsanen, sometimes
called Jacob van Amsterdam
(Oostsanen lies a few miles
north of Amsterdam), and is
obviously the central panel
of a triptych. Only a dozen
dated pictures by van
Oostsanen are extant, and
the discovery of this work
adds considerably to our
understanding of the artist's
style at the beginning of his
known career. By 1507 van
Oostsanen was about 37
years old and must already
have established an artistic
reputation: in addition to
paintings, he is also known
to have illustrated books,
painted choir vaults and
made designs for stained
glass, embroidery and
prints. Amsterdam was,
until the time of his arrival,
almost utterly devoid of an
artistic tradition. It may
well be that he was the
earliest artist of note to
work in the city. (LEFT)

NICOLAS POUSSIN
Rest on the Flight into Egypt
OIL ON OAK PANEL, 46 x 31cm (18⅛ x 12¼in)
Monaco FF3,663,000 (£449,400:$672,100).
2.VII.93

Until the recent reappearance of this
work (for which previously only
photographs were available) its
attribution to Poussin was disputed. The
evidence provided by the painting itself,
however, leaves no doubt that this is an
important early work by the master
dating from around 1627, the same time
as the celebrated painting, the *Death of
Germanicus*. Undoubtedly painted in
Rome, the style of the work is vigorous,
direct and yet romantic, for the painter
was clearly still preoccupied with the
breadth and warmth of the art of
Renaissance Venice. (RIGHT)

LAURENT DE LA HYRE
Landscape with Two Women at a Fountain
SIGNED AND DATED *1653*, OIL ON CANVAS,
63.5 x 88.3cm (25 x 34¾in)
New York $415,000 (£266,026). 20.V.93
From the Estate of Paul Henreid

Laurent de la Hyre has been considered
a quintessential Parisian artist of the first
half of the seventeenth century despite
the fact that he did not study with
Vouet, the leading painter of the day.
He received sacred commissions from
the Capucins and the Jacobins and, by
the mid 1630s, Cardinal Richelieu had
become his fervent protector. This work
is a major addition to his late œuvre – a
time when his attention was turning
increasingly to landscape. It reveals the
artist gently eliminating traces of the
'literary' and concentrating instead on
the 'natural', absorbing the lessons of
the Parisian community in Rome
(especially Claude), but allying them
with a direct feeling for nature. (BELOW)

ANASTASIO FONTEBUONI
Troilo Orsini, who brings Aid from Cosimo I de' Medici for King Charles IX
OIL ON CANVAS, 179 x 245.5cm (70½ x 96¾in). London £1,651,500 ($2,493,700) for seven paintings. 21.IV.93

This is one of a series of paintings commissioned by Marie de' Medici in 1623 for the *Cabinet Doré* of the Luxembourg Palace in Paris. Following Henri IV's death in 1610, Marie had acted as Regent for their eldest son until he was able to assume the throne in 1617 as Louis XIII. By 1623, following a period of exile, Marie was anxious to re-establish her position. Her plans for the decoration of the Palace were intended to help achieve this and to serve as a reminder of France's debts to the Medici. The series was to be a history of the Medici family, seen in terms of the marriages that had allied it to various European royal families. The pictures, by several Florentine artists, were delivered to Paris by the end of 1627. In 1803 seven of them were bought by the Earl of Elgin and removed to Fife, where they stayed until this sale. (ABOVE)

JUAN DE ARELLANO
Still Life of Flowers
in a Basket
SIGNED, OIL ON CANVAS,
81.9 x 102.9cm (32¼ x 40½in)
New York $1,102,500 (£706,731).
20.V.93.

Juan de Arellano was the
most important painter of
floral still lifes in Spain in the
seventeenth century. His
fame was considerable during
his own lifetime, most of
which he spent in Madrid.

The present work, dating
from 1670-6, is undoubtedly
among the finest of its kind.

It is possible that it was
conceived as one of a series of
floral still lifes. (RIGHT)

JAN DAVIDSZ. DE HEEM
Still Life with Grapes,
Peaches, Oysters and a
Glass of Wine
SIGNED, OIL ON PANEL,
39.7 x 47cm (15⅝ x 18½in) New York
$1,542,500 (£1,008,170). 15.I.93

Although there is a dearth of
dated works by de Heem after
1655, it is likely that this
painting was executed in the
early 1670s. The artist was
born in Utrecht, where he
studied under Balthasar van
der Ast. He is renowned for
sumptuous flower pieces and
large compositions of richly
laid tables which exude the
full opulence of Flemish
Baroque painting. (BELOW)

JACOB VAN HULSDONCK
**Still Life of Oranges,
Lemons and
Pomegranates in a
Blue and White Bowl**
SIGNED, OIL ON PANEL,
32 x 42.5cm (12½ x 16⅝in)
Amsterdam Dfl759,000
(£279,000:$421,600). 11.XI.92
This work had been in the
possession of the family
who consigned it to
Sotheby's for sale since at
least the beginning of the
century. Its directness and
immediacy are beautifully
complemented by the
intimacy of its small scale.
(RIGHT)

PHILIPS DE KONINCK
**A Panoramic River
Landscape**
SIGNED AND DATED *164...*,
OIL ON CANVAS, 86 x 121cm
(33 x 47½in) London £990,000
($1,554,300). 9.XII.92
From the Collection of the
Rt Hon. the Earl Mountbatten
of Burma.
It is possible that Philips
de Koninck was a pupil
of Rembrandt in Amster-
dam. His panoramas
convey a unique vision of
his native land, in which
towns, villages, rivers and
signs of human activity
are encompassed in a
broad sweep. (BELOW)

FRANÇOIS BOUCHER
The Marriage of Cupid and Psyche
OIL ON PAPER LAID ON CANVAS, 44.8 x 56.8cm (17½ x 22¼in)
London £221,500 ($332,200). 7.VII.93

The story of Cupid and Psyche was very popular among Italian Renaissance artists, and its high drama contributed to a vogue for the theme in eighteenth-century France. In 1744, Boucher executed a painting of *The Marriage of Cupid and Psyche* (recently acquired for the Louvre) for which this picture would appear to be a preparatory oil sketch. (RIGHT)

GIOVANNI ANTONIO CANALE, CALLED CANALETTO
A View of Riva degli Schiavoni, Venice, Looking East
OIL ON CANVAS, 57.2 x 92.7cm (22½ x 36½in)
New York $2,642,500 (£1,693,910). 20.V.93

This panoramic work by Canaletto is one of only two known depictions of this view in which both the column of the Lion of Saint Mark and that of Saint Theodore appear. Only in this canvas, however, did Canaletto depict work in progress on the *fondamenta* in the foreground. It has been suggested that the painting dates from the late 1730s. (BELOW)

FRANCISCO DE GOYA
Bullfight. Suerte de Varas
OIL ON CANVAS, 50 x 60cm (19¾ x 23½in) London £4,950,000 ($7,771,500). 9.XII.92
From the Collection of Marquesa de la Gándara.

With the restoration of King Ferdinand VII of Spain in November 1823, Goya felt politically insecure and, in June 1824 at the age of 78, moved to Paris, where he executed this important work. The composition echoes that of one of the prints in his *Tauromaquia* series, issued in 1816. The bull has gored two horses and now stands impassively in the arena, eyeing the picador whose own horse has a gaping wound. X-rays have revealed that originally the horse was blindfolded, as in the *Tauromaquia* print; Goya's decision to paint out the bandage has heightened the poignancy of the physical encounter between these two animals. The freedom of Goya's technique in this work, using a palette knife as well as a brush (and maybe even his fingers and a rag), reveals an extraordinarily modern sensibility. The work is a formidable demonstration of the artist's creativity at the end of a long and courageous career. (ABOVE)

OLD MASTER DRAWINGS

JEAN-BAPTISTE GREUZE
The Departure for the Wet-Nurse
BLACK AND GREY INK AND WASH
OVER BLACK CHALK,
38.4 x 50.7cm (15⅛ x 20in)
New York $151,000 (£97,419).
13.I.93

This impressive work is characteristic of Greuze's genre and moralizing subjects. The topic of wet-nurses and the raising of children was hotly discussed in eighteenth-century France. This drawing is a study for one of a series of paintings the artist intended to execute, but never completed.
(RIGHT)

JEAN-HONORÉ FRAGONARD
The Garden of an Italian Villa with a Gardener and Two Children Playing
BROWN WASH OVER BLACK CHALK,
33.8 x 45.1cm (13½ x 18in)
New York $343,500 (£221,600).
13.I.93

This drawing is likely to have been made during or soon after Fragonard's second Italian journey of 1773-4, a period considered to be a watershed in the artist's career. In this work Fragonard reveals himself to be preoccupied with atmospheric effects, built up through tones of wash.
(BELOW)

BENOZZO GOZZOLI
Study of a male nude
PEN AND BROWN INK
ON PAPER WASHED PINK,
diameter 9.3cm (3⅝in)
London £28,750 ($43,400). 5.VII.93

Drawings by Gozzoli appear very rarely on the market and it has not been possible to connect this drawing with a surviving work or even be sure for what purpose it might have been intended. The naturalism of the figure suggests that it was drawn from life, while the refined facial type is one that can be seen in a number of the artist's works. (ABOVE)

**PAOLO CALIARI, CALLED
IL VERONESE**
The Rest on the Flight into Egypt
BROWN WASH HEIGHTENED WITH
WHITE ON PAPER WASHED BLUE-GREY,
40.8 x 41.8cm (16 x 16⅜in)
London £177,500 ($268,000).
5.VII.93

Veronese made a large number of *chiaroscuro* drawings that are generally complete compositions and are thought to have been executed as independent works rather than as preparatory studies for paintings. Many may have been kept in the artist's studio for the use of his pupils and so their dating is problematic; they are, nevertheless, highly prized by collectors. (LEFT)

BRITISH PICTURES 1500 – 1850

POMPEO BATONI
Portrait of Sir Charles Watson, Bt
SIGNED AND DATED *1775*,
OIL ON CANVAS,
97 x 73.5cm (38¼ x 29in)
London £463,500
($690,600).14.VII.93
Batoni was one of the most successful (and ostentatious) painters of the eighteenth-century Roman School. He executed a large number of religious and mythological pieces, but achieved greatest renown for his portraits of British nobility making the Grand Tour. The sitter in this work, who is wearing van Dyck dress, was the son of Vice-Admiral Charles Watson, former Commander-in-Chief of the Fleet in the East Indies. (LEFT)

WILLEM WISSING
Portrait of Queen Anne, when Princess of Denmark
SIGNED AND DATED *1687*, OIL ON CANVAS, 124.5 x 101cm (49 x 39¾in)
London £54,300 ($80,900). 14.VII.93

Having studied and worked in Holland, Wissing came to London to work in Lely's studio in 1676. On Lely's death in 1680 he took over much of his master's thriving and fashionable practice. The sitter in this work, the future Queen Anne, was the second daughter of James II. In 1683 she married Prince George of Denmark, and bore him seventeen children, only one of which – William, Duke of Gloucester – survived infancy. She succeeded the throne on the death of William III in 1702. (ABOVE)

SIR PETER LELY
Portrait of Mary II, when Princess of Orange
OIL ON CANVAS, 214.5 x 99cm (49 x 39in)
London £54,300 ($80,900). 14.VII.93

Lely came to London from the Low Countries in around 1643 and by 1650 he had built up a considerable practice as a portrait painter. At the Restoration in 1660 he became Principal Painter to Charles II. He was knighted in 1679 and died a year later. The sitter of this work, the future Mary II, was the eldest daughter of James II. In 1677 she married William of Orange and moved to Holland. In 1689 James II fled the kingdom, leaving no male heir, and William and Mary were invited to rule jointly in his place. (ABOVE)

WILLIAM ASHFORD
Carton, the seat of the Duke of Leinster – a horse-drawn carriage crossing the bridge
SIGNED AND DATED *1779*, OIL ON CANVAS, 110 x 150cm (43 x 59in)
London £84,000 ($125,100). 14.VII.93

Although commissioned by the 2nd Duke of Leinster, this painting testifies to the extraordinary creation at Carton of his father James, 20th Earl of Kildare and 1st Duke of Leinster (1722-73), and his wife Emily. It was they who, in the 1750s and 60s, transformed the formal gardens into a vast picturesque landscape. Amongst other improvements, a series of dams was built to create a lake and serpentine river. Other features included a shell house, an ornamental bridge and an ornamental dairy. (ABOVE)

THOMAS GAINSBOROUGH
Portrait of Peter Darnal Muilman, Charles Crockatt and William Keeble
OIL ON CANVAS, 75 x 62cm (29½ x 24½in) London £1,079,500 ($1,608,400). 14.VII.93

This fine conversation piece, dating from around 1753-55 when the artist was still in his early twenties, represents an ideal fusion of portraiture and landscape. It is one of a very small group of portraits of local friends and landowners which Gainsborough painted in his native Suffolk shortly after his return from London in 1748; portraits in which his natural gifts are shown unclouded by the requirements of fashion. While in London the artist had studied the works of the great Dutch seventeenth-century naturalistic painters, whose influence can be detected in parts of this work. (RIGHT)

JOHN FERNELEY, SNR
**Lord Robert Manners, Lord Charles and the
5th Duke of Rutland hunting at Belvoir Castle**
SIGNED AND DATED *1838*, OIL ON CANVAS, 89 x 142.4cm (35 x 55¼in)
London £132,400 ($198,600). 6.IV.93
In 1814, John Ferneley set up a succesful practice at
Elgin Lodge in Melton Mowbray, painting society figures
who hunted with the Quorn and the Belvoir. (RIGHT)

SIR EDWIN HENRY LANDSEER
**Alpine Mastiffs Reanimating
a Distressed Traveller**
OIL ON CANVAS, 188 x 236cm (74 x 93in)
New York $525,000 (£347,600). 4.VI.93
Property of the Warner Collection of Gulf States Paper Corporation
This work of 1820, when Landseer was 18, was his most
ambitious picture to date, and was rapturously received at
its exhibition at the British Institution. (BELOW)

BRITISH WATERCOLOURS

SAMUEL PALMER
Oxen Ploughing at Sunset
SIGNED, WATERCOLOUR OVER PENCIL AND RED CHALK,
39.5 x 27cm (15½ x 10½in)
London £60,500 ($90,150). 15.VII.93

The distant mountains in this watercolour of 1863 are reminiscent of the Apennines, through which Palmer and his wife travelled on their honeymoon in Italy in 1837-9. The classically composed figure of the woman with an earthenware vase on her head on the right of the work is probably based on the antique gem carvings in which Palmer was interested.

The composition of the piece is one that Palmer returned to many times in later work, and close comparisons can be made with etchings such as *The Morning Spread upon the Mountains* and *The Early Ploughman*. (RIGHT)

JOSEPH MALLORD WILLIAM TURNER
Lichfield, Staffordshire
WATERCOLOUR, 28.6 x 43.8cm (11 x 17in)
London £187,000 ($286,000). 19.XI 92

The first of Turner's works to be exhibited at the Royal Academy, in 1790, was a watercolour, and it was for his work in this medium that the artist first achieved public acclaim. *Lichfield, Staffordshire* dates from between 1830 and 1835, when Turner's popularity was at its zenith, and shows Lichfield Cathedral from the south-west. This work was intended to form part of the *Picturesque Views in England and Wales*, the most important series of engravings with which Turner was involved. The series was commissioned from the artist by Charles Heath in 1825, though was not completed until 1837. (ABOVE)

JOHN ROBERT COZENS
Vesuvius from Sir William Hamilton's Villa at Portici
WATERCOLOUR OVER PENCIL, 36 x 52.5cm (14¼ x 20⅝in)
London £140,600 ($209,000). 15.VII.93

The majority of John Robert Cozens' watercolours are connected with the journeys
he made to Switzerland and Italy between 1776 and 1783. He did not confine
himself to topographical exactitude and often transposed landscape features in the
interests of a more lyrical composition. Some of his Italian travels were made in the
company of William Beckford, whom Alexander Cozens, John's father, had once
instructed. It was Beckford who introduced John Cozens to Sir William Hamilton.
This work is based on a drawing made in August 1783. (ABOVE)

THOMAS GAINSBOROUGH
Wooded Landscape with Drover and Packhorses
SIGNED, WATERCOLOUR AND
BODYCOLOUR OVER PENCIL,
28.3 x 34.2 cm (11¼ x 13½in)
London £88,000 ($134,500). 19.XI.92

It was between 1760 and 1774, during his sojourn in Bath, that Gainsborough used watercolour most extensively, turning to the local countryside for inspiration. This drawing, which dates from around 1765 and comes from a group of presentation drawings probably intended for sale, was first owned by the Hon. Mrs Graham, a famous beauty whose portrait Gainsborough painted many times. It is a fine example of the artist's increasing interest in *chiaroscuro* and the effects of light on his subject.
(LEFT)

JOHN CONSTABLE
Helmingham Dell, Suffolk
PENCIL AND GREY WASHES,
53.3 x 66.4cm (21 x 26⅛ in)
London £98,000 ($147,000). 1.IV.93

In 1800, the year in which this drawing was executed, Helmingham Hall in Suffolk was the seat of Wilbraham Tollemache, 6th Earl of Dysart. Constable was not introduced to the Earl until 1807 and it therefore seems that this work was not linked to any commission. The dell is still identifiable, although the wooden footbridge was replaced by a stone bridge in 1815. Constable executed a number of drawings at Helmingham Park, this work being on a far more ambitious scale than the others. It was to form the basis for four oil versions of the subject, one of which is now in the Louvre.
(RIGHT)

BRITISH PICTURES FROM 1850

SIR FRANK DICKSEE
The Mirror
SIGNED AND DATED *1896*,
OIL ON CANVAS,
95.3 x 118.1cm (37½x 46½in)
New York $725,000
(£467,700). 17.II.93

This work was exhibited
to considerable critical
acclaim at the Royal
Academy in 1896, and
shows Dicksee's passion
for the contemporary
taste amongst London
artists for exotic subjects.
It also displays his
virtuoso handling of
texture, not least in the
depiction of the mother-
of-pearl inlay that
embellishes the sitter's
silver throne. (RIGHT)

SIR FRANK DICKSEE
Leila
SIGNED AND DATED *1892*,
OIL ON CANVAS,
101.5 x 127cm (40 x 50in)
London £793,500 ($1,190,200).
8.VI.93

In 1905 Dicksee's
biographer Dibdin
wrote of his subject's
'lovingly elaborated
decoration of surfaces'
and his 'delight in rich
colour combinations'.
No work demonstrates
this more eloquently than
Leila. The subject of the
work is the heroine of the
Arabian love story
Layla and Majnun, which
dates from the seventh
century AD. (LEFT)

SIR EDWARD COLEY BURNE-JONES
Portrait of Amy Gaskell
SIGNED AND DATED *1893*, OIL ON CANVAS, 96.5 x 52cm (38 x 20½in)
London £496,500 ($744,700). 8.VI.93

Amy Gaskell was the daughter of Helen Mary Gaskell,
with whom in 1892 Burne-Jones entered into a close
friendship. This sombre portrait was first exhibited at
the New Gallery, London, in 1894, and was seized
upon by the critic of *The Art Journal* as 'one of the
most masterly works produced by this artist'. The
picture was sold with letters from Burne-Jones to Amy
Gaskell containing his plans for the portrait. (BELOW)

DANTE GABRIEL ROSSETTI
La Ghirlandata
SIGNED AND DATED *1873*, COLOURED CHALKS, 90.5 x 76cm (35½ x 30in)
London £463,500 ($695,200). 8.VI.93

La Ghirlandata is literally 'she who is adorned with garlands of flowers'. The drawing
was executed at Kelmscott Manor in the summer of 1873 as the cartoon for Rossetti's
oil painting of the same title, now in the Guildhall Art Gallery, London. The sitter
was Alexa Wilding, and William Morris's daughter May appears twice in the picture
(as both angels). Rossetti seems to have worked further on the drawing after the
painting was completed. (ABOVE)

EDWARD LEAR
The Pyramids Road, Giza
SIGNED AND DATED *1873*, OIL ON CANVAS, 53 x 104cm (21 x 41in)
London £232,500 ($348,700). 8.VI.93

In his diary entry for 14 October 1872 Lear described the scene depicted in this painting: 'Nothing in all life is so amazingly interesting as this new road & avenue – literally all the way to the Pyramids.... The effect of this causeway in the middle of wide waters is singular... & were one sure of quiet, there is much of poetry in the scene, but it wants thought and arrangement.' The avenue of trees that lined the Pyramids Road had been planted three years earlier to celebrate Empress Eugenie's visit for the opening of the Suez Canal. (ABOVE)

DAVID ROBERTS
The Island of Philae, Nubia
SIGNED AND DATED *1843*, OIL ON CANVAS, 77 x 153.5cm (30¼ x 60in) London £177,500 ($266,250). 8.VI.93

David Roberts was the first British oil painter of any standing to travel up the Nile. He landed at Alexandria on 24 September 1833, and a fortnight later was on his way up the river, writing in his journal 'I am the first artist at least from England who has been here and there is much in this.' He returned home in July 1839, having traversed Egypt, the Holy Land, Syria and the Lebanon. By that time he had 272 sketches and three full sketchbooks, one of the single greatest bodies of work from any artist's journey. (LEFT)

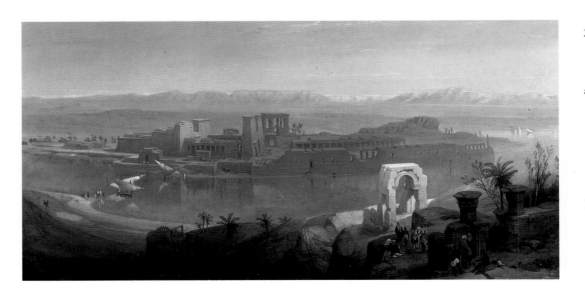

ARCHIBALD THORBURN
Voices of the Forest – Red Deer
SIGNED AND DATED *1912*, WATERCOLOUR, 53.5 x 74cm (21 x 29¼in)
London £69,500 ($102,500). 31.III.93
From the collection of the Thorburn Museum

Like many painters of his time, Thorburn was the son
of an artist. His father Robert, a successful miniaturist
patronized by Queen Victoria, was his first teacher
and a stern critic. (RIGHT)

ARCHIBALD THORBURN
Woodcock and Chicks
SIGNED AND DATED *1932*, WATERCOLOUR, 19 x 28cm (7½ x 11in)
London £30,000 ($44,500). 31.III.93
From the collection of the Thorburn Museum

In 1930 Thorburn underwent an operation for cancer
and his final years were accompanied by almost
continuous pain. The work of those years was gentler
and on a smaller scale, often repeating the theme of
hen birds and their young. (BELOW)

ARCHIBALD THORBURN
The Close of a Winter's Day
SIGNED AND DATED *1905*, WATERCOLOUR, 67.5 x 161cm (26½ x 63½in)
London £100,500 ($148,500). 31.III.93
From the collection of the Thorburn Museum

The Close of a Winter's Day is generally considered to be one of Thorburn's finest
achievements and took three weeks to complete. He generally worked at an amazing
pace, rising early and preceding his labours with a cold bath, a bowl of porridge oats
and a walk in his garden in Hascombe, Surrey, where he moved in 1902. (BELOW)

MODERN BRITISH PAINTING

SIR WILLIAM ORPEN
The Roscommon Dragoon
SIGNED, OIL ON CANVAS, 76 x 63.5cm (30 x 25in)
London £139,000 ($209,800). 30.VI.93

Painted in 1913, this work and its companion piece, *The Irish Volunteer*, are generally considered to be the artist's two most famous portraits. They are the culmination of a series of pictures of Vera Hone, a celebrated beauty of the time. *The Roscommon Dragoon* shows the sitter dressed in an Armagh Infantry militia tunic, evoking the sort of Irish stock figure which Orpen had portrayed in a number of earlier self-portraits. (ABOVE)

SIR ALFRED MUNNINGS
Dragoon Guard on a Dappled Horse, facing left
(one of a pair)
SIGNED, OIL ON CANVAS, 81.3 x 69.9cm (32 x 27½in)
New York $288,500 (£191,000) for the pair. 4.VI.93
Property of Senator John W. Warner

This is one of a pair of canvases of the same subject (the other is a view from the back of the dragoon). Munnings' skill in the traditional specialization of horse portraiture brought him considerable fame and success with the British public and the London art establishment, and in 1944 he was elected President of the Royal Academy. (ABOVE)

GRAHAM SUTHERLAND
Palm Palisade
SIGNED AND DATED *1948*, OIL ON CANVAS, 112 x 90cm (44 x 35½in)
London £74,800 ($166,600). 4.XI.92

In 1947 the artist visited the South of France, returning every
summer thereafter. The luxuriant flora of the area transformed his
work, allowing the introduction of new local subjects – palm fronds,
vine trellises, banana leaves and cicadas – and a fresh palette: hot
pinks, reds, yellows and vibrant acidic greens applied straight from
the tube. As Sutherland turned to these new tones, his forms became
simpler with the picture plane flattening dramatically. This was
also the period when he began to invest organic forms with a
quasi-mechanistic quality. (ABOVE)

SIR STANLEY SPENCER
The Temptation of Saint Anthony
OIL ON CANVAS, 122 x 91.5cm (48 x 36in)
London £297,000 ($463,300). 4.XI.92

Executed in 1945, this painting was the result of a competition run
by an American film studio to find a picture on the theme of Saint
Anthony to appear in the film of Maupassant's novel *Bel Ami*. Eleven
artists took part, including Dali, Delvaux and Ernst. The subject
matter, with its story of self-denial and chastity, was radically
reworked by Spencer: those from whom the saint turns away are seen
not as evil, but as representative of the artist's philosophy of free love
uniting Man, Woman and God. Elements of this painting, including
the thinly applied pale colours, mark it as the first of Spencer's late
works, prefiguring some of the great pictures of the 1950s. (ABOVE)

NINETEENTH–CENTURY EUROPEAN PAINTINGS

JOAQUIN SOROLLA Y BASTIDA
Oxen in the Sea, study for *Afternoon Sun*
SIGNED AND DATED *1902*, OIL ON CANVAS, 96 x 135.5cm (37¾ x 53¼in)
London £848,500 ($1,272,750).16.VI.93

From 1900 onwards Sorolla abandoned painting for the Salons and International
Exhibitions, looked to Velázquez for inspiration and began work on large outdoor
canvases that display broad, vigorous brushwork. This work is the most important of
the artist's preparatory pieces for his famous *Sol de Tarde* (Afternoon Sun), from
1903, now with the Hispanic Society of America in New York. It is widely agreed
that these paintings mark the point at which Sorolla achieved the pinnacle of his
artistic development. (ABOVE)

JEAN-AUGUSTE-DOMINIQUE INGRES
Don Pedro of Toledo Kissing the Sword of King Henry IV
SIGNED AND DATED *1820*, OIL ON PANEL, 48 x 40cm (19 x 15¾in) London £628,500 ($942,750). 16.VI.93

Ingres was greatly inspired by the figure of Henry IV and planned to illustrate many episodes from his life. This is one of four versions of the subject, dating from 1814 to 1831. The 1814 version is now lost; the 1819 version is in a private collection in France; and the 1831 version is in the Louvre. The appearance at auction of this work, from 1820, was a rare event. (ABOVE)

Jean-Léon Gérôme
La Reception de Condé à Versailles
SIGNED, OIL ON CANVAS, 96.5 x 139.7cm (38 x 55in)
New York $800,000 (£516,129). 26.V.93

In November 1674 the Duke of Condé was received in great honour by Louis XIV at the Palace of Versailles. Infirm from an attack of gout, Condé paused on his way up the stairs, for which the king excused him: 'Do not hurry yourself, cousin. It is not surprising that you can scarcely walk, loaded as you are with laurels.' In executing this work, Gérôme was realizing a long-held ambition to illustrate the anecdote and was undoubtedly proud of the result. He wrote: 'I have worked upon it without intermission to reach the desired end.' (ABOVE)

William Adolphe Bouguereau
The Virgin, Child and Saint John the Baptist
SIGNED AND DATED *1875*, OIL ON CANVAS,
200.7 x 121.9cm (79 x 48in)
New York $690,000 (£445,161). 26.V.93

To the studied synthesis of Byzantine and High Renaissance elements in this important work, Bouguereau brings a sculptural consciousness recalling the forms of Michelangelo and Bernini. The artist balances the rigid symmetry of the architectural background with flowing linear arabesques and, from a psychological point of view, the innocence and joy of the children with the Virgin's expression of melancholy and foreboding. (LEFT)

JAMES-JACQUES-JOSEPH
TISSOT
La Mondaine
SIGNED, OIL ON CANVAS,
147.3 x 101.6cm (58 x 40in)
New York $1,982,500
(£1,295,700). 17.II.93
From the Joey and Toby
Tanenbaum Collection

From 1882 to 1885
Tissot executed fifteen
large canvases, *La
Femme à Paris*, that
illustrate *parisiennes*
of various classes at
their vocations and
amusements. Common
to this series was the
emphasis on fashion,
beauty and the
increasingly complex role
of women in society.
Such scenes of modern
life were intended to
attract wealthy art
patrons of the *haute
bourgeoisie* and the risqué
subject matter of this
canvas may have been
calculated to quicken the
pulse of the elderly art
buyer. (LEFT)

IMPRESSIONIST AND MODERN ART

PIERRE-AUGUSTE RENOIR
Femmes dans un Jardin
SIGNED, OIL ON CANVAS, 54.6 x 65.4cm (21½ x 25¾in) New York $6,712,500 (£4,358,700). 11.V.93
Renoir and Monet worked together frequently in 1872-3, and the extent of Monet's influence is shown
clearly in this work of 1873 in the dominance of landscape over figures. The force of this work lies in the
dramatic brushwork: quick dashes of paint describe the flowers reflecting in the sun, long drags of wet
pigment form the trees, dark pigments crushed into the surface create the deep recesses and a brilliant
daub of pure white depicts the sun glinting off the white parasol. (ABOVE)

PAUL CÉZANNE
Nature Morte: les Grosses Pommes
SIGNED, OIL ON CANVAS, 45.7 x 54cm (18 x 21¼in) New York $28,602,500 (£18,573,000). 11.V.93

'Cézanne made a living thing out of a teacup or, rather, in a teacup he realized the existence of something alive. He raised still life to the point where it ceased to be inanimate. He painted things as he painted human beings.... He achieved expressive colour and a form that harmonizes this colour with an almost mathematical abstraction. A man, a tree, an apple are not represented but used by Cézanne in building up a painterly thing called a "picture".' (Wassily Kandinsky, *Concerning the Spiritual in Art*, 1912.) (ABOVE)

AUGUSTE RODIN
Eve
WHITE MARBLE, height 76cm (30in)
London £429,000 ($664,900). 1.XII.92

This figure was conceived as one of a pair (with Adam)
to flank the *Gates of Hell,* a vast Romantic creation for
the Musée des Arts Décoratifs that took over twenty
years to complete. It was first executed in a life-size
version, but it was the half-size reduction that was
exhibited publicly and quickly became one of Rodin's
most popular works. The model was Mme Abruzzezzi,
whom Rodin described – literally – in glowing terms:
'The dark one had sunburned skin, warm, with the
bronze reflections of the women of sunny lands... and
that perfect equilibrium, that simplicity of bearing
which makes great gesture.' (RIGHT)

CLAUDE MONET
Femme à l'Ombrelle
SIGNED, BLACK CRAYON WITH *GRATTAGE,* 30.5 x 23.5cm (12 x 9¼in)
London £353,500 ($537,300). 22.VI.93
From the Collection of Marie-Louise Durand-Ruel.

This sensitive drawing of 1890 is a *reprise* after Monet's
painting *Essai de Figure en Plein Air (vers la droite)* of
1886, and was commissioned by Paul Durand-Ruel to
accompany Octave Mirbeau's article on Monet in
L'Art dans les Deux Mondes, 7 March 1891. Independent drawings are rare in Monet's œuvre, and the
majority were made after paintings for publication in
journals. The subject had a special significance for the
artist as the model was Suzanne Hoschedé-Butler, his
step-daughter and favourite model, who died in 1899
at the age of 33. Monet kept the painting in her
memory until his own death in 1926. (FAR RIGHT)

WASSILY KANDINSKY
Sketch 1 for Composition VII
SIGNED AND DATED *1913*, OIL ON CANVAS, 78 x 100cm (30¾ x 39⅜in) London £5,500,000 ($8,525,000). 1.XII.92

Executed in Munich in November 1913, this painting is the most definitive of six oil studies for *Composition VII* (Tretiakov Gallery, Moscow), considered to be the most important of the artist's pre-War works. From 1911 until 1933, Kandinsky shared a close friendship with the artist Paul Klee, and they frequently exchanged paintings. *Sketch I* was given to Klee in around 1925, and had remained in the Klee family until this sale. (BELOW)

HENRI MATISSE
L'Asie
SIGNED AND DATED *46*, OIL ON CANVAS, 116.2 x 81.3cm (45¾ x 32in) New York $11,000,000 (£7,284,700). 10.XI.92
From the Estate of Mollie Parnis Livingston.

L'Asie was painted in Vence in 1946. The orientalizing arabesques evoke the exotic subjects of Matisse's Moroccan period of 1911-12. As in many of the artist's late works, the light emanates directly from the brilliance of the colour, the perspective being flattened out to obtain decorative, semi-abstracted qualities from the image. (RIGHT)

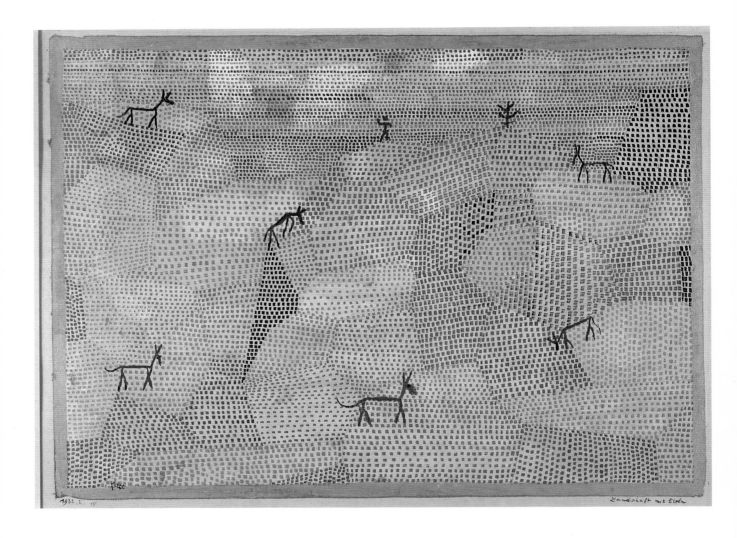

PAUL KLEE
Landschaft mit Eseln
SIGNED AND DATED *1932*, PENCIL, WATERCOLOUR AND GOUACHE ON COTTON, 41.4 x 55.6cm (16¼ x 21⅞in)
London £1,013,500 ($1,489,800). 22.VI.93
This painting is from a series of works by Klee of the early 1930s, executed in a
method the artist described as 'so-called pointillism'. The colours and imagery loosely
refer to Klee's visit to Egypt in the winter of 1928-29 and the work is in keeping with
the mysterious and poetic compositions that the artist produced during his period at
the Düsseldorf Academy. (ABOVE)

EGON SCHIELE
Youth in a Sailor Suit
SIGNED AND DATED *1914*,
WATERCOLOUR AND GOUACHE,
47.8 x 31.2cm (18 x 12¼in)
London £429,000 ($664,900).
1.XII.92

This work is thought to depict
Paul Erdmann, Schiele's
nephew. Erdmann appears in
a number of works of this
period, either alone or with
the artist's wife, Edith. Jane
Kallir has pointed out that
'the drawings of Edith with
her nephew, Paul Erdmann,
achieve an unprecedented and
bizarre degree of erotic
ambiguity. At times the
Edith/Egon representations
seem to merge with the
Edith/Paul pictures, and it is
impossible to be sure who the
subjects are.' In this work,
however, Erdmann is alone
and Schiele seems more
interested in the youthful
contraposto of the child's body
than in its erotic charge.
(RIGHT)

WASSILY KANDINSKY
Milieu Accompagné (Centre with Accompaniment)
SIGNED WITH THE MONOGRAM AND DATED *37*, OIL ON CANVAS, 114 x 146cm (44⅞ x 57½in)
London £3,026,500 ($4,600,200). 22.VI.93
From the Collection of Monsieur and Madame Adrien Maeght

When the Nazis closed the Bauhaus in 1933 Kandinsky moved to Paris, where he
joined a number of artist friends, including Arp, Duchamp, Ray and Miró. One of
Kandinsky's finest paintings of this period, *Milieu Accompagné* testifies to the artist's
closeness to Miró, whose contemporary work undoubtedly helped to suggest the
stylized organic forms floating across the plane of the picture surface. (BELOW)

HENRI MATISSE
La Mulâtresse Fatma
OIL ON CANVAS, 146.1 x 61cm (57½ x 24in)
New York $14,302,500 (£9,287,300). 11.V.93
From the Collection formed by Joseph Müller

This work was painted on the second of two trips
to Morocco. The first, in the early part of 1912, had
been marred by bad weather, but Matisse returned
in October the same year to stay for four months.
His fascination with Morocco, which had a lasting
influence on his work, was due in part to the artist's
admiration for the painter Eugène Delacroix, who
had visited the country in 1832. *La Mulâtresse Fatma*
can be seen as a direct descendant of the work of the
Orientalist painters of the nineteenth century. The
artist used a number of models while in Morocco,
of whom Fatma was perhaps the least favourite –
he found her 'irritating'. (LEFT)

PAUL DELVAUX
La Joie de Vivre
SIGNED AND DATED *1–38*,
OIL ON CANVAS,
101.5 x 120cm (40 x 47¼in)
London £1,013,500
($1,540,500).22.VI.93
Painted a year after the death of the artist's father and in the first year of his marriage to Suzanne Purnal, this painting has an audacity and directness in its imagery that mark a new phase in the artist's work. The barriers of non-communication between the sexes, so apparent in Delvaux's earlier work, are beginning to be demolished: the naked woman and dark-suited man – both recurrent Delvaux images – here touch as they have never done before. (LEFT)

SALVADOR DALI
La Montre Molle
SIGNED AND DATED *49*,
OIL ON CANVAS,
21 x 25.4cm (8¼ x 10in)
New York $662,500 (£430,100).
11.V.93
This is surely one of the most widely known images to have been created by this most successful of surrealist painters. Dali's 'soft watch' imagery is best known from his masterpiece, *The Persistence of Memory* of 1931. *La Montre Molle* is a later variation of that work.
(RIGHT)

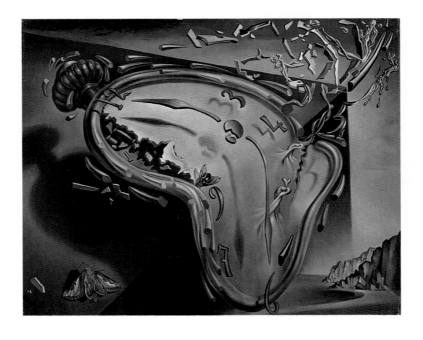

MAX ERNST
The King Playing with the Queen
INSCRIBED *Max Ernst*, BRONZE,
height 97.8cm (38½in)
New York $1,210,000
(£801,325). 10.XI.92
From the Collection of Mr and Mrs Joseph Randall Shapiro
This sculpture was executed in plaster in 1944 from which an edition of nine bronzes was cast. Ernst may have been influenced by native American art in his adoption of 'primitive', elemental forms. (RIGHT)

CONTEMPORARY ART

ROY LICHTENSTEIN
Girl with Piano
SIGNED AND DATED *63*, MAGNA ON CANVAS,
172.7 x 121.9cm (68 x 48in)
New York $1,815,000 (£1,194,079). 17.XI.92
This work is an early example of
Lichtenstein's famous cartoon
paintings, which are recognized as
major landmarks in the history of
American Pop Art, and can be
considered as distillations of the artist's
major artistic concerns. In common
with other Pop artists of the day,
Lichtenstein focused on the
transformation of objects from popular
culture into high art, employing a style
and medium directly related to
contemporary popular media. (RIGHT)

ANDY WARHOL
Marilyn x 100
SIGNED AND DATED *1962*, INK AND
SYNTHETIC POLYMER PAINT ON CANVAS,
205.7 x 567.7cm (81 x 223 ½ in)
New York $3,740,000 (£2,460,500). 17.XI.92
Marilyn x 100 is the largest version of
the artist's serial image of the movie
star. These posthumous portraits are
perhaps the most famous result of the
combination of Warhol's pioneering
use of the photographic silkscreen and
his discovery of media icons as subject
matter. It was the public viewing of
his first Marilyn paintings at the
Stable Gallery, New York, in
November 1962, which included this
work, that finally brought the artist
serious critical attention and
widespread recognition. (BELOW)

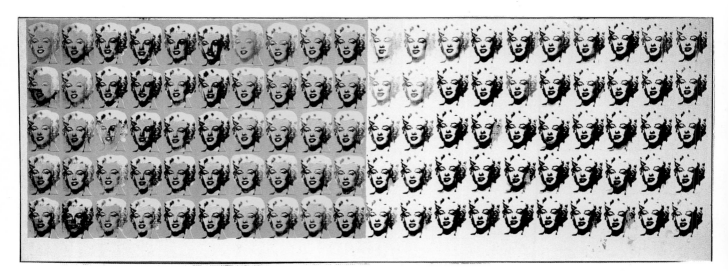

DAVID HOCKNEY
Henry Geldzahler and Christopher Scott, 1968-9
ACRYLIC ON CANVAS, 213.4 x 304.8cm (84 x 120in)
New York $1,100,000 (£723,684). 17.XI.92
From the collection of Mrs Harry N. Abrams and Mr Robert E. Abrams

Henry Geldzahler and Christopher Scott, 1968-9 is a double portrait of two of the
artist's closest friends. Having recently arrived in New York in 1964, Hockney had
attended a party at Andy Warhol's studio, where he met Geldzahler, a curator of
twentieth-century art at the Metropolitan Museum of Art, who was subsequently to
appear in a large number of the artist's sketches and paintings. Hockney was
intrigued by the pictorial possibilities of double portraits, and had just completed a
major work of Christopher Isherwood and Don Bachardy, a similarly grand and
rigorously symmetrical work. (ABOVE)

FRANCIS BACON
Study for a Portrait
OIL ON CANVAS,
51 x 41cm (20 x 16in)
London £562,500 ($826,800).
24.VI.93
This previously
unrecorded work is
closely related to a group
of four *Studies for a
Portrait* made in the
summer of 1952, which
were to lead to the
famous *Study for a
Portrait* of 1953 now in
the Kunsthalle in
Hamburg. The work does
not depict a specific
person; it is more a
statement about mankind
itself, where the figure
becomes a symbol of
human fate. Bacon once
said to David Sylvester:
'When I look at you
across the table I don't
only see you but I see a
whole emanation which
has to do with personality
and everything else. And
to put that over in a
painting... means that it
would appear violent in
paint.' (RIGHT)

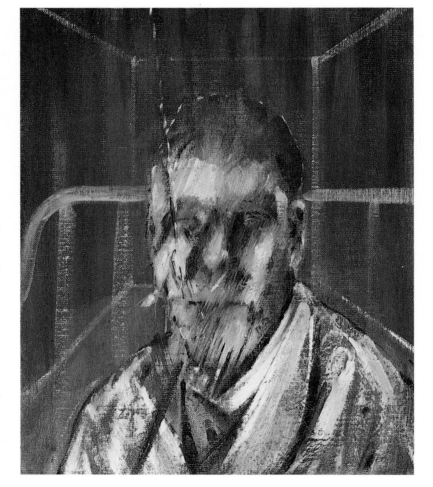

LEON KOSSOFF
**Children's
Swimming Pool,
11 O'Clock Saturday
Morning, August
1969**
SIGNED AND DATED *August 1969*,
OIL ON BOARD,
152.5 x 205cm (60 x 81in)
London £209,000 ($323,900).
3.XII.92
This work belongs to an
important series of
paintings from the late
1960s and early 70s, in
which the artist depicted
everyday places and
activities in order to seize
the beauty of ordinary
life. The influence of
Monet has been noted in
Kossoff's paintings of this
period, which can be seen
as true developments of
early Impressionism,
concentrating on the
importance of light and
its effect at specific times
of the day. (ABOVE)

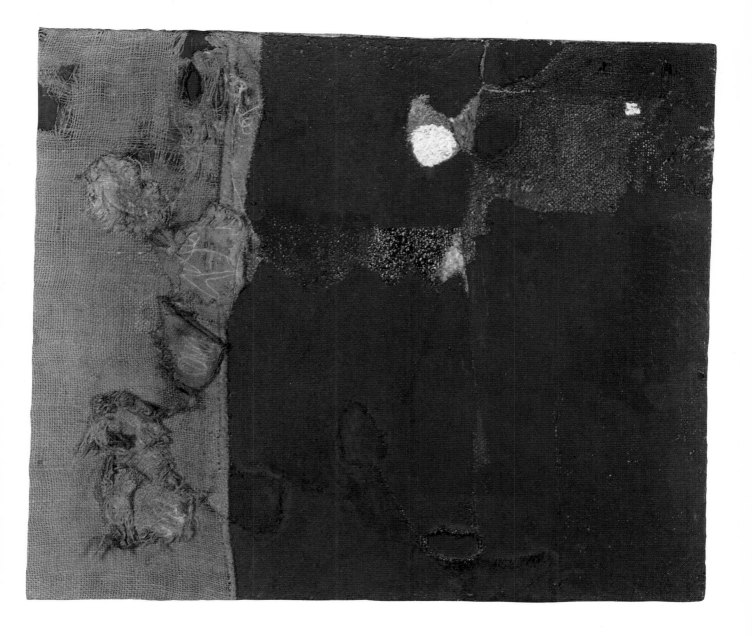

ALBERTO BURRI
Sacco e Oro
SIGNED AND DATED *Roma 53*, OIL, BURLAP AND GOLDLEAF, 86.4 x 101cm (34 x 39⅜in)
London £309,000 ($454,965). 24.VI.93
Burri first started to use old sacking in a prisoner-of-war camp, where it was the only material
available. It was then that he realized its capacity to stretch, its subtle variations of tone and
irregular texture, and began to sew the 'sacco' together in different patterns, as a surgeon would
sew wounds. (Burri had studied medicine before joining the Italian army.) *Sacco e Oro* belongs
to the celebrated group of *Sacchi*, in two of which gold is used as an additional medium,
in striking contrast to the background. (ABOVE)

GERHARD RICHTER
Neger (Nuba)
SIGNED, OIL ON CANVAS, 145 x 200cm (57⅛ x 78¾in)
London £320,500 ($471,100). 24.VI.93

Early in the 1960s Richter began using press photographs as the direct visual source for his
paintings, and those produced between 1962 and 1965 often openly display these origins, as
they include captions or margins. This canvas, painted in 1964, is one of a group of paintings
based on travel photographs (in the same year Richter also painted the Great Sphinx). Whereas
many of the early pictures are painted in monochromatic hues of grey, *Neger* employs a much
wider palette, a reflection of the artist's desire to 'add more to the painting'. (ABOVE)

ANSELM KIEFER
Dein Goldenes Haar, Margarethe!!
SIGNED AND DATED *1981*, OIL AND MIXED MEDIA ON BURLAP, 170 x 190cm (67 x 74in)
London £309,500 ($454,900). 24.VI.93
This work belongs to Kiefer's *Margarethe und Shulamith* series which was inspired by Paul
Celan's poem *Death Fugue*. The poem, which Celan wrote in a concentration camp in 1945,
contrasts Margarethe, the blond German, with the Jewish Shulamith – inseparably bound
together in the cycle of life and death. Kiefer chose to represent Margarethe through the
application of straw, reminiscent of her blonde hair, and the presence of the Jewish Shulamith
by the black shadows behind the straw. (ABOVE)

CY TWOMBLY
Untitled
SIGNED AND DATED *1956*, OIL, CRAYON AND PENCIL ON CANVAS, 117.5 x 175.3cm (46¼ x 69in)
New York $2,145,000 (£1,411,184). 17.XI.92
An outstanding example of Twombly's gestural paintings of the 1950s,
Untitled is characteristic of the artist's all-over compositions of linear 'writing'
on a luminous ground. (ABOVE)

BRUCE NAUMAN
One Hundred Live and Die, 1984
NEON TUBING MOUNTED ON FOUR PANELS, 299.7 x 335.9 x 53.3cm (118 x 132¼ x 21in)
New York $1,925,000 (£1,266,447). 17.XI.92
This is an extraordinarily ambitious neon sculpture comprising a list of a
hundred commands. The commands can be switched on and off to form
different visual arrangements and combinations of meaning. (RIGHT)

LIVE AND DIE
DIE AND DIE
SHIT AND DIE
PISS AND DIE
EAT AND DIE
SLEEP AND DIE
LOVE AND DIE
HATE AND DIE
FUCK AND DIE
SPEAK AND DIE
LIE AND DIE
HEAR AND DIE
CRY AND DIE
KISS AND DIE
RAGE AND DIE
LAUGH AND DIE
TOUCH AND DIE
FEEL AND DIE
FEAR AND DIE
SICK AND DIE
WELL AND DIE
BLACK AND DIE
WHITE AND DIE
RED AND DIE
YELLOW AND DIE
LIVE AND LIVE
DIE AND LIVE
SHIT AND LIVE
PISS AND LIVE
EAT AND LIVE
SLEEP AND LIVE
LOVE AND LIVE
HATE AND LIVE
FUCK AND LIVE
SPEAK AND LIVE
LIE AND LIVE
HEAR AND LIVE
CRY AND LIVE
KISS AND LIVE
RAGE AND LIVE
LAUGH AND LIVE
TOUCH AND LIVE
FEEL AND LIVE
FEAR AND LIVE
SICK AND LIVE
WELL AND LIVE
BLACK AND LIVE
WHITE AND LIVE
RED AND LIVE
YELLOW AND LIVE
SING AND DIE
SCREAM AND DIE
YOUNG AND DIE
OLD AND DIE
CUT AND DIE
RUN AND DIE
STAY AND DIE
PLAY AND DIE
KILL AND DIE
SUCK AND DIE
COME AND DIE
GO AND DIE
KNOW AND DIE
TELL AND DIE
SMELL AND DIE
FALL AND DIE
RISE AND DIE
STAND AND DIE
SIT AND DIE
SPIT AND DIE
TRY AND DIE
FAIL AND DIE
SMILE AND DIE
THINK AND DIE
PAY AND DIE
SING AND LIVE
SCREAM AND LIVE
YOUNG AND LIVE
OLD AND LIVE
CUT AND LIVE
RUN AND LIVE
STAY AND LIVE
PLAY AND LIVE
KILL AND LIVE
SUCK AND LIVE
COME AND LIVE
GO AND LIVE
KNOW AND LIVE
TELL AND LIVE
SMELL AND LIVE
FALL AND LIVE
RISE AND LIVE
STAND AND LIVE
SIT AND LIVE
SPIT AND LIVE
TRY AND LIVE
FAIL AND LIVE
SMILE AND LIVE
THINK AND LIVE
PAY AND LIVE

AMERICAN PAINTINGS

ALBERT BIERSTADT
An Indian Encampment
SIGNED AND DATED *'61*, OIL ON CANVAS, 33.7 x 47.6cm (13¼ x 18¾in)
New York $695,500 (£445,830). 27.V.93

Bierstadt made his first trip west with Colonel Frederick Lander's US Government expedition in 1859. It was during this foray along the Platte River to the Wind River Mountains, Nebraska, that the artist first encountered the western landscape and the lifestyle of the native Americans. The artist wrote to *The Crayon* from the Rocky Mountains: 'We often meet Indians, and they have always been kindly disposed to us and we to them; but it is a little risky, because being very superstitious and naturally distrustful, their friendship may turn to hate at any moment.' This work is one of a small group of encampment scenes completed on the artist's return from the 1859 journey. (ABOVE)

WINSLOW HOMER
The Unruly Calf
SIGNED AND DATED *1875*,
OIL ON CANVAS,
61.6 x 97.8cm (24¼ x 38½in)
New York $1,210,000
(£775,640). 3.XII.92
Property from the
Pauline Woolworth Trust
The Unruly Calf was
painted during Homer's
visit to Petersburg,
Virginia, in the summer
of 1875. Much of the
artist's work at this time
developed subjects con-
nected with rural child-
hood, but the paintings
of this and other trips to
Virginia also tackled
themes sympathetic to
the social conditions of
the newly emancipated
southern black
population. (RIGHT)

WINSLOW HOMER
Looking Out to Sea
SIGNED AND DATED *1872*,
OIL ON CANVAS,
39.4 x 57.2cm (15½ x 22½in)
New York $706,500
(£452,800). 27.V.93
This newly discovered
work by Homer relates
to three other known
paintings by the artist
executed in 1872, all
sharing compositional
elements such as the
positioning of a flower
pot or pots on the sill
and a blonde young
woman gazing out of the
window. At the time this
work was painted,
Homer's subjects were
dominated by scenes
with a latent narrative
force taken from
memories of his boy-
hood and images of
country life. (RIGHT)

CHILDE HASSAM
The Room of Flowers
SIGNED AND DATED *1894*, OIL ON CANVAS, 86.4 x 86.4cm (34 x 34in) New York $5,502,500 (£3,527,200). 27.V.93
From the Collection of Arthur G. Altschul
Childe Hassam was one of America's leading 'Impressionist' painters. This work was painted as a tribute
to the poet, writer and gardener Celia Thaxter, who ran a summer resort on Appledore Island in New
Hampshire in the 1890s which attracted a wide circle of artists, writers and musicians. The guests were
invited to informal salons in the parlour of Mrs Thaxter's cottage, the room depicted in this painting.
Hassam regarded *The Room of Flowers* as 'one of my best things'. (ABOVE)

WILLIAM MERRITT CHASE
Peonies
SIGNED, PASTEL ON PAPER, 121.9 x 121.9cm (48 x 48in) New York $3,962,500 (£2,540,000). 27.V.93
The general scheme of *Peonies* might have been inspired by Whistler's painting *Symphony in White No. 2: The Little White Girl* (Tate Gallery, London), although it is hard to establish any direct precedent. William Merritt Chase (1849-1916) recognized the influence of a variety of contemporary painters while strongly preserving his own distinctive artistic qualities through a mastery of technique. He favoured pastels from early on in his career, a medium rarely used by his professional American counterparts. *Peonies* is exceptionally large for a pastel study and vivid proof of the artist's technical skills. (ABOVE)

CHARLES DEMUTH
Welcome to Our City
SIGNED AND DATED 1921, OIL ON
CANVAS, 63.5 x 50.8cm (25 x 20in)
New York $825,000 (£528,850).
3.XII.92

Charles Demuth (1883-1935) spent his entire life in Lancaster, Pennsylvania. Until 1920 he restricted his talents to the execution of delicate watercolour studies, but a subsequent change in his choice of subject matter encouraged him to turn to oil and tempera. His work of this period portrays architectural and industrial scenes of his native town, often incorporating cryptic letters and fragments of words. *Welcome to Our City* features the dome of the Lancaster courthouse, a distinguished mid-nineteenth-century landmark. The subtle anthropomorphism of the dome itself, a device Demuth periodically employed, hints at the artist's doubts about industrial progress and development. (RIGHT)

MARSDEN HARTLEY
Abstraction
OIL ON CANVAS,
119.4 x 100.3cm (47 x 39½in)
New York $1,155,000 (£750,300).
3.XII.92
Property of Robert E. Abrams
and Michael D. Abrams

This painting of 1913 belongs to a group of innovative works executed by Marsden Hartley in the years 1913-15 which show the strong impact of his first experiences abroad. Foremost among the new stimuli was Wassily Kandinsky, who Hartley had first heard about in 1912, shortly after settling in Paris. His interest in Kandinsky was developed by *Der Blaue Reiter*, which Kandinsky had edited with Franz Marc, as well as by Kandinsky's treatise *Concerning the Spiritual in Art.* Early in 1913 Hartley travelled to Germany to meet Kandinsky in order to learn more about his new ideas. *Abstraction* was painted later that year. (RIGHT)

EDWARD HOPPER
Gloucester Houses
SIGNED, WATERCOLOUR,
40.6 x 55.2cm (16 x 21¾in)
New York $330,000
(£211,540). 3.XII.92

Hopper sold his first painting at the Armory Show in New York in 1918, but it was not until the 1930s that he came to be hailed as a leading exponent of the new realism in American painting. Between 1912 and 1928 Hopper spent several summers in Massachusetts, devoting much of his time to painting the local New England architecture. (RIGHT)

LATIN AMERICAN PAINTINGS

RUFINO TAMAYO
Mujer en éxtasis
SIGNED AND DATED *0-73*, OIL AND SAND ON CANVAS, 130.5 x 194.6cm (51⅜ x 76⅝in) New York $1,485,000 (£976,900). 23.XI.92
The property of Robert E. Abrams

Female sexuality is one of the dominant themes of Rufino Tamayo's work. In this picture he seems to be celebrating the power of female eroticism, which he sees as something that needs to be deciphered in the springtime of life – hence the vivid yellow background, the yellow that he described as 'tender sun on a spring day'. (ABOVE)

FERNANDO BOTERO
La casa de las gemelas Arias
SIGNED AND DATED *73*, OIL ON CANVAS, 229 x 188cm (90 x 74in) New York $1,540,000 (£1,013,100). 23.XI.92 The property of Robert E. Abrams

Botero is one of this century's most cosmopolitan artists, yet all his work is suffused with the spirit of his native Colombia and most of his paintings display a reaction to the most exaggerated elements of South American life. This work is one of a series executed in the early 1970s on the theme of prostitutes and brothels. (LEFT)

MATTA
Psychological Morphology No. 14 (Personnages et automobile)
SIGNED, GRAPHITE, CRAYON
AND COLOURED PENCIL,
31.6 x 47.9cm (12½ x 18⅞in)
New York $104,250 (£67,600).
18.V.93

Matta was born in Chile in 1911 and trained as an architect, first in Santiago and then in Paris under Le Corbusier. In 1937 he turned to painting. He was a friend of Marcel Duchamp and an active member of the Surrealist movement, exerting a strong influence on Ernst, Tanguy, Breton and Masson. (LEFT)

JOSÉ CLEMENTE OROZCO
Acordada (Caballos y Zapatistas)
SIGNED, OIL ON CANVAS,
66 x 81.9cm (26 x 32¼in)
New York $374,000 (£246,000).
23.XI.92

The subject matter of this picture derives from pre-revolutionary Mexico. *Acordadas* were the henchmen of the landed classes, often employed to conscript farmers into slave labour. This practice led to a confrontation between the President of Mexico and the peasant leader, Emiliano Zapata, whose oppressed followers Orozco depicts here. The artist was a participant in the revolution, which broke out in 1910. (LEFT)

ARMANDO MORALES
Trois nus et voiture à cheval
SIGNED AND DATED 85, OIL ON CANVAS, 161.8 x 129.9cm (63⅗ x 51⅛in) New York $376,500 (£244,400). 18.V.93
Armando Morales was born in Nicaragua in 1927. His first one-man exhibitions were in Brazil and Peru
and in 1969 he moved to New York. His work of the 1960s incorporated informalist abstraction with
the use of canvas collage but after 1968 he returned to a more representational style, placing his figures
in semi-abstract environments which integrated volume and background. (ABOVE)

CANADIAN ART

CORNELIUS DAVID KRIEGHOFF
A Gentleman's Cutter
SIGNED, OIL ON CANVAS, 36.6 x 53.3cm (14 x 21in)
Toronto CN$49,500 (£25,390:$39,000). 19.V.93

Cornelius Krieghoff (1815-72) was an itinerant German artist who was resident in
French Canada from around 1840 to 1866. He settled first in Montreal and latterly
in Quebec, long enough to portray the landscape and the life of its people in great
detail. His paintings were sought after as souvenirs by English garrison officers, many
of whom were amateur painters themselves and responsible for much of the early
landscape art to emerge from the country. (ABOVE)

AUSTRALIAN ART

NORMAN ALFRED
WILLIAMS LINDSAY
Captured
SIGNED AND DATED *1938*,
OIL ON CANVAS,
159 x 129.5cm (63½ x 51⅛in)
Sydney AUS$145,000
(£65,300:$99,200). 22.XI.92
The work of Norman
Lindsay dominated the
closing years of Australia's
Victorian age. He was a
champion of the creative
imagination and the joys
of the flesh, and took on
his puritan detractors with
gusto. The battle was as
much concerned with
morals as with aesthetics
and, owing to Lindsay's
tireless activity, the role of
the artist in Australian
society became a matter of
vehement public debate.
Captured is a late example
of the artist's vivid fantasy.
(RIGHT)

PRINTS

REMBRANDT
HARMENSZ VAN RIJN
Jan Six
ETCHING, DRYPOINT AND BURIN,
FOURTH (FINAL) STATE,
24.4 x 19.1cm (9⅝ x 7½in)
New York $618,500 (£404,248).
13.V.93
From the Collection of
Dr Otto.Schäfer

Although he had known
members of the Six family
for some time, Rembrandt
became friends with Jan Six
during the course of etching
his portrait in 1647. It was a
time-consuming project,
requiring three separate
preparatory drawings, but
the final work is a triumph
of the printmaker's art.
Rembrandt combined
etching, engraving and
drypoint in so sophisticated
a manner that it is almost
impossible to distinguish
the different techniques. On
the plate he worked from
dark to light, using a single
point of illumination, the
window, as a frame for the
portrait. (RIGHT)

GIOVANNI BATTISTA PIRANESI
The Man on the Rack,
plate XV from *I Carceri
d'Invenzione*, from a
collection of nineteen
volumes of the
artist's work
ETCHING, 57.1 x 42cm (22½ x 16½in)
London £199,500 ($297,200) for the
collection. 29.VI.93
Piranesi's hallucinatory visions
of imaginary gaols, etched with
unprecedented energy, form
part of a collection of nineteen
volumes containing nearly all
of the artist's work. The
volumes were assembled by his
family in Rome shortly after
the artist's death in 1778 and
are in exceptionally fine
condition. Such sets formed
part of the libraries of many
aristocrats who had made the
Grand Tour, but most have
been broken up over the years.
(LEFT)

FRANCISCO JOSÉ DE
GOYA Y LUCIENTES
Plates from
Los Caprichos
ETCHINGS WITH AQUATINT, folio
London £111,500 ($166,100).
29.VI.93

These four etchings are
from the set of eighty
plates from a fine early
copy of *Los Caprichos*
(The Caprices), before
certain changes made for
the first edition of 1799.
Etched with the most
delicate tones of aquatint
– which soon wore out –
the fantastical and
nightmarish nature of the
images satirized the
corruption of society and
the Church in Spain.
Goya was forced to
withdraw the series from
circulation almost
immediately and only
about 300 copies were
printed in his lifetime.
(RIGHT)

El de la rompia)

Tantalo.

Aquellos polbos.

Que pico de Oro!

ALEXANDER
RODCHENKO
Plate from
Gravyuri
Rodchenko 1919,
from a complete
portfolio
LINOCUT, 15.7 x 11.1cm
(6½ x 4⅜in)
London £52,100 ($78,600)
for the portfolio. 30.VI.93
This work is from an
exceptionally rare
complete portfolio
of nine prints which
were executed at an
important stage in
the artist's career,
when he was begin-
ning to turn away
from two-dimen-
sional painting to
focus on the three-
dimensional design of
objects for everyday
use. Apart from a
few artist's proofs,
an edition of only
ten copies of the
portfolio was issued
at the request of the
Museum of Painterly
Culture (set up to
train and support
artists as well as to
promote the arts and
crafts design move-
ment). Of these ten,
only four complete
copies are known to
have survived. (LEFT)

MARY CASSATT
Woman Bathing or La Toilette
DRYPOINT AND AQUATINT PRINTED IN COLOURS, 47.4 x 31.3cm (18⅝ x 12⅜in)
New York $288,500 (£187,300). 13.V.93

Although born in America, Cassatt chose to spend most of her working life in Paris. She is particularly renowned for her extraordinarily fresh, direct coloured prints (this example is from 1890-1), which reveal her interest in Japanese woodblock prints as well as her indebtedness to Degas. Cassatt's links with Degas were strong, and it was he who persuaded her to exhibit with the Impressionists. (ABOVE)

HENRI DE TOULOUSE-LAUTREC
Reine de Joie
LITHOGRAPH PRINTED IN COLOURS, 149 x 96.2cm (58⅝ x 37⅞in)
Tokyo ¥5,500,000 (£26,400:$45,400). 14.X.92

Toulouse-Lautrec's lifelong fame and success rested entirely on his work in poster design rather than on his painting or graphic art. This work, executed in 1892, is one of his more controversial images.
Baron Rothschild, who believed himself portrayed as the main character of the book which this poster advertized, attempted to have the edition suppressed. (ABOVE)

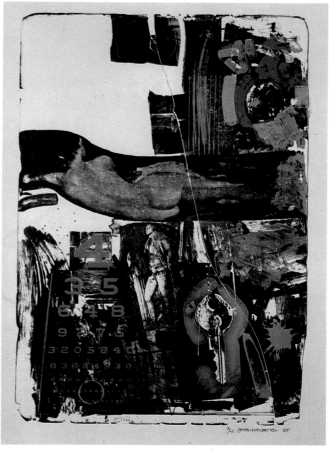

FRANK STELLA
Talladega Three II
SIGNED AND DATED *1982*, RELIEF PRINTED IN COLOURS, 168 x 132cm (66⅛ x 52in)
New York $61,600 (£40,261). 7.XI.92

Printed on handmade, hand-coloured paper, this work is from the suite *Circuits*. The cursive black lines to which the colour appears to cling, are made from the laser cuts left in the wood which was used as a backboard in the foundry where Stella's large cut-out constructions are made. When he saw the design left by the random marks overlaid one on another, he decided to use the wood as the surface from which this large graphic work is printed. (ABOVE)

ROBERT RAUSCHENBERG
Breakthrough II
SIGNED AND DATED *1965*, LITHOGRAPH PRINTED IN COLOURS,
111.8 x 78.5cm (30⅞ x 30⅞in)
New York $33,350 (£21,941). 15.V.93

After completing the first impression of this image in 1965, Rauschenberg went on a worldwide tour with the Merce Cunningham Dance Company and upon his return again took up the stone, adding three colours and rotating the orientation by 45 degrees. By this time the stone had begun to disintegrate rapidly, so each impression of *Breakthrough II* is slightly different. (ABOVE)

PHOTOGRAPHS

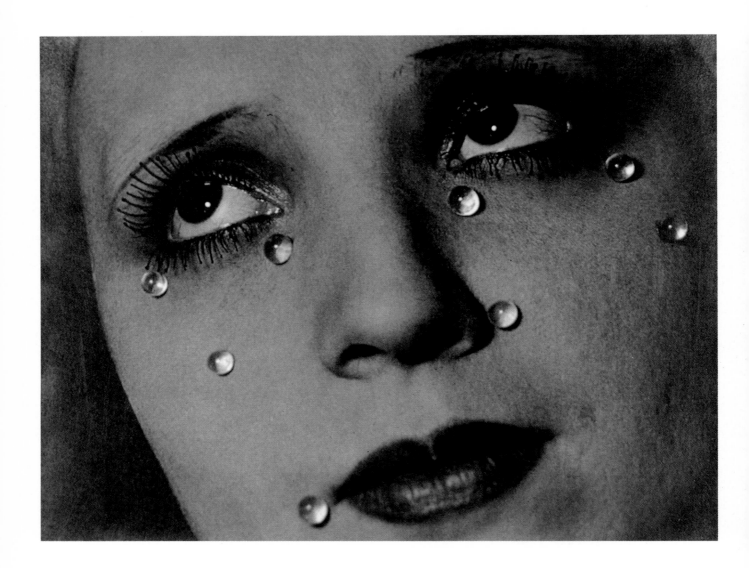

MAN RAY
Glass Tears
MONOGRAMMED, *c.*1930, SILVER PRINT, 22.8 x 29.8cm (9 x 11¾in)
London £122,500 ($190,100). 7.V.93
This work, dating from around 1930, is a little-known variant of a
more tightly cropped image that has been widely published and
exhibited. Its sale on 7 May 1993 achieved a record auction price
for a single photograph. (ABOVE)

ROBERT MAPPLETHORPE
Calla Lily
SIGNED AND DATED *1987,* PLATINUM PRINT ON LINEN,
50 x 50cm (19¾ x 19⅜in)
New York $63,250 (£37,426).16.X.92
This characteristic work is one in a series of studies of single
blooms made by Robert Mapplethorpe during the late 1980s.
(RIGHT)

quodammi aibiaiui omnus
quod humile erat in latitua
predix' quaturor .x. ibi multi
bx; in oione constant' plau
induhis. tamen post mat

LITERARY PROPERTY *by Paul Needham*

L iterary Property at Sotheby's is a broad umbrella, covering the written and printed culture of the Western world and Near East from ancient times to the present; and also the associated fields of illumination and illustration, calligraphy, fine printing and fine book bindings. The enormous variety of people, times, places and events encompassed by Literary Property is the key to its fascination for those involved in these specialist areas. The material at hand may be at one moment an early Qur'an fragment, at another a finely illuminated Book of Hours, at another an elegant binding commissioned by a Renaissance collector, at another Einstein's desk set of scientific offprints, at another an early version of the game of Monopoly, and so on; each piece contributing to our collective knowledge of the human past.

Last year, we lamented the relative dearth of single owner sales; this year there was a 'good plenty' leading to the production of a number of catalogues with a continuing reference value because of their unifying themes. Single owner sales included: Darwin's Century: The Jeremy Norman Collection (£177,600); The Jeffrey Young Collection (£441,100); The Sammlung Rudolf von Gutmann (£1,035,000); The Otto Kallir Collection of Aviation History ($1,014,000); The Library of Camille Aboussouan (£1,113,000) and the Library of Alan G. Thomas (£1,531,000).

One private treaty sale deserves special notice. The entire manuscript library of the Princes von Fürstenberg was sold through the mediation of Sotheby's to the state of Baden-Württemberg, Germany. The Donaueschingen Collection of some 1,200 items includes fragments dating to the seventh century, and integral codices from the twelfth century onwards. A forte of the collection is a group of medieval German literary manuscripts. The reported sale price was DM48 million, establishing this as one of the largest single book transactions in history.

An area so extensive as Literary Property inevitably breaks down into smaller, more or less discrete collecting markets, each with its own history.

The Helmingham Breviary (detail)
*c.*1420, NORWICH, IN LATIN, ILLUMINATED MANUSCRIPT ON VELLUM, 205 LEAVES, 42.2 x 29cm (16⅝ x 11½in)
London £100,500 ($147,700). 21.VI.93
From the Library of the late Alan G. Thomas. (LEFT)

A miniature of St Bartholomew from an illuminated manuscript Passionary
THIRD QUARTER OF THE TWELFTH CENTURY, TUSCANY, 20.2 x 10.4cm (8 x 4⅛in)
London £67,500 ($99,200). 21.VI.93
From the Library of the late Alan G. Thomas. (ABOVE)

La Description des
Douzes Cesars
Abregees avecques
leurs Figures Faictes
et Portraictes
*c.*1520, Tours, in French,
illuminated manuscript
on vellum, 24 leaves,
21.1 x 13.8cm (8¾ x 5⅜in)
London £165,000 ($259,000).
7.XII.92 (Above)

The field of English Literature and History, which last year was somewhat thin, came back in force this season with the July London sale exceeding its high estimate. Highlights included a letter by Charlotte Brontë (£66,000), the Book of Fame *of Hannah More (£126,900), and the Reformation Collection formed by George Goyder (£313,800).*

Early printing, a traditionally strong area, showed less certainty this season, though with gratifying results for several unusually rare and fine items. In December we offered an illuminated vellum copy of the 1462 Bible, in a well-preserved contemporary Erfurt binding. Despite lacking some 26 leaves, it found strong competition, being knocked down finally at $286,000.

Travel Maps and Atlases continued the resilience noted last year, the major item being a superb copy of Blaeu's Atlas Major *in a contemporary cabinet which realized £170,000. In the sale of the late Alan G. Thomas's Collection, his copy of Stuart & Revett's* The Antiquities of Athens *made £89,500.*

In music, the season was dominated by manuscripts and letters of the great composers of the Austro-German tradition, including works by J. S. Bach, Haydn, Mozart, Beethoven, Gluck, Schubert, Brahms, Brückner and Richard Strauss. Among the highlights were the famous letter by Leopold Mozart discussing Haydn's praise of the young Wolfgang Mozart (£133,500, a record for a letter by a musician) and the autograph of Haydn's last string quartet, Op. 103 (£155,500). The market for printed music continues to hold strong; the first edition of Bach's Goldberg Variations *(Nuremberg 1714) made £18,700, and Orlando di Lassus'* Missae posthumae *(Münich 1610) £29,000 — both record prices for printed works by these composers.*

Apart from the en bloc *Donaueschingen sale already cited, Western Manuscripts and Miniatures had relatively few high profile items during the*

JOSEPH HAYDN
Autograph
manuscript of the
final unfinished
String Quartet,
Opus 103
SIGNED AND DATED *1803*,
VIENNA, 6 PAGES,
oblong folio,
London £172,500 ($265,700).
28.V.93. (ABOVE)

season, yet more modest offerings attracted considerable competition. One consignor had particularly good fortune. In February 1993 he purchased for £20 at a country house auction a miniature manuscript Psalter of the fifteenth century, which he brought to Bond Street for further study and appraisal. It was placed in our 22 June sale, and was knocked down at £9,000.

The Oriental manuscripts and miniatures market showed a steady recovery during the past season. One of the most interesting manuscripts was an early vellum palimpsest Qur'an leaf dating from the mid-seventh century, which brought £159,500.

Undoubtedly, the strongest single market within Literary Property this season was Americana, the colossus being Abraham Lincoln, whose autograph manuscripts dominated New York's auctions of Americana in December and May. Both of the two major Lincoln leaves in these sales came out of the almost legendary 'Grimsley carpetbag'.

Perhaps the most important leaf from what Lincoln called his 'literary bureau' was hitherto unrecorded and contains the earliest known formulation of Lincoln's 'House Divided' doctrine, the most historically significant Lincoln autograph to have been discovered this century. Three bidders in the 16 December 1992 sale were still active when the pre-sale high estimate was doubled at $1,000,000. The leaf was finally knocked down at $1,540,000, establishing a new auction record for any American historical document.

The second carpetbag manuscript of the season was sold in our May Americana auction. The only surviving page from a speech Lincoln gave between 1857 and 1859, this leaf last appeared on the market in 1952 when it made $1,850. This time it was sold to the purchaser of the 'House Divided' leaf for $992,500.

GEORG BRAUN AND
FRANZ HOGENBERG
Civitates Orbis
Terrarum,
volumes I-IV
1588, COLOGNE, IN LATIN,
COLOURED IN A CONTEMPORARY
HAND, 236 DOUBLE-PAGE
ENGRAVED PLATES,
39.5 x 28.5cm (15½ x 11¼in)
London £77,000 ($117,800).
19.XI.92. (BELOW)

PRINTED BOOKS & AUTOGRAPH MANUSCRIPTS

JAMES STUART AND NICOLAS REVETT
The Antiquities of Athens
VOLUMES I TO III, FIRST EDITIONS,
RED MOROCCO WITH GILT INLAY, folio
London £89,500 ($131,500). 22.VI.93
This binding represents the first
neo-classical example of its type and
has been attributed to James 'Athenian'
Stuart, making it the earliest English
binding known to have been designed
by an architect. In 1748 Stuart, along
with Nicolas Revett, discussed the idea
of publishing measured drawings of views
of Athenian buildings. The first volume
of the resulting *The Antiquities of Athens*
appeared in 1762. The works proved to
be an important early influence on the
Greek Revival movement in England.
(RIGHT)

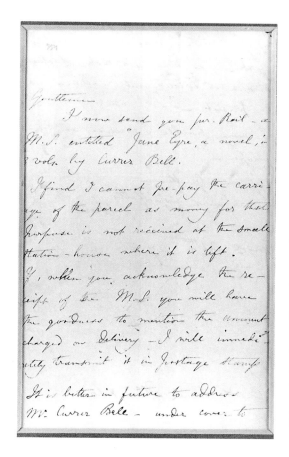

CHARLOTTE BRONTE
Autograph letter
DATED *24 August [18]47,* 2 PAGES, 8vo
London £66,000 ($102,300). 14.XII.92
From the Jeffrey Young Collection.

This letter was sent by Charlotte Brontë to her future publishers, Smith, Elder & Co, with the manuscript of *Jane Eyre*. The reaction of the firm's reader, William Smith Williams, has become legendary: he embarked on it after breakfast, broke for a sandwich and a glass of wine at lunch, cancelled an afternoon engagement to go riding, bolted his dinner and did not go to bed until it was finished. *Jane Eyre* was published on 16 October 1847 and was sensationally received, marking the beginning of Brontë's fame as a novelist. (ABOVE)

Nine first edition twentieth-century novels
STELLA GIBBONS Cold Comfort Farm (LONGMANS, GREEN AND CO., 1932)
CHRISTOPHER ISHERWOOD Goodbye to Berlin (HOGARTH PRESS, 1929)
ALDOUS HUXLEY Brave New World (CHATTO & WINDUS, 1932)
EVELYN WAUGH Vile Bodies (CHAPMAN & HALL, 1930)
EVELYN WAUGH Decline and Fall (CHAPMAN & HALL, 1930)
GEORGE ORWELL Nineteen Eighty-Four (SECKER & WARBURG, 1949)
ERNEST HEMINGWAY The Old Man and the Sea (CHARLES SCRIBNER, 1952)
MARGARET MITCHELL Gone with the Wind (MACMILLANS, 1936)
KAREN BLIXEN Out of Africa (PUTNAM, 1937)
London £6,369 ($9,999) for nine lots in total. 14.XII.92
From the Jeffrey Young Collection. (ABOVE)

ALBERT EINSTEIN
Autograph quotation beneath an early image of Einstein
DATED *1924*, 24.2 x 15.3cm (9½ x 6⅛in)
New York $66,000 (£41,700). 17.XII.92

The translation of this quotation is as follows: 'No human society can stay healthy without a common goal. This must be taken into consideration in order to understand the supreme importance of Palestine for all Jews.' In his early years, Einstein showed little interest in Judaism, but with the spread of anti-Semitism in post-First World War Germany he became a strong supporter of the Zionist movement. A committed pacifist, he opposed nationalism and thus adopted Zionism spiritually whilst rejecting its political ideologies. (RIGHT)

JOHN TALMAN
One of a collection of drawings of the various insignia of the Pontificate and other subjects
ITALY, 1702-21, TWO HUNDRED AND TWO DRAWINGS MOUNTED INTO TWO ALBUMS, folio
London £166,500 ($249,700). 2.IV.93

John Talman (1677-1726) was the son of the influential Baroque English architect William Talman. In 1710 he was in Rome with William Kent and it was then that he began collecting architectural and antiquarian drawings. The selection represented here contains examples commissioned by Talman as well as those by his own hand. It is remarkable that Talman, as an English Protestant, should have been given access to, and have been allowed to draw, objects that included those from the Pope's Secret Sacristy. (RIGHT)

LUDWIG WITTGENSTEIN
Autograph letter to C. K. Ogden
DATED *1922*, TWENTY-SIX PAGES, 4to
London £19,500 ($29,100). 20.VII.93

This letter provides detailed comments on the English translation of *Tractatus Logico-Philosophicus*, the only work by Wittgenstein (barring one short paper) to be published in his lifetime. The letter is written to the Cambridge linguistic psychologist and editor C. K. Ogden, who undertook the translation of the work. The *Tractatus* explored the dilemmas inherent in logic, which had previously exercised Bertrand Russell with whom Wittgenstein had studied, and was published in 1918 with an intro-duction by Russell himself. (RIGHT)

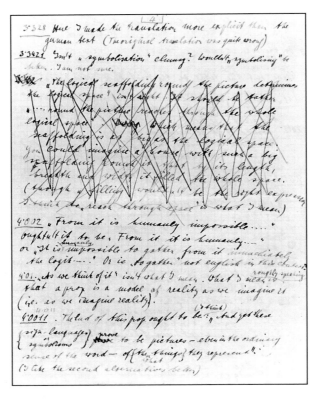

JOHANNES BLAEU
A Dutch-text edition of the *Atlas Major*
ELEVEN VOLUMES CONTAINED IN A CONTEMPORARY DUTCH WALNUT CABINET, 1649, folio
London £170,000 ($260,100). 19.XI.92

Copies of the Dutch-text edition of Johannes Blaeu's atlas are extremely rare. As with this example, they are sometimes augmented by the addition of the Dutch-text edition of Blaeu's celebrated *Townbooks of the Netherlands*. Sixteen sets have been identified within the Netherlands but only a small number exist outside the country. When coloured by a contemporary hand, as here, they form some of the most lavishly illustrated books produced in Amsterdam in the seventeenth century. (RIGHT)

ABRAHAM LINCOLN
Autograph manuscript
*c.*1857–59, 24.9 x 19.4cm (9¾ x 7⅞in)
New York $992,500 (£644,400). 21.V.93

This extract from one of Lincoln's most passionate indictments of slavery contains the lines: '... although volume upon volume is written to prove slavery a very good thing, we never hear of the man who wishes to take the good of it, by being a slave himself.' It dates to within a year of Lincoln's acceptance of the Illinois Republican nomination as candidate for the United States Senate. The manuscript is from the Grimsley Carpet Bag, which contained all of Lincoln's non-legal pre-presidential writings that he did not take to Washington. The bag was entrusted to Elizabeth Todd Grimsley, a cousin and friend of Mrs Lincoln. (ABOVE)

ABRAHAM LINCOLN
Autograph manuscript, a leaf from a speech
DECEMBER 1857
New York $1,540,000 (£974,600). 16.XII.92
Property of a descendant of Elizabeth Todd Grimsley.

This leaf can be regarded as the most historically significant autograph manuscript by Abraham Lincoln to have been discovered this century. Written in late December 1857, as Lincoln was emerging from relative obscurity to national fame, this represents the earliest surviving formulation of his 'House Divided' doctrine. The leaf is another important survival from the Grimsley Carpet Bag, most of the contents of which were widely dispersed after Lincoln's death. This leaf, however, had been kept by a member of Elizabeth Todd Grimsley's family. (ABOVE)

Dear Sir Paris May 17. 1788.

I have at length an opportunity of acknoleging the receipt of your favors of Feb. 8 & Mar. 14. and of congratulating you on your resurrection from the dead among whom you had been confidently entombed by the news-dealers of Paris. I am sorry that your first impressions have been disturbed by matters of eti-quette, where surely they should least have been expected to occur. these disputes are the most insusceptible of determination, be-cause they have no foundation in reason. arbitrary & senseless in their nature they are arbitrarily decided by every nation for itself. these decisions are meant to prevent disputes, but they produce ten where they prevent one. it would have been better therefore in a new country to have excluded etiquette altogether; or if it must be ad-mitted in some form or other, to have made it depend on some [illegible]stance founded in nature, such as the age or stature of the parties. — however you have got over all this, and I am in hopes have been able to make up a society suited to your own dispo-sitions. your situation will doubtless be improved by the adop-tion of the new constitution, which I hope will have taken place before you receive this. I see in this instrument a great deal of good. the consolidation of our government, a just representation an administration of some permanence and other features of great value, will be gained by it. there are indeed some faults which re-

His Excellency the Count de Moustier.

La machine s'eleva avec les applaudissement general de toute l'assemblée c'etoit bien le spectacle le plus imposant de voir un corps aussi voluminaux s'elever majestueusement par sa propre puissance. comme on avoit pas dessein de la perdre on ne l'a voit point fermée par en bas de sorte qu'a mesure qu'elle s'elevoit elle perdoit de l'air qu'elle contenoit elle ne s'eleva donc qu'a la hauteur de trois cent toises en decrivant une ligne courbe et fut tomber a trois quart de lieue de l'endroit d'ou elle etoit partie. le tems de sa course fut de dix minutes pendant deux desquels elle resta presque la même place on pouvoit juger qu'elle vouloit toujours s'elever mais comme elle perdoit continuellement de son gaz elle s'affoiblissoit, et le vent qui souffloit fort alors précipita sa chute.

On y avoit attaché au bout d'une corde d'environ quinze pieds une cage d'osier dans laquelle on avoit mis un mouton, un cocq, et un canard qui sont revenus tres bien portant. le public qui avoit vû disparoitre le globe du champ de Mars ne voyant point disparoitre cette machine cy crut que c'etoit une experience manquée parce qu'on ignoroit qu'elle fut ouverte. mais comme on se propose de repetter ces experiences et qu'il en couteroit trop de refaire chaque fois de ces machines on ne veut pas courir le risque de la perdre. il suffit de savoir qu'elle peut s'elever dans l'air et parcourir l'espace en proportion de l'air ou gaz qu'elle perdra et lors qu'on voudra qu'elle disparoisse absolument on la fermera entierement.

Cette machine etant remplie de gaz ou air inflamable pese dix cent et s'enleve par une force de dix huit cent c'est a dire qu'elle pourroit emporter avec elle un poid de [illegible] cent. chose etonnante! car enfin qu'on lance dans l'air un corps quelquonque il ne s'y elevera qu'en raison de la force avec laquelle on l'aura lancé et retombera avec encore plus de vitesse qu'il n'a eté elevé. au lieu que cette machine ne craint rien tant que de toucher la terre elle bondit elle roule tant qu'il lui reste un peu de son gaz ce n'est que par sa perte totale qu'elle reste sans mouvement.

Si tu me temoigne que cela t'amuse je te ferai part de ce que je saurai des autres experiences qu'on fera par la suite. adieu.

Cette machine contient quarante mille pieds cube de gaz, ou air inflamable.

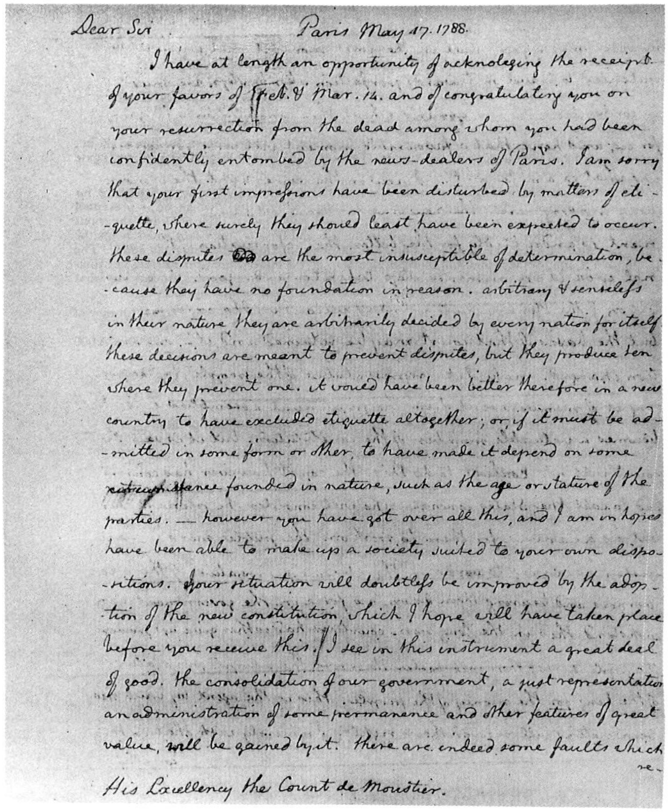

THOMAS JEFFERSON

Autograph letter

DATED *1788*, THREE PAGES, 4to

New York $200,500 (£130,100). 24.V.93

Jefferson's letter was written from Paris, during his term as Minister to France, to the Comte de Moustier, his French counterpart in America. He commiserates with Moustier on the rigours of the six-day crossing from Le Havre to New York, and politely defends his compatriots from the charge of deficiency in etiquette with which Moustier had taxed them. Most significantly, Jefferson gives his approbation of the US Constitution, which was just approaching ratification: 'we must be contented to travel on towards perfection, step by step.' (ABOVE)

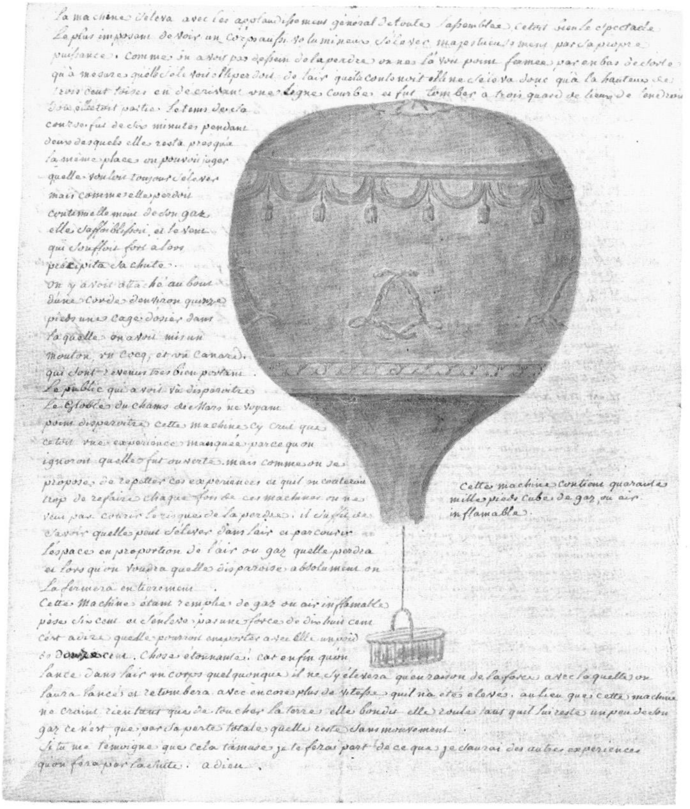

PHILIPPE LESUEUR

Autograph letter

DATED *1783*, FOUR PAGES, 4to

New York $20,700 (£13,500). 14.VI.93

From the Otto Kallir Collection of Aviation History.

Philippe Lesueur's letter gives an exceptionally detailed account of two famous early balloon ascents: the hot-air ascent of J. A. C. Charles from the Champs de Mars, Paris, on 27 August 1783; and the hydrogen ascent of Joseph Montgolfier from Versailles on 19 September 1783. The letter includes a fine watercolour rendition of the Montgolfier balloon. (ABOVE)

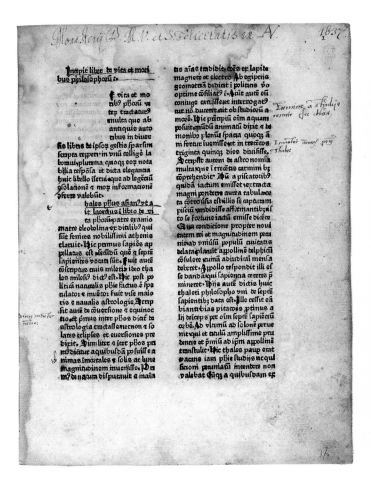

WALTER BURLEY
De Vita et Moribus Philosophorum
COLOGNE, WILLIAM CAXTON, *c.*1471-72, folio
New York $54,625 (£33,900). 14.VI.93

Burley's collection of stories about the ancient philosophers was
possibly the first book financed and published by William Caxton.
It was printed in Cologne, where Caxton lived in exile for a period of
some eighteen months, having previously spent most of his adult life
as a merchant adventurer in Bruges. The book was produced in
collaboration with the so-called Printer of Dares, Johann Schilling,
with whom Caxton formed an association that resulted in the
production of three editions. This is apparently the first copy of the
Burley tractate to appear at auction since a sale in our rooms of 1928.
(ABOVE)

Part of the library of Lord William Howard
TWO HUNDRED AND FIFTY-ONE VOLUMES (PLUS FIFTEEN PRINTED AFTER 1640)
London £35,000 ($54,900). 15.XII.92

Lord William Howard was a seventeenth-century bibliophile and
the owner of Naworth Castle in Cumbria. His library was housed
in the Castle tower and in 1844 narrowly escaped destruction from
a disastrous fire. The fire did not reach the tower, but many of the
books were thrown out of the window. Fortunately, the volumes
survived and were restored. The library has remained complete and
in situ ever since, and mainly consists of religious works, but
also includes books on history, language, poetry, science and law.
(ABOVE)

A 1462 Latin Bible

PRINTED ON VELLUM, TWO VOLUMES, Royal folio
New York $286,000 (£181,000). 17.XII.92

Despite missing leaves, this is one of the largest, freshest and most elaborately decorated surviving copies of the famous 1462 Bible printed in Mainz by Johann Fust and Peter Schoeffer, former partners of the inventor of printing, Johann Gutenberg. The contemporary binding comes from Erfurt, the probable source of the Bible's finely wrought illuminations. (LEFT)

MUSIC MANUSCRIPTS

JOHANNES BRAHMS
Autograph manuscript of the sixteen waltzes
for piano duet, Opus 39
DATED *[1]866*, 16 PAGES, large oblong folio, London £100,500 ($155,700). 28.V.93
Brahms composed this famous set of waltzes in the mid-1860s, after
his move to Vienna. He had always been attracted to the waltz
rhythm and he admired the music of Johann Strauss, although what
is distinctive about Brahms' treatment of the form is the way in which
he succeeded in investing it with a serious content. (ABOVE)

LEOPOLD MOZART
Autograph letter to his daughter Nannerl
VIENNA, DATED *1785*, 3 PAGES, 4to, London £133,500 ($205,500). 28.V.93
This celebrated and much-quoted letter from Leopold Mozart to his
daughter contains among other things the glowing testimonial of
Joseph Haydn for Wolfgang Mozart: 'I tell you before God, as an
honourable man, your son is the greatest composer known to me by
name or in person'. Haydn was at the time at the peak of his success,
and his judgement was greatly valued. (RIGHT)

Mittagmahl bis Keeß. Den auch tag bis Freyhling, und am Freytag um 5 uhr war wir in der Schillerstraße N°: 846, im zweyten Stock. der weeg war durchaus abscheulich dorthin zu gehen, kahl und rauch, und aller Orth weeg arbeiten. das die Bruder schöne quartier mit aller Zimmer Bequemlichkeit hat mögt ihr daraus schlüßen, weil er 4 hundert Gulden Hauszins zahlt. Den nämlich freytag abends fuhren wir um 6 uhr in sein erstes subscriptions Concert, wo eine große Versammlung von Menschen von Rang war. und die franken zahlt für die 6 Fasten Concert nur Souverain d'or. Es ist auf die Musik und im zahlt für den Eintritt insgemein nur ein halb Souverain d'or. das Concert war unvergleichlich, das Orchester vortrefflich, außer den Symphonie sung eine Sängerin von welscher Theater 2 Arien. Dan war ein neues vortreffliches Clavier Concert vom Wolfgang, wo der Copist, da wir noch nicht einmahl Zeit hatte, weil er die Copiatur übersetzen müste.

Herr Haydn sagte mir: ich sage ihnen vor Gott, als ein ehrlicher Mann, ihr Sohn ist der größte Componist, den ich von Person und dem Nahmen nach kenne. er hat geschmack, und über das die größte Compositionswissenschaft. Den Sonntag abends war im Theater die accademie der ital: Sängerin Laschj, die itzt nach Italien reiset. Sie sang 2 Arien, es war ein Violoncello Concert, ein Tenor und Baßsänger sung eine Aria.

WESTERN MANUSCRIPTS

Hebrew manuscript of
festival prayers, biblical and
other readings for the
liturgical year
PESARO, DATED *1480*, ILLUMINATED
MANUSCRIPT ON VELLUM,
18.2 x 12.5cm (7 x 4⅞in)
Tel Aviv $1,157,500 (£751,600). 15.IV.93
This is an exceptionally rich and
lavishly illuminated Hebrew
manuscript which bears
comparison with some of the
finest examples to emerge from
the Italian Renaissance. It was
commissioned by Elijah ben
Schlomo, a native of Ferrara on
the Adriatic coast. Both Ferrara
and Pesaro had flourishing Jewish
communities in the fifteenth
century which dominated
financial operations and
stimulated fruitful patronage of
the arts in both cities. (RIGHT)

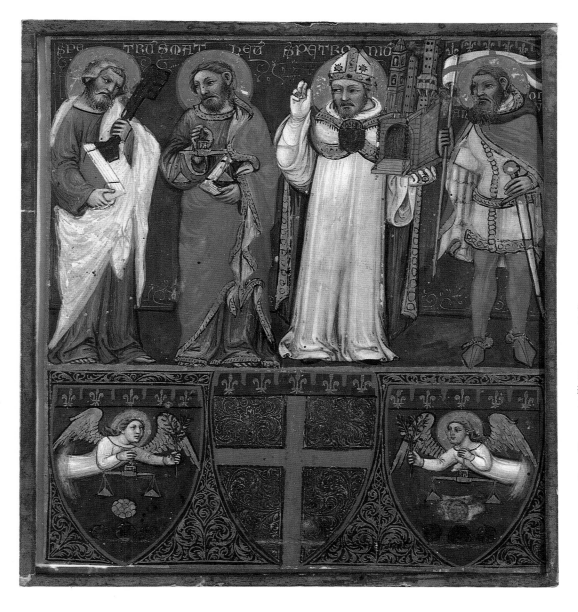

NICOLO DA BOLOGNA
Frontispiece from a register of the Guild of Money Changers of Bologna
BOLOGNA, c.1390-5,
ILLUMINATED MANUSCRIPT
ON VELLUM,
19.3 x 17.5cm (7½ x 6¾in)
London £45,500 ($63,300).
22.VI.93

Nicolò da Bologna was highly regarded and immensely successful during his lifetime. By the late 1380s he had been appointed illuminator to the Corporation of Bologna, and was also Mayor of the district of Zappolino and Special Counsellor to the Bolognese booktrade. This miniature was painted in his official capacity as city illuminator and evidently illustrated a register of the Money Changers' Guild. It depicts Saints Peter, Matthew, Petronius (a fifth-century Bishop of Bologna) and Florian (a fourth-century Roman martyr). (LEFT)

A Book of Hours, in Latin and French

DIJON OR BESANÇON, *c.*1430-50, ILLUMINATED MANUSCRIPT ON VELLUM, 22.4 x 15.8cm (8½ x 6in) London £89,500 ($132,400). 22.VI.93

After the fall of Paris in 1420, many manuscript illuminators appear to have fled to the provinces. One group or workshop evidently settled in Besançon in eastern France, bringing with them the pattern sheets and training of the Bedford and Egerton Masters' styles. This Book of Hours, apparently unrecorded and of high quality and great richness, is an excellent example of the imported Parisian style. The folio shown here depicts Saint Thomas the Apostle dressed as a traveller (he went to India) with staff and book. (RIGHT)

Wycliffite New Testament, in Middle English
FIRST HALF OF FIFTEENTH CENTURY, MANUSCRIPT ON VELLUM, 9.2 x 6cm (3¼ x 2⅜in)
London £95,000 ($140,600). 22.VI.93

This Wycliffite Bible is remarkable not only for the fact that it is virtually complete
but also for its microscopic script. The scribe has written fourteen lines to the inch
and the entire New Testament is thus contained within 157 leaves. The book
resembles the smallest thirteenth-century Bibles, with their miniature scripts, no
longer fashionable by the fifteenth century. This could have been a deliberate attempt
to avoid prosecution: the book is small enough to be easily concealed. (ABOVE)

ORIENTAL MANUSCRIPTS

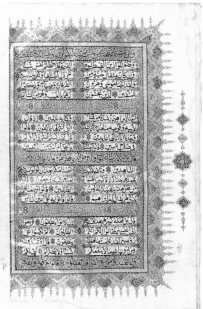
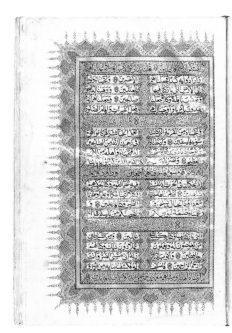

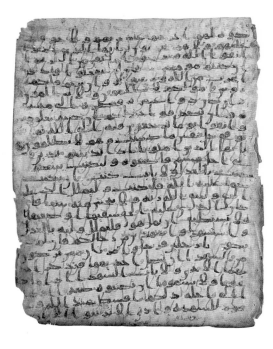

An Indian Qur'an

NORTH INDIA, PROBABLY ALWAR,
EARLY NINETEENTH CENTURY,
ARABIC MANUSCRIPT ON PAPER,
48 x 29.5cm (18½ x 11⅝in)
London £106,000 ($165,300). 28.IV.93

Alwar, the Muslim state midway
between Delhi and Jaipur, was situated
on an important trade route and was an
active centre of craftsmanship. This
manuscript was possibly commissioned
from the Alwar court. By the time of its
production the mobility of artists within
the Indian sub-continent had given rise
to a relatively homogeneous style of
manuscript illumination, and the
decoration of this example owes much
to the contemporary Delhi style, itself a
descendant of the seventeenth-century
Moghal tradition. (ABOVE)

A leaf from the Qur'an

MID-SEVENTH CENTURY AD,
HIJAZI SCRIPT ON VELLUM,
36.6 x 28.2cm (14 x 11in)
London £159,500 ($258,300). 23.X.92

This leaf is one of the earliest fragments
of the Qur'an in existence. It may well
have formed part of one of the earliest
canonized copies and was quite possibly
written by one of the companions of the
Prophet Muhammad. It provides a rare
and fascinating insight into both the
early collections of the written Qur'an
and the early development of the Arabic
script, and its religious significance is of
the utmost importance. (LEFT)

A Pair of Lovers Watching the Approaching Rains
KANGRA, *c.*1820, GOLD MARGINS, 22.9 x 16.8cm (9 x 6⅝in)
New York $26,450 (£17,400). 17.VI.93
This painting is an illustration from a *Baramasa* series depicting the month of *Bhadon* (August/September). The poet Keshav Das describes the rainy month: 'The purple clouds are gathering, the thunder rolls and rain pours in torrents, / The wind blows fiercely, the cicadas chirp, the lions roar, and elephants fell the trees. / The day is dark like the night, and one's own home is the best. / Pray leave me not in the month of Bhadon for separation pains like poison.' (Randhawa, *Kangra Paintings on Love*.) (ABOVE)

ATTRIBUTED TO SAJNU
The Hour of Cowdust
MANDI, *c.*1810, GOUACHE WITH GOLD ON PAPER, 30.2 x 21.3cm (11⅞ x 8⅜in)
New York $30,800 (£19,700). 5.XII.92
The artist Sajnu came to Mandi from Kangra in the first decade of the nineteenth century, completing a *Hamir Hath* series for his new patron, Raja Isvari Sen of Mandi, in 1810. The work shown here depicts cattle being taken to water before their return home to the village for the night: the 'Hour of Cowdust', one of the most evocative moments of the day in Indian village life. Also shown is the figure of Krishna playing his flute. (ABOVE)

A portrait bust from an album of watercolours
QAJAR, EARLY NINETEENTH-CENTURY, COLOURED DRAWINGS ON PAPER,
the album 19.3 x 11.2cm (7½ x 4in)
London £26,400 ($41,100). 23.X.92
This album contains sixty-one watercolours
depicting a variety of subjects ranging from formal
portraits of rulers, officials and grandees to lively
genre scenes. The portrait shown here depicts a lady
wearing an elaborate head-cloth and an unbuttoned
green tunic. (ABOVE)

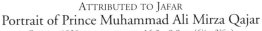

ATTRIBUTED TO JAFAR
Portrait of Prince Muhammad Ali Mirza Qajar
QAJAR, c.1820, OIL ON CANVAS, 16.3 x 9.8cm (6¼ x 3¾in)
London £73,000 ($113,800). 28.IV.93
Muhammad Ali Mirza (1788-1821) was the eldest son of Fath Ali Shah, who
succeeded Agha Muhammad Khan, the founder of the Qajar dynasty. Ali Mirza's
mother, however, was a Georgian and his half-brother, Abbas Mirza, whose mother
was a Qajar princess, therefore became heir to the Qajar throne. (ABOVE)

SCHOOL OF BIHZAD
Manuscript decorated with miniatures
HERAT, LAST QUARTER OF THE FIFTEENTH CENTURY,
GOLD-SPRINKLED PAPER, each page 23.3 x 15.8cm (9 x 6in)
London £20,700 ($32,290). 28.IV.93

Illustrated manuscripts produced at Herat during the reign of Sultan Husain Mirza are considered to be among the finest achievements of Persian miniature painting. This is a leaf from an example consisting of 40 leaves and the miniature depicted is one of three by the school of the renowned painter Bihzad. The calligrapher for this manuscript was Sultan Ali al-Mashhadi, who often worked together with Bihzad on poetical manuscripts. (LEFT)

A leaf from one of the 'Leningrad' albums
MOGHAL, c.1660-80, GOUACHE WITH GOLD ON PAPER,
album page 47 x 32.5cm (18 x 12½in)
London £13,200 ($21,285). 23.X.92

Most of the 'Leningrad' albums are preserved in the Institute for the Peoples of Asia in St Petersburg. Russian sources indicate that the album to which this leaf belongs was purchased in Tehran for Tsar Nicholas II. The albums were originally compiled in 1739 after Nadir Shah had sacked Delhi and returned to Persia with a hoard of manuscripts and treasure, including the legendary Peacock Throne. (LEFT)

THE DECORATIVE ARTS *by Philippe Garner*

A bronze figure of The Young Hercules Reading *by the Italian Renaissance sculptor Antico achieved £1,266,500 (London, July 1993); an Iznik pottery candlestick set a record for an Islamic work of art at £617,500 (London, April 1993); an Archaic Chinese bronze ritual vessel sold for £925,500 (London, June 1993); an Egyptian head of a queen or goddess made $451,000 (New York, December 1992); a Korean screen sold for $332,500 (New York, June 1993) and a fine Louis XVI* bureau plat *by Weisweiler from the estate of Hélène de Beaumont made FF8,436,000 (Monaco, December 1992). This season has seen strong prices and new records in most areas of the Decorative Arts, with fine works and impressive collections being brought to auction. Underlying the pleasing high prices for outstanding works, however, is a statistical shift which provides much comfort after a period of upheaval and uncertainty. Whilst the volume of sales may not have significantly increased, and in a business focused on the rare this should not be cause for alarm, there has been an encouraging fall in the 'bought-in' percentages.*

There have also been larger numbers of bidders taking part in the sales, with quantifiable developments in various areas of interest. Japanese buyers, for example, are again making their presence felt in the Art Nouveau glass market. Meanwhile, Chinese works of art spokesman Julian Thompson was pleased to confirm that there were no less than five bidders over £600,000 for the Archaic bronze vessel cited above. Significantly, these were from four different locations: Japan, Hong Kong, Continental Europe and London, an indicator of real depth to the market.

As an auctioneer one is uniquely placed to identify a mood swing in the market place. A price list never tells the full story. Was there only one bidder, bidding against the reserve? Were there two bidders or were there several attempting to catch the auctioneer's attention on a given lot? During the past

'Hammersmith'
hand-knotted carpet
(detail)
BY WILLIAM MORRIS, *c*.1895,
342 x 497cm (134 x 194in)
Melbourne A$352,000
(£158,400:$246,400). 24.V.93
From the Collection of Mrs
Tom Barr Smith. (LEFT)

A fragmentary
chalcedony
female head
ROMAN, 1st CENTURY AD,
height 8cm (3⅛in)
London £44,400 ($66,100).
8.VII.93. (ABOVE)

Grisailles-painted
demi-lune
commode
BY RENÉ DUBOIS,
*c.*1775, PARIS,
length 141cm (55¼in)
Monaco FF2,331,000
(£286,000:$427,700). 4.XII.92
From the Estate of Mme
Hélène Beaumont. (ABOVE)

season I for one have become increasingly aware of an upturn in the number of participants; I was frequently obliged to ignore bids, since an auctioneer should only take bidding up between two people at once, returning to an eager third bidder only once one of the contestants has stopped. There is no better measure of a healthy market place than this kind of multiple interest.

It would be foolhardy, however, to expect a resurgence comparable to that which peaked in 1989–90. We are evolving towards a new market, naturally limited by the scarcity of fine property, but driven by the scholarship of collectors and specialist dealers. Connoisseurship plays a greater role in such a market. Speculative buying will find no easy rewards. There is much reference from auctioneers in their press releases to buyers being keen but 'selective'. This is precisely what buyers should be, as indeed should auctioneers, in so far as it is in their power to control the flow and the quality of what they offer. The desirable factors remain constant whether trading in or collecting works of art – quality, rarity and provenance.

The sale of fine French furniture and furnishings from the estate of Mme Hélène Beaumont well demonstrated these ingredients. Fine pieces by Riesener, Peridiez, Dubois, Weisweiler and RVLC boasted provenances which traced their history back through very few hands over a century and a half or more. Here was the ideal mix of works of the finest quality, with specific and fascinating provenances, never before available to even the most senior of today's generation of buyers. Understandably, the auction was highly successful, with 98.4% of the works selling and a total of over FF30 million.

In the field of antiquities provenance is of particular importance because of the problems of establishing lawful origins for excavated works. The success of the sale of Important Antiquities from the Norbert Schimmel Collection, and that of works from the estate of the late Humfry Payne, doubtless owed much to the associations of these names.

Considerable interest was aroused in Melbourne with the sale of a group of carpets and furnishings from Morris & Co. These had the added appeal of being offered for sale by the Barr-Smith family, direct descendants of the Barr-Smiths who had originally commissioned these furnishings from William Morris and his company. One carpet sold for (A$352,000), and the group totalled (A$818,400).

The Decorative Arts category embraces furniture of all types, tapestries and carpets, ceramics and glass, European works of art including nineteenth-century sculpture and garden statuary, American decorative arts and American Indian and Pre-Columbian art, Islamic and Indian art, Chinese, Korean, Japanese and tribal art, and twentieth-century applied arts. In many of these fields the season has been spiced with single-owner sales. Collections of note, in addition to those already mentioned, included the Japanese sword collection formed by Field Marshal Sir Francis Festing, one of which set a new record at £265,500. The sale in New York of much of the stock of Barry Friedman, a dealer in twentieth-century works of art, attracted great interest. A dealer selling stock lacks the appeal of a collector releasing hitherto unavailable works. However Friedman's reputation is such that the sale bore no negative connotations. The results were highly satisfactory with several gratifying prices, notably the $187,000 paid for a table by Hector Guimard.

Continued success for the Decorative Arts market will depend on a rigorous approach to the selection process and on a realistic attitude towards pricing. Vendors have for the most part come to accept the need for prudent estimates to stimulate buyer interest. The great satisfaction of the 1992–93 season has been to witness so many prices set after multiple-party bidding battles. This is the surest sign of a strengthening market.

KATSUKAWA SHUN'EI
Ichikawa Danzo IV in 'Shibaraku' attire
SIGNED AND DATED 1798,
33 x 14.4cm (13 x 5⅝in)
London £5,175 ($7,810).
11.VI.93
From the Collection of the late
Prof. H. R. W. Kühne. (ABOVE)

An Adam Revival cabinet on stand
BY J. G. CRACE AND SONS,
1867, LONDON,
height 213cm (84in)
New York $244,500
($176,700). 17.IV.93. (BELOW)

ISLAMIC AND INDIAN ART

A Safavid tile mosaic panel
PERSIA, SIXTEENTH CENTURY, 171 x 161cm (67¼ x 63½in)
London £275,000 ($445,500). 22.X.92

At the close of the Middle Ages, the Islamic world saw the emergence of new, well-organized states. Sixteenth-century Persia was ruled by the Safavids, who gave much encouragement to the arts. The art of Islam was dominated by religion, and the ornamentation of palaces and mosques often incorporated passages from the Qur'an. In this example of painted tilework, which would originally have decorated an ornamental arch, two verses from the Qur'an are contained within the broad border surrounding the central design. (RIGHT)

A Mamluk marble and stone mosaic fountain
EGYPT, FIFTEENTH CENTURY,
approx. 430 x 430cm (170 x 170in)
London £166,500 ($259,700). 29.IV.93

The Mamluks ruled Egypt from 1450 to 1550. This spectacular fountain is said to have come from a palace in Cairo and dates from the reign of Sultan Qaitbay (1468-96). It is complete and consists of three tiered octagons with a domed superstructure and eight water-jets emanating from eight columns at each level. Fountains of this type were usually incorporated into a domestic interior where they provided a focal point for household and social gatherings. (RIGHT)

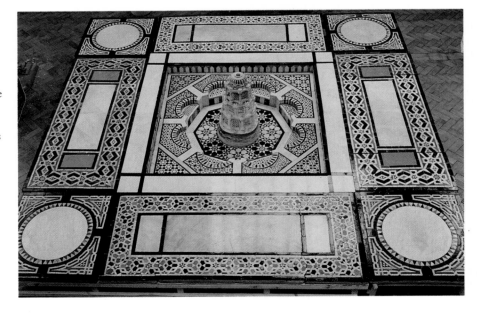

An Iznik blue and white candlestick

TURKEY, *c*.1480, height 25cm (9in)
London £617,500 ($963,300). 29.IV.93
Early monochrome blue and white Iznik pottery is extremely rare and, with this exception, all the finest examples are in museums. The piece dates from the time of Sultan Mehmed II, who, having conquered Constantinople in 1453, founded Istanbul in the ruins of the Byzantine city. Mehmed was well known for his patronage of the arts and it was in response to the demands of his court that the kilns at Iznik took on a new lease of life. (LEFT)

A Khmer sandstone balustrade finial

ANGKOR PERIOD, LATE TWELFTH CENTURY, height 123cm (48¼in)
New York $68,500 (£45,000). 17.VI.93

In the Hindu religion each of the many gods is
associated with a particular animal, which accompanies
them as an attendant or simply as a vehicle on which
the god may ride or travel. This sculptural fragment
depicts Garuda, half-man, half-bird, who was the
faithful carrier of Vishnu the Preserver. (RIGHT)

A Tibetan polychrome wood figure of the Adibuddha Vajrasattva

LADAKH, LATE ELEVENTH/EARLY TWELFTH CENTURY,
height 52.4cm (20⅝in) New York $71,250 (£46,800). 17.VI.93

Very few examples of Tibetan wood sculpture from the
eleventh or twelfth centuries survive, particularly in the
intact state of this figure. This piece retains much of its
original colouring, and depicts a Bodhisattva, the
Buddhist equivalent of a Christian saint. (ABOVE)

A Gandhara figure of Buddha

NORTH-WEST PAKISTAN, THIRD/FOURTH CENTURY, height 153cm (60¼in)
London £38,900 ($60,600). 29.IV.93

Buddhism was founded in northern India in around 500BC when Siddharta
Gautama, who was born a prince but renounced material life to embark on a quest
for spiritual perfection, achieved enlightenment. Gandhara, the region between the
Upper Indus river and Kabul, was one of the richest sources of Buddhist art during
the third and fourth centuries, art acquired by means of the vast wealth amassed by
the Kushan dynasty from trade between the Middle East, India and China. (LEFT)

A Tamil Nadu bronze figure of Siva Nataraja

THIRTEENTH TO FIFTEENTH CENTURY, height 65cm (25½in) London £44,000 ($71,200). 22.X.92

The god Siva manifested himself in a multitude of ways. Here he is seen depicted as
Nataraja, the Lord of the Dance, whose dancing shook the universe and created the
world. Siva – Creator and Destroyer – is probably the most important god in the
Hindu pantheon and this image, which represents the five divine acts of creation,
protection, solace, the dispelling of ignorance and the destruction of the universe,
is one of the best-known in Indian art. (ABOVE)

ORIENTAL CARPETS AND RUGS

An Anatolian dragon and phoenix carpet fragment
FIRST HALF OF THE FIFTEENTH CENTURY OR EARLIER,
approx. 66 x 48cm (26 x 19in)
New York $68,500 (£38,600).
17.IX.92

This fragment is probably the oldest example of Eastern knotted-pile weaving ever to have been offered at auction. Whilst the pattern is interpreted in a purely Turkish style, the dragon and phoenix design is probably borrowed from motifs in Chinese art. Unearthed during the 1935-36 excavations at Fostat in Old Cairo, this fragment provides a significant addition to the body of historical knowledge on early Turkish carpet production. (LEFT)

A Mamluk rug
EGYPT, c.1500,
approx. 188 x 145cm (74 x 57in)
New York $275,000 (£177,400).
10.XII.92

The Mamluk Turks were the rulers of Egypt from 1450 until 1550, when they were deposed by the Ottoman Turks. During this time the Mamluk Sultanate established court manufactories to produce the deeply coloured red, green and blue octagonal medallion rugs that bear its name. These rugs are among the oldest surviving complete carpets in the world and they rarely appear on the commercial market. (RIGHT)

An Azerbaijani rug
EAST CAUCASUS, EIGHTEENTH CENTURY, 210 x 133cm (83 x 52in)
London £26,450 ($41,300). 28.IV.93

During the early sixteenth century, the region of Azerbaijan, sandwiched between the Safavid and Ottoman empires, was an area of continual conflict and changed hands frequently. By 1588 it was firmly under Safavid control and it was Shah Abbas I who, consistent with his policy of establishing weaving centres throughout Persia, founded the textile and carpet workshops that were to embody the weaving tradition of which this rug is an example. (ABOVE)

A Tabriz silk carpet
NORTH-WEST PERSIA, 343 x 269cm (135 x 106in)
London £73,000 ($113,800). 28.IV.93
This exemplary north-west Persian carpet illustrates the high-point of nineteenth-century
Persian silk weavings. The linked double floral medallion is an unusual feature, as is the
depiction of a variety of naturalistically-drawn mythical beasts. The carpet dates from the
third quarter of the nineteenth century. (ABOVE)

CHINESE ART

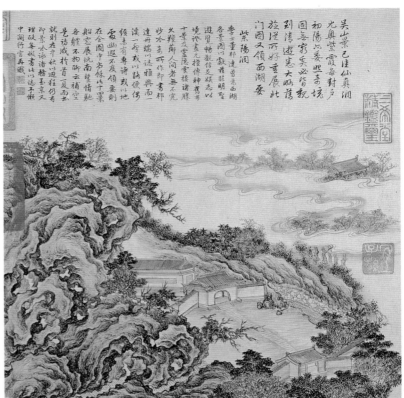

BADA SHANREN
Album of various subjects
SIGNED, INK ON PAPER, SEVEN LEAVES, each 35 x 29.2cm (12 x 11½in)
New York $332,500 (£214,500). 1.VI.93

Bada Shanren (1626-1705), a scion of the fallen
Ming imperial family, was forced to take refuge in
the Buddhist church for his personal safety. An
extremely educated and talented man, he created
a highly individual painting style noted for its
startling juxtapositions and abstracted brushwork.
His work is an important influence on twentieth-
century painting. (ABOVE)

DONG BANGDA
Forty Views of West Lake
c.1750, INK AND COLOUR ON PAPER, SET OF FOUR ALBUMS OF FORTY LEAVES,
each 31.5 x 30.8cm (12⅜ x 12⅛in)
Hong Kong HK$3,320,000 (£272,100:$431,100). 29.IV.93

Dong Bangda was a native of Fuyang in Zhejiang province. As well as being highly
regarded as a painter and calligrapher, he was a successful scholar and official in the
imperial court. The pictorial series *Forty Views of West Lake* was commissioned by the
Qianlong emperor. West Lake, in Dong's province, was a famous beauty spot and
the artist's treatment of the subject seems to have been appreciated by his patron. The
set of albums remained in the imperial collection until the fall of the Qing dynasty.
(ABOVE)

FU BAOSHI
Playing Go at the Water Pavilion
INK AND COLOUR ON PAPER, HANGING SCROLL,
117.5 x 67.3cm (46¼ x 26½in)
New York $134,500 (£89,600). 16.VI.93
From the Robert Hatfield Ellsworth Collection.

One of the great literati painters, Fu Baoshi (1904-65)
specialized in moody, atmospheric landscapes. Fu
studied Western watercolour techniques in Japan and
used these principles in conjunction with traditional
Chinese subject matter and brushwork. This painting,
which the artist considered one of his best, is typical
of Fu Baoshi's romantic style. (LEFT)

GAO QIFENG
An album of birds and flowers
SIGNED, INK AND COLOUR ON PAPER, TWELVE LEAVES,
each 26 x 35.5cm (10¼ x 14in)
Hong Kong HK$1,650,000 (£135,200:$219,000). 29.X.92

One of the salient features of the Chinese painting
tradition is its veneration of the past and its stylistic
emphasis on calligraphic techniques. It was not until
the early 1900s that artists in China began to free
themselves from the restrictions imposed by traditional
training and to experiment with a more Western
approach. This nineteenth-century album of bird and
flower paintings combines Western perspective and
shading with traditional Chinese brushwork, colour
and attention to detail. (ABOVE)

A jadeite snuff bottle
1780-1850, height 5.1cm (2in)
Hong Kong HK$396,000 (£32,400:$52,400). 28.X.92
From almost gem-quality jadeite, as here, to porcelain, to mammoth ivory or to dried tangerine skin, snuff bottles exhibit a greater diversity of constituent material than any other category of Chinese art. (LEFT)

A jadeite ring
The stone approx. 2.5 x 1.9 x 1.4cm (1⁵⁄₁₆ x ¾ x ⁹⁄₁₆in)
Hong Kong HK$4,970,000 (£318,500:$477,700). 28.IV.93
Jadeite has been popular in China as jewellery since the latter part of the Qing dynasty. This magnificent emerald-green cabochon ring of exceptional translucency is mounted on reeded, eighteen-carat gold. (ABOVE)

A pair of imperial jadeite lanterns
1736-95, QIANLONG MARKS AND PERIOD, height 41.3cm (16¼in)
New York $332,500 (£214,500). 1.VI.93
From the Collection of Mr and Mrs Bernard K. Crawford.
These lanterns may well have been made for one of the Buddhist chapels built in the Forbidden City during the reign of the Emperor Qianlong. Qianlong had an interest in the decorative arts and many pieces of the finest quality were crafted in the palace workshops on his instructions. (ABOVE)

An archaic bronze ritual food vessel, the Bo Ju *gui*

*c.*1050-975BC, EARLY WESTERN ZHOU DYNASTY, height 23.6cm (9¼in)
London £925,500 ($1,388,500). 8.VI.93

The Bo Ju *gui*, so named after the pictographic inscription cast on its interior, is remarkable
not only for the quality of its casting but also for the number of directions from which its
ornament is intended to be read: from the front or back the large-eyed masks are prominent;
from the oblique angles the dragons on the corners of the base join to form masks, and from
the sides pairs of birds flank the now foreshortened handles. (ABOVE)

A *wucai* wine jar and cover
1522-66, JIAJING MARK AND PERIOD, height 45.4cm (17⅞in)
New York $2,860,000 (£1,845,200). 1.XII.92
From the J. M. Hu Family Collection.
The sale of this piece in December achieved the world record auction price for a
piece of Chinese (or any other) porcelain. Large jars painted in overglaze enamels
using the five-colour *wucai* palette are considered to be among the most impressive
pieces from the Jiajing period. (ABOVE)

A Ming blue and white stembowl

1426-35, XUANDE MARK AND PERIOD, width 15.6cm (6⅛in)
Hong Kong HK$3,080,000 (£252,400:$406,300). 27.X.92

Stembowls like this one belong to an elite family of
early Ming blue and white porcelain on which the
principal decoration of dragons is executed in deep
cobalt-blue and set against the lighter blue background of a turbulent sea. The number of dragons
varies, from nine, as here, to two or five. The
interior has further dragons in *anhua* ('secret
decoration'), the fineness of which is only revealed
by holding the bowl up to a strong light. (ABOVE)

An imperial *famille rose* vase

1736-95, QIANLONG SEAL MARK AND PERIOD,
height 51.4cm (20¼in)
New York $374,000 (£241,300). 1.XII.92

The 'nine peach' subject painted on this vase in
famille rose enamels was reserved for the Emperor.
The ability to execute such a complex design on a
three-dimensional object was one of the great
achievements of the Palace Workshops under the
Emperor Qianlong, whose reign dominated most
of the eighteenth century. (LEFT)

KOREAN ART

ANONYMOUS
Ten Symbols of Long Life
INK AND COLOUR ON SILK, TEN-FOLD SCREEN,
166 x 356cm (65½ x 140in)
New York $332,500 (£221,700). 18.VI.93

The subject of this nineteenth-century
screen lies at the core of Korean art and
culture. The theme of longevity is derived
from traditional Korean nature-worship
as well as from Taoist beliefs and the
Chinese legends of the immortals. The
scene depicts the ten symbols of long life
in a continuous landscape reminiscent of
Pong Nae, the mythical island stronghold
of the gods. Symbolic dragons, qilins,
phoenix, peacocks and mandarin ducks
wander freely through the island paradise.
(ABOVE)

YANG KI-HUN
Geese in a Marsh (detail)
SIGNED, EMBROIDERY ON SILK, TEN-PANEL SCREEN,
276 x 389cm (108½ x 153in)
New York $167,500 (£111,700). 18.VI.93

Yang Ki-hun (1843-98) came from
northern Korea and spent much of his
time at the court in Seoul. He enjoyed a
good reputation as a painter and
calligrapher and it is likely that this screen
was produced for the royal palace. The
artist would have applied the ink painting
to the screen and then turned it over to
the court embroiderers, the region being
famous for its needlework and for the
high quality of the silk thread produced
there. The inscription is a prose poem
and is signed 'Your Majesty's subject,
Yang Ki-hun'. (LEFT)

JAPANESE ART

A group of two wrestlers
c.1680, PORCELAIN, height 31.8cm (12½in) New York $143,000
(£89,300). 4.XII.92 From the Collection of William S. Paley.
This rare pair of Sumo wrestlers was made during the
last quarter of the seventeenth century when the export
of Japanese porcelain via the Dutch East India
Company was at its height. It was around that time
that the 2,000 year-old martial art of Sumo wrestling
became a professional sport. Only a few other examples
of the subject are known. (ABOVE)

A pair of Kakiemon-style candlesticks
c.1670-90, height (excluding pricket) 34.2cm (13½in)
London £144,500 ($216,700). 10.VI.93
Kakiemon is the name given to a style of porcelain
decoration conceived by Sakaida Kakiemon in
around 1650. Its attenuated, asymmetrical designs in
yellow, turquoise, red and blue enamels are particularly
distinctive and were later much copied by European
porcelain makers. (ABOVE)

UNNO MORITOSHI
An inlaid shibuichi and silver tokuri
1834-96, OZEKI COMPANY, height 19.3cm (7⅝in) London £84,000 ($124,300). 31.III.93
This double-gourd wine-bottle, or *tokuri,* is inlaid in silver and shibuichi (a metal
alloy). The lower section shows the *Rokkasen,* six celebrated poets from the ninth
century. The piece bears the inscription 'Muzashiya', the contemporary name for
the part of Tokyo in which the Ozeki company was then situated. (RIGHT)

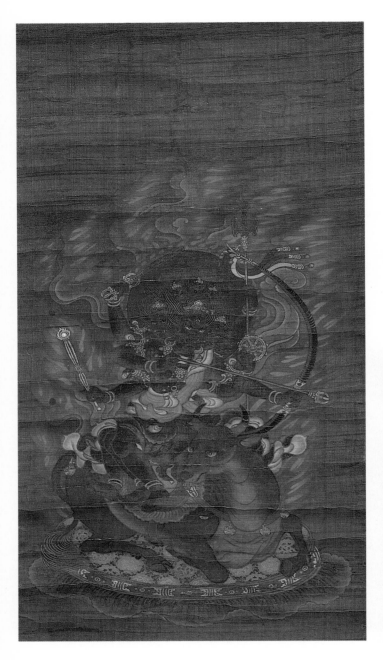

UTAGAWA HIROSHIGE
Sixty-Nine Stations of the Kiso Highway: Seba
SIGNED, WOODBLOCK PRINT, 23.8 x 35.8cm (9⅜ x 14⅛in)
New York $34,500 (£23,000). 18.VI.93
Utagawa Hiroshige is regarded as one of the great Japanese print
masters, and is particularly known for his landscape series illustrating
famous views from various regions of Japan. This print is the most
sought-after composition taken from a series featuring all the stops
along the well-travelled Kiso Highway. (RIGHT)

ANONYMOUS
Daitoku Myo-o
MUROMACHI PERIOD, HANGING SCROLL, INK, COLOUR AND GOLD ON SILK,
68.9 x 36.8cm (27⅛ x 14½in) New York $23,000 (£15,300). 18.VI.93
This work depicts one of the Four Great Wisdom Kings in wrathful
incarnation. It is an image of Esoteric Buddhism, often called 'Secret
Buddhism', as it was passed secretly from teacher to pupil. This form
of Buddhism came to Japan via China in the ninth century. (ABOVE)

RIMPA SCHOOL
Scene from the Tale of Ise
TWO-PANEL SCREEN, INK, COLOUR AND GOLD ON PAPER, 171 x 184cm (67½ x 74½in)
New York $48,875 (£35,500). 18.VI.93 From the Estate of Baron Hisaya Iwasake.
The last great flowering of Japanese art took place during the Edo
period (1615-1868). A truly Japanese style is reflected in the works
produced by the Rimpa School throughout the Edo period, which
derive their inspiration from nature and literature. (ABOVE)

KATSUSHIKA HOKUSAI
Interior of a Theatre with a Play in Progress
SIGNED AND DATED 1788,
26 x 38.8cm (10¼ x 15⅛in)
London £14,950 ($22,500).
11.VI.93

This print falls into the category of *ukiyo-e*, which translates as 'Pictures of the Floating World' and was a popular movement in Japanese genre painting in the Tokugawa period. Theatre scenes were a favourite subject, arising from the development of *kabuki* theatre in the seventeenth century. (BELOW)

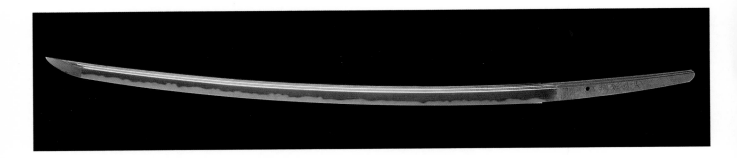

A black lacquer inro with metal inlay

BY HARA YOYUSAI AND HARUAKI HOGEN, NINETEENTH CENTURY,
length 8.5cm (3⅜in) London £52,100 ($77,100). 31.III.93
An inro is a seal case and comprises a box of vertically-
arranged fitted trays threaded down each side by a cord
which in turn manipulates the opening and closing
actions by means of a bead, or *ojime*. (ABOVE)

YAMAURA MASAYUKI
A Shinshinto
Musashi Katana

DATED 1839, 69.6cm (27⅜in)
London £265,500 ($392,200).
1.IV.93
From the Collection of Field
Marshal Sir Francis Festing.
Japanese sword-making
has been developed over
1,500 years. In the
nineteenth century a
revival of traditional
methods produced several
masters, the most famous
of whom was Yamaura
Masayuki. A Japanese
sword is appreciated both
as a weapon and as a work
of art. (ABOVE)

Figure of Raigo
Kannon

GILTWOOD, KAMAKURA PERIOD,
height 46.4cm (18¼in)
New York $30,800 (£19,200).
4.XII.92
'Pure-Land Buddhism',
which centres on the
Buddha Amitabha, Lord
of the Western Paradise,
first came to Japan in the
tenth century. One of the
most recurring images is
that of the *raigo*
(or heavenly descent) in
which Amitabha is flanked
by his two Bodhisattvas
leading a heavenly retinue
to welcome and guide the
soul of the dying to
paradise. (LEFT)

TRIBAL ART

A Raratonga Island staff god section
Height 89.5cm (35¼in)
New York $165,000 (£110,800). 24.XI.92

Raratonga, one of the Cook Islands, was converted to Christianity in 1927. John Williams, a leading missionary, claimed to have destroyed most of the indigenous religious artifacts in his crusade to eradicate pagan worship. Fortunately, Williams' purge was not as effective as he maintained, and fifteen complete staff gods are known to exist, as well as a number of end-sections, including this piece. The emergence of these sculptures suggests that a quantity of staff gods was hidden from Williams by the islanders. (ABOVE)

A Hawaiian bowl
Greatest diameter 45cm (17⅜in)
London £6,900 ($10,100). 21.VI.93
Property of Susan Mast

It was a tradition within Hawaiian communities to congregate for meals in a communal tent and to share what was known as a community bowl. The piece shown here is important in that it is considerably larger than the standard bowl used for this purpose. The particularly rich and glossy patina is also exceptional. (RIGHT)

A Solomon Islands seated female figure
Height 10cm (4in)
London £3,080 ($4,840). 7.XII.92 From the Peter Hallinan Collection

This figure, fashioned from betelnut, once surmounted a limestick, a splinter of which was once attached to the base. Limesticks were used in the Solomon Islands to extract lime from containers in order to make a substance that featured regularly in Melanesian ceremonial rituals. Mixing the lime with betel vine and saliva resulted in a concoction that induced a slightly stimulating effect on the brain. (ABOVE RIGHT)

A Tellem figure
Height 34cm (13½in)
London £20,700 ($30,400).
21.VI.93
The gesture of this figure has been interpreted in different ways. The most obvious relates to its use on ancestral altars, but it has also been suggested that it could refer to the most crucial moment in the induction ritual for a Binu priest. At the high point in the ceremony the postulant would kneel before two officiating priests who would pour chicken blood and millet over a pendant held above his head. With these sacrificial liquids streaming over him the new priest would then kneel and raise his hands to wipe them away. (RIGHT)

**A Fang male
reliquary figure**
Height 44.5cm (17½in)
New York $206,000
(£133,700). 18.V.93
From the Alexander S. Honig
Collection.

The reliquary figure was
of great significance to
the Fang and embodied
considerable power. In
this example the variant
surface textures of the
sculpture attest to years
of ritual use. The
sculptural strength of the
figure can be detected in
the strong horizontal
lines, which rhythmically
break up the length of
the torso, giving it a
unity and plasticity
which is achieved in the
round by a series of
corresponding lines and
volumes. It was formerly
in the collection of Serge
Brignoni, a noted pre-
War collector. (LEFT)

PRE-COLUMBIAN ART

A Mochica wood portrait mask
*c.*100BC-AD300, NORTH COAST, width 26.4cm (10⅜in)
New York $104,000 (£68,400). 23.XI.92
Ceramic portraits are one of the hallmarks of Moche art, but this sculpted example in wood
may be unique. The expressive and clearly defined features, together with the rich colours and
ornamental detail, suggest that it might originally have been the property of a high-ranking –
possibly royal – individual. (ABOVE)

A Tiahuanaco gold beaker
*c.*AD900-1100, COASTAL TIAHUANACO, height 11.1cm (4⅜in)
New York $79,500 (£51,600). 17.V.93
The Tiahuanaco region was in the southern highlands of the Andes
on the Bolivian/Peruvian border. This example of gold repoussé
work, which would have been inlaid with semi-precious stones,
depicts a puma-headed deity towering over two captives. (ABOVE)

An Olmec blackware vessel
*c.*1150-550BC, CHALCATZINGO, height 45.1cm (17¾in)
New York $233,500 (£151,600). 17.V.93
The Olmec region was on the Gulf Coast of Pre-Columbian Mexico.
The Olmec were the first Pre-Columbian culture to combine realism
with religious symbolism. This piece is a fine example of symbolic
decoration, and includes the profile of a grimacing deity. (ABOVE)

AMERICAN INDIAN ART

A pair of quilled hide moccasins
NORTH-EASTERN, POSSIBLY RED RIVER METIS OR CREE,
length 25.7cm (10⅛in) New York $46,750 (£30,500). 12.XI.92
Property of the Earl of Harrowby
Moccasins were perhaps the most significant item of Indian cloth-ing. This pair, made of soft hide with quillwork decoration, prob-ably dates from the middle of the eighteenth century. (BELOW)

A pair of quilled hide moccasins
EASTERN GREAT LAKES, HURON, length 25.4cm (10in)
New York $77,000 (£50,300). 12.XI.92
Property of the Earl of Harrowby
These fine early moccasins were originally acquired by
the first, or possibly the second, Earl of Harrowby,
both of whom were travellers, art collectors and
diplomats of distinction during the nineteenth century.
The moccasins remained in the family and were
offered for sale by the present Earl. (ABOVE)

A polychrome coiled seed jar
PANAMINT SHOSHONE, diameter at shoulder 20.3cm (8in)
New York, $13,800 (£8,900). 25.V.93
From the Charlotte Butler Skinner Collection
This unusual example of Panamint Shoshone basket-work comes from the collection of Charlotte Butler Skinner, who, in 1905, settled in Owens Valley, California, and during the years that followed filled her house with Indian baskets, many of which she acquired from Panamint Shoshone women camping nearby.
Early basketry from this tribe is highly varied in its decoration, the result of regular contact with the basket-makers of neighbouring tribes. (RIGHT)

A tradecloth and beadwork panel bag

NORTH-EASTERN, RED RIVER METIS OR CREE, length 60.3cm (23¾in)
New York $41,800 (£27,300). 12.XI.92 From the Collection of the Earl of Harrowby

The Red River Metis wore caps and top hats encircled with silk ribbons, knee-length leggings worn over trousers, and coats bound with sashes. The panel bag was normally attached to the sash and was commonly used as a tobacco pouch. The ornamentation was standard: a panel of woven beadwork attached to the bottom, surrounded by woollen tassels on long strings of beads. The beadwork design was geometric and often quite complex. (ABOVE)

A cloth and quillwork neck pouch

EASTERN GREAT LAKES, PROBABLY EASTERN OJIBWA, total length 80cm (31½in)
New York $71,500 (£46,700). 12.XI.92 From the Collection of the Earl of Harrowby

Pouches such as this were worn suspended from a strap around the neck. The rectangular form decorated with two parallel bands of woven quillwork is typical of the work of the natives of the central Subarctic. Such bags were widely traded, and examples similar to the one shown here have been dated to the late eighteenth century. Watercolours of the 1820s by the artist Peter Rindisbacker depict neck pouches in use at that time. (RIGHT)

ANTIQUITIES

An Egyptian crystalline limestone head
1323-1292BC, EIGHTEENTH DYNASTY, REIGN OF AY/HOREMHAB,
height 25.6cm (10⅛in)
New York $451,000 (£287,200). 16.XII.92
From the Norbert Schimmel Collection.

The horizontal bands incised across the forehead of this piece are the remains of a headdress worn by queens, goddesses, or queens in the guise of goddesses. This head would have surmounted a monumental statue, possibly of Horemhab's queen, Mutnodjmet. Horemhab served as a general under Tutankhamun and his successor King Ay, finally assuming the throne himself as the last king of the Eighteenth Dynasty. (LEFT)

A Roman marble figure of Pan

c. MID-SECOND CENTURY AD, ANTONINE, height 67.6cm (26⅝in)
New York $176,000 (£110,400). 17.XII.92
This statue is a copy of a lost Hellenistic original of
the third/second century BC, and is a fine
representative of the baroque currents in the art
of the period. (RIGHT)

An Egyptian alabaster jar

*c.*2965-2705BC, EARLY DYNASTIC PERIOD, height 57.8cm (22¾in)
London £28,750 ($41,300). 8.VII.92

The Egyptians, like the Greeks, had no specific word
for 'art' and did not distinguish it from handicraft.
Hence the ancient Egyptian craftsman's feeling for
materials and his instinctive sense of form and
proportion are often revealed most graphically in
the applied arts. The flowing lines and classically
simple definition of this jar are a clear illustration of
the beauty that could be invested in an entirely
functional utensil. (RIGHT)

An Attic white-ground *lekythos* fragment
NEAR THE THANATOS PAINTER, *c.*440BC, height 18.1cm (7⅛in)
London £20,900 ($32,600). 10.XII.92

Attic, or Athenian, vase-painting is stylistically most
readily identified by its black- and red-figure work,
but there was also a white-ground style, of which
this fragment is a fine example. The white slip appears
to have been most commonly applied to *lekythoi*,
elongated funerary vessels normally decorated with
scenes of domestic life or farewell. The white-ground
style invited a softer, more fluid draughtsmanship than
the black- and red-figure styles, and allowed a wider
range of colours for drapery. (LEFT)

EUROPEAN WORKS OF ART

A Florentine ormolu-mounted and
pietra dura **ebonized mahogany casket**
31 x 52.7 x 45.7cm (12¼ x 20¾ x 18in)
New York $21,850 (£14,180). 12.I.93
This Florentine casket was reputedly formerly in the
collection of Empress Eugenia de Montijo of France.
The interior of the casket is fitted with red velvet trays.
(BELOW)

A north German bronze aquamanile
*c.*1200, height 29.8cm (11¾in)
London £660,000 ($1,029,600). 10.XII.92
Although a few northern European water vessels were fashioned in the shape of
equestrian knights, it is rare to find one sporting a nasal helm. Most horse-and-rider
aquamaniles therefore had flat-topped helmets, some of which were adapted into
hinged lids to receive the water. (ABOVE)

One of three north German wood reliefs of saints

*c.*1490-1500, height 103cm (41½in)
London £52,100 ($79,700) for the three. 22.IV.93

This piece and its two companion pieces have been attributed to the workshops of Hans Klocker, a renowned craftsman resident in Brixen at the end of the fifteenth century. The attribution is based on comparable works by Klocker, such as his figure of St. George, now in the Deutsches Museum, Berlin, which reveals a marked similarity in the detailing of the hands, the facial expression and the workmanship of the hair. (RIGHT)

A Paduan bronze figure of a satyr

EARLY SIXTEENTH CENTURY, height 24.6cm (9⅝in)
New York $46,000 (£29,800). 12.I.93

This piece might have served a utilitarian purpose – the figure originally supporting a standing vase in its right hand that would probably have been used as an inkpot or pen holder. (LEFT)

One of a pair of Florentine terracotta angels

SECOND QUARTER OF THE SIXTEENTH CENTURY, height 72.4cm (28½in)
New York $51,750 (£33,600) for the pair. 12.I.93

Whilst this figure is largely in keeping with the traditions of late fifteenth- and early sixteenth-century Florentine terracotta sculpture, the drapery, the style of the hair and the somewhat mannered pose suggest a date closer to the middle of the sixteenth century. (LEFT)

PIER JACOPO
ALARI-BONACOLSI,
CALLED ANTICO
**A bronze figure of
the young Hercules,
reading**
*c.*1495, MANTUA, height
22.9cm (9in)
London £1,266,500
($1,887,000). 8.VII.93

One of the great Italian
Renaissance sculptors,
Antico was born in
Mantua in around 1460.
The ruling family of the
city at that time, the
Gonzagas, were avid
patrons of the arts, and
Antico was to serve three
generations of the family
before his death in 1528.
The small bronzes
produced by Antico
adhered closely to the
forms and ideals of the
Hellenistic Roman
sculptures being
excavated at that time.
(RIGHT)

CLAUDE MICHEL, CALLED CLODION
A terracotta group celebrating the ascension of the Montgolfier brothers' hot-air balloon
SIGNED, *c*.1785, height 53.5cm (21in)
London £397,500 ($592,200). 8.VII.93

As one of the most accomplished of late eighteenth-century French sculptors, Clodion was patronized by such figures as Catherine the Great and Louis XVI, who in 1778 made him *Sculpteur du Roi*. His reputation and popularity survived the upheavals of the French Revolution, to the extent that in 1791 he was created *Sculpteur de Paris*. This allegorical work celebrates the invention of the hot-air balloon by the Montgolfier brothers, and the first-ever ascents made in the autumn of 1783. (LEFT)

NINETEENTH-CENTURY SCULPTURE

CHARLES SUMMERS
Cupid whispering to Venus
SIGNED AND DATED *1875*,
WHITE MARBLE,
height without column 77cm (30¼in)
London £30,800 ($48,000). 30.IV.93

Charles Summers showed at the Great Exhibition of 1851 and in the same year became the first Royal Academy student to win the Silver and Gold medals simultaneously. In 1853 he left for Australia to prospect for gold. After a sad lack of success in this venture he returned to art and achieved a formidable reputation as Australia's leading sculptor. He went back to Europe in 1867, establishing a flourishing studio in Rome. (BELOW)

SIR ALFRED GILBERT
Perseus Arming
BRONZE WITH BLACK PATINA, height including base
73cm (28¾in) London £33,000 ($51,500). 30.IV.93

At the time the model for this bronze was made Gilbert was living in Rome. It was the first of an autobiographical trilogy, the others being *Icarus* and *Comedy and Tragedy*. (ABOVE LEFT)

SIR ALFRED GILBERT
Comedy and Tragedy: 'Sic Vita'
BRONZE WITH BLACK PATINA, height including base
78.5cm (31in) London £27,500 ($42,900). 30.IV.93

The composition of the allegorical *Comedy and Tragedy*, a dancing figure looking askance from the mask it holds before its face, is one of self-parody. (ABOVE RIGHT)

GIOVANNI GIUSEPPE FONTANA
Cupid captured by Venus
*c.*1870, WHITE MARBLE, height 132cm (52in)
Sussex £15,400 ($23,250). 1.VI.93

Giovanni Giuseppe Fontana, sculptor and watercolourist, was born in Carrara in 1821 and died in London in 1893. He specialized in classical and allegorical groups and exhibited at the Royal Academy and the New Watercolour Society. Examples of his work can be seen in the collection of the Walker Art Gallery, Liverpool. (ABOVE)

GARDEN STATUARY

CARL DORN
Leda and the Swan
*c.*1897, BRONZE,
height 193cm (76in)
New York $50,600 (£33,500).
1.VII.93
Carl Dorn was born in
1831 and exhibited
regularly at the Berlin
Academy. Mythological
subjects such as this
example were extremely
popular with sculptors and
their patrons during the
late-nineteenth century,
although Dorn's particular
specialization was in busts
and portrait reliefs. (RIGHT)

RAFFAELE MARINI
**Figure of a
nude female**
SIGNED, LATE-NINETEENTH
CENTURY, MARBLE,
196 x 92.7cm (77 x 36½in)
New York $31,900 (£17,800).
16.IX.92
Raffaele Marini was born in
Naples in 1868 and studied
at the city's Institute of Fine
Art, where he exhibited
from 1888 onwards. Marini
specialized in groups and
figures from Roman
antiquity. This figure,
prostrate in a field covered
with fruit and flowers, was
probably intended to
represent Persephone.
(RIGHT)

ATTRIBUTED TO EMANUELE CARONI
A female figure
THIRD QUARTER OF THE NINETEENTH
CENTURY, MARBLE, height including base
187cm (73½in)
New York $101,500 (£70,000). 18.III.93
The surge of nationalistic fervour
which swept America after the Civil
War created a demand for
monumental works of sculpture.
This work attributed to Emanuele
Caroni (born in 1826) represents the
Continent America. (LEFT)

ENGLISH FURNITURE

A Queen Anne japanned bureau bookcase

SIGNED AND DATED *1713*, height
257cm (101in)
New York $231,000 (£142,593).
24.X.92
Property of Mr and Mrs Douglas Dillon
This gilt-decorated, black-
japanned bureau bookcase has
a double dome surmounted
by three giltwood finials
representing a crowned
maiden, a water bearer and a
trumpeter. Despite this
classical detailing and the use
of Corinthian pilasters, the
ornamentation is consistent
with the contemporary taste
for *chinoiserie*: the fall-front,
for example, is decorated with
a procession of Chinese
dignitaries. (LEFT)

A pair of George I walnut side chairs

FIRST QUARTER OF THE EIGHTEENTH CENTURY
New York $198,000 (£122,222). 24.X.92

These substantial burr-walnut chairs have vase-form splats with carved foliage 'spilling' from their tops. The cabriole legs are carved with classical motifs: shells at the knee and lion's-paw feet. The floral needlepoint seats, in tones of green and pink on a brown ground, are a fitting complement to the rich, mottled tones of the wood. (ABOVE)

A Queen Anne walnut wing chair

c.1705
New York $231,000 (£142,593).
24.X.92

This rare walnut chair is upholstered with fine eighteenth-century needlepoint, probably original, depicting a seated maiden holding aloft a cluster of grapes accompanied by a recumbent deer and leopard. The sides, too, are richly embellished with depictions of flora and fauna, and the seat bears images of a male and female, possibly Adam and Eve. The cabriole legs are carved at the knees with shells and foliage, and end in pad feet. (LEFT)

ATTRIBUTED TO
GEORGE BULLOCK
**An oval oak dining
or breakfast table**
*c.*1815,
top 200 x 180cm (78¾ x 71in)
London £110,000 ($168,300).
27.XI.92
Although not known to
be part of any recorded
Bullock commission, this
piece relates closely to
other attributable works
by him. (RIGHT)

ATTRIBUTED TO
THOMAS CHIPPENDALE
**A George III
lacquer-mounted
commode**
*c.*1775, height 90cm (35½in)
London £194,000 ($302,600).
14.V.93
Conceived in the
chinoiserie style of the
early 1770s, this com-
mode is related to a
small group of japanned
and lacquered com-
modes by, or attributed
to, Thomas Chippendale.
An extensive mountain-
ous landscape is depicted
on the top and a more
intimate village scene on
the panelled doors. The
four gilt-brass pilasters
have swagged rams'
heads and hoof feet.
(RIGHT)

ATTRIBUTED TO JOHN CHANNON
A George II brass-inlaid circular tripod table
*c.*1740, height 71cm (28in)
London £67,500 ($100,500). 9.VII.93

John Channon, who had established himself in St Martin's Lane by the mid 1730s, produced furniture that was strikingly Germanic in character, and it is possible that he employed German cabinet-makers in his workshop. This table has an intricate ten-lobed top with a central cinquefoil surrounded by engraved brass shells and mother-of-pearl buds. The plain baluster stem is supported by cabriole legs, with engraved brass leaf mounts. (RIGHT)

SEDDON, SONS AND SHACKLETON
The top of one of a pair of George III D-shaped painted satinwood card tables
1793, width 100cm (39¼in)
London £67,500 ($100,500) for the pair. 9.VII.93

This card table (one of a pair) was supplied to Richard Hall Clarke of Bridwell House, Devon, as part of a commission that included chairs, a sofa, tripods and even window cornices – all intended for a suite of state rooms. Seddon established his cabinet-making business in Aldersgate Street, London, in the early 1750s and by 1786 had over 400 employees. (ABOVE LEFT)

SEDDON, SONS AND SHACKLETON
A George III painted satinwood Pembroke table
1793, top when open 81 x 95cm (30 x 37½in)
London £41,100 ($61,200). 9.VII.93

This Pembroke table is from the same commission as the satinwood card table captioned above. (LEFT)

CONTINENTAL FURNITURE

A Louis XV secrétaire à abattant, incorporating lacquer panels
STAMPED *BVRB JME*, MID-EIGHTEENTH CENTURY, width 105cm (41¼in)
London £496,500 ($713,600). 11.VI.93
Bernard van Riesenburg was the son of a Dutch merchant and cabinet-maker who had moved to Paris in 1694. He enjoyed a considerable reputation, and was probably the first Parisian *ébéniste* to inset Sèvres plaques into furniture, a fashion that acquired great popularity during the reign of Louis XVI. It is likely that he also initiated the trend for end-cut marquetry, in which the inlaid decoration was cut across the grain to give a distinctive finish. (LEFT)

A Louis XVI ormolu-mounted mahogany bureau-plat, inset with painted panels
STAMPED *WEISWEILER*, *c.*1788-90,
width 117cm (46⅛in)
Monaco FF8,436,000
(£968,100:$1,519,900). 4.XII.92
From the estate of
Mme Hélène Beaumont.
The discoveries of
Pompeii and Herculan-
eum in the mid-eighteenth
century led to the growing
adoption of classical styles
and ideals. One of those
who capitalized on
this new taste was the
German cabinet-maker
Adam Weisweiler, whose
veneered pieces are
notable for their finely
figured wood and ormolu
mounts. (LEFT)

A Louis XVI japannned commode
STAMPED *LEVASSEUR*, *c.*1770-90,
width 122.5cm (49in)
Monaco FF6,660,000
(£817,100:$1,222,000). 3.VII.93
Japanning as an
embellishment to furniture
was immensely popular in
France throughout the mid-
eighteenth century, and
Etienne Levasseur (1721-98)
was one of the master
exponents of the style. The
commode shown here is an
important example of
Levasseur's work. (RIGHT)

A Louis XV marquetry cylinder bureau

STAMPED *J.F. LELEU, c.*1770, height 109cm (41in)
London £265,500 ($400,900). 11.VI.93

Jean-François Leleu (1729-1807) was apprenticed in the
workshop of the master *ébéniste* Jean-François Oeben,
whose furniture is renowned for the excellence of its
marquetry. After Oeben's death, Leleu's career went
from strength to strength. His patrons included the
Prince de Condé, for whom he created a marquetry floor
in the Palais de Bourbon, and Madame du Barry. He
also produced furniture for the Baron d'Ivry at the
Château d'Hénonville and probably for the Marquis
de Marigny at Menars. (LEFT)

Two from a set of six Louis XV giltwood fauteuils à la reine

SIGNED *TILLIARD,*
MID-EIGHTEENTH CENTURY,
New York $825,000 (£528,800).
31.X.92

Louis XV's preference for
living in the intimate
surroundings of the *petits
appartements* in Versailles
as opposed to the vast and
imposing state rooms did
much to encourage the
development of more
informal furniture. Design
conceits still prevailed,
however, and chairs were
often styled to stand in a
specific position in the
room in order that the
shape of their backs and
their carved decoration
could reflect that of the
panelling behind. (RIGHT)

A German painted and parcel-gilt commode

MID-EIGHTEENTH CENTURY,
width 165cm (65in)
New York $253,000
(£172,100). 27.III.93

This commode probably comes from Munich. During the eighteenth century Germany was divided into a number of separate courts, each ruled by an elector, bishop or prince. Contemporary furniture was thus extremely diverse in style. The south, and in particular the great palaces such as Würzburg and Nymphenburg, produced furniture which was frequently based on French prototypes, such as this piece. (LEFT)

A pair of Louis XVI ormolu five-light bras de lumière

LAST QUARTER OF THE EIGHTEENTH CENTURY,
height 68.6cm (27in)
New York $396,000
(£253,800). 31.X.92

The fashion for ormolu in France began in the 1660s, when most art and decoration became focused on the glorification of the nation and of its ruler Louis XIV.

By the eighteenth century gilded metal-work had come to be virtually synonymous with the refinement of the French nobility. The design of these wall-lights is almost identical to two pairs currently in the Petit Trianon at Versailles. (LEFT)

An Italian ormolu, burr-walnut and fruitwood marquetry commode
MID-EIGHTEENTH CENTURY, height 87.6cm (34½in)
New York $88,000 (£56,400). 26.IX.92

The *bombé* commode is perhaps the most familiar example of rococo furniture. This piece comes from Lombardy in northern Italy and was most likely made in Milan, the design elements being typical of the mid-eighteenth century in that city. The gilt-metal mounts, which completely encase the legs and then follow the outline of the apron frieze, are a particularly unusual feature. (BELOW)

An Italian walnut-veneered bureau-cabinet
SECOND QUARTER OF THE EIGHTEENTH CENTURY,
height 238cm (95¼in)
Milan L180,000,000 (£83,100:$130,500). 3.XII.92

The rococo in Italy, which was at that time still divided into independent states, was most immediately apparent in the north. In Rome, where the prime concern of the nobility was with dignity and ceremony, it was less easy to distinguish from the baroque, residual vestiges of which remained long after the formal end of the movement itself. (ABOVE)

A Neapolitan suite of painted and parcel-gilt furniture
*c.*1800, the table diameter 72cm (28½in)
London £95,000 ($146,300). 28.V.93

This suite was reputedly made for Napoleon's second wife, the empress Marie-Louise, the link with the city of Naples possibly having been formed through the city's queen, Napoleon's sister, Caroline Murat. (RIGHT)

NINETEENTH-CENTURY FURNITURE

An oak dining table
PHILIP WEBB, *c*.1864, length 260cm (102¼in)
London £26,400 ($40,300). 12.II.92
Philip Webb was a close associate of William Morris, with whom he was a founding partner
of Morris, Marshall, Faulkner and Co. This oak dining table was one of the company's
commissions, and is here seen with the appropriate accompaniment of a collection of
William de Morgan ceramics. (ABOVE)

One of a pair of
German carved
ivory wall plaques
*c.*1860, width 129cm (50¾in)
London £78,500 ($119,300)
for the pair. 2.IV.93
The pair of wall plaques
of which this is one are
after the work of the
early seventeenth-
century sculptor and
ivory carver Gerard van
Opstal, who worked
under Richelieu, and
eventually became *Sculp-
teur du Roi*. Examples of
original ivory carving by
van Opstal are in the
Louvre and the Rijks-
museum. The pair
represented here show
such subjects as the
Triumph of Bacchus and
the Sacrifice to Priapus.
(RIGHT)

A pair of figural
candelabra
EUGENE DELAPLANCHE,
DATED *1885*, MARBLE AND GILT-
BRONZE, height 285cm (112in)
New York $165,000 (£92,100).
16.IX.92
Eugene Delaplanche
exhibited at the Paris
Salon in 1861, winning
the Prix de Rome three
years later. He is well
known for his portrait
and allegorical sculpture,
of which these large
figures are a good
example. Each is raised
on a violet marble base
and each supports tiered,
foliage-cast candle
branches hung with
glass drops. (LEFT)

A French marquetry occasional table

*c.*1855, Paris,
height 72cm (28½in)
London £33,350 ($51,000).
21.V.93

This occasional table has been attributed to Joseph Cremer, one of the most celebrated *marqueteurs* of the opulent Second Empire period. He supplied furniture to Louis-Philippe in 1844, also to the King of Holland, and exhibited at the 1852, 1855 and the 1862 International exhibitions. (Left and Right)

AMERICAN DECORATIVE ARTS

A 'Chippendale' wing armchair
*c.*1770, PHILADELPHIA
New York $321,500 (£211,500). 30.I.93

Thomas Chippendale's book of furniture designs, *The Gentleman and Cabinet-maker's Director*, was published in England in 1754, and a revised edition became available in Philadelphia in 1762. The book made a significant impression on tastes in furniture design in late eighteenth-century America, especially with New England cabinet-makers. (LEFT)

A 'Chippendale' side chair
*c.*1770, PHILADELPHIA
New York $156,500 (£102,900). 30.I.93

The rise in popularity in New England of Chippendale-style pieces of furniture encouraged an accompanying rise in the quality of workmanship. This can clearly be seen in this rare dining chair made in Philadelphia in around 1770. It is identical to two other chairs, one in the Henry Ford Museum and the other in the Karolik Collection at the Museum of Fine Arts in Boston. (RIGHT)

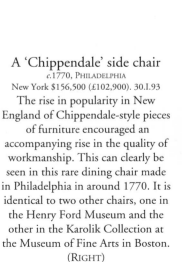

A Queen Anne-style balloon-seat side chair
*c.*1755, NEW YORK
New York $189,500 (£124,600). 30.I.93

On the whole the rococo movement made little impact on eighteenth-century American cabinet-makers although there is some evidence of its serpentine lines in their design of chair splats, as can be seen here. This chair is part of an original set of eight, one now being in the Metropolitan Museum of Art, New York, four in the private collection of Bernard Levy and one (previously owned by Cora Ginsburg) in another private collection. (ABOVE)

An ormolu-mounted lighthouse clock
*c.*1825, MASSACHUSETTS,
height 63.5cm (25in)
New York $200,500
(£136,300). 23.VI.93
The lighthouse clock was
an invention of Simon
Willard and this fine and
rare example is inscribed
Simon Willard's Patent.
It is of a type often
referred to as an
Eddystone lighthouse
clock, taking its name
from the Eddystone
lighthouse in Plymouth,
England. (LEFT)

The Martin van Buren dining table
1800-10, NEW YORK, length
fully extended 474cm (186½in)
New York $189,500
(£128,900). 23.VI.93
The accordion-action
construction of this rare
table is based on a patent
of 1800 of Richard
Gillow of London and
Lancaster. Most tables of
this form are believed to
be the work of New
York cabinet-makers.
This particular table was
made for Martin van
Buren, President of the
United States. (RIGHT)

An American eagle
*c.*1880, PENNSYLVANIA, height 35.6cm (14in)
New York $38,500 (£23,700). 25.X.92
This stylized piece of American folk art was made by
Wilhelm Schimmel of the Cumberland Valley,
Pennsylvania, in around 1880. Decorated with paint
and gesso, the eagle has a yellow comb, red mouth
and yellow feet. (RIGHT)

A painted dower chest
DATED *1778*, SCHOHARIE COUNTY, NEW YORK, length 119cm (47in)
New York $46,000 (£30,200). 30.1.93
In 1710, as part of an experiment sponsored by the
British Government, 2,400 Germans arrived in the
Hudson River Valley. They settled in the Schoharie
and Mohawk valleys of New York, and produced
fine-quality furnishings for their houses, including
decorated marriage chests. (BELOW)

Afbeelding van een Huis in Oost Jersey aan de Pesayack
Rivier, twintig mylen N.W. van Nieuw York, en Sestien mylen N.O. van Morris Town.

PETER BUDENAARDE
**A House in
East Jersey on the
Passaic River**
DATED *1786*, WATERCOLOUR,
PEN AND INK ON PAPER,
20.3 x 26.7cm (8 x 10½in)
New York $26,450 (£17,400).
30.I.93
On a present-day map of
New Jersey, the area
depicted in this work is
twenty miles north-west
of New York City. It was
a region which was
heavily settled by old
New Jersey Dutch
families. Visitors to
neighbouring Bergen
County in the late-
eighteenth century noted
the use of the Dutch
language, both spoken
and written. (ABOVE)

CARL E. MUNCH
**A fraktur birth-
letter for Salome
Holtzmann**
SIGNED AND DATED *1810*,
WATERCOLOUR, PEN-AND-INK
AND GRAPHITE ON PAPER,
31.8 x 38.1cm (12½ x 15in)
New York $55,000 (£33,900).
25.X.92
Carl E. Munch was born
in Germany in 1769. In
1798 he emigrated to
America where he
became a teacher, first at
Schaefferstown and then
at Rehrersburg. In 1804
he moved across the
mountains to the Lykens
Valley. This painted
birth-letter shows angels
with a cornucopia of
flowers, wreaths and
flower-filled vases. (LEFT)

EUROPEAN TAPESTRIES

A northern Swiss tapestry fragment
c.1440-50, PROBABLY BASEL,
50.5 x 49.8cm (19⅞ x 19⅝in)
New York $101,500 (£65,900). 24.V.93
This early fragment depicts a lady and a gentleman in conversation and clad in courtly attire. The lady upholds a bunch of flowers, and the background is filled with scrolling vines. (RIGHT)

A London seasons tapestry
EARLY EIGHTEENTH CENTURY,
295 x 427cm (116 x 168in)
London £33,000 ($51,800). 11.XII.92
This tapestry is from a set of the seasons and depicts the months of Summer. Another version of the work is known, which is inscribed 'Julius/Augustus/September'. The two tapestries are now ascribed to the London workshop of John Chabanex, a Huguenot refugee working in England in the early eighteenth century. (BELOW)

A Brussels mythological tapestry
LATE SEVENTEENTH CENTURY,
339 x 263cm (133½ x 103½in)
New York $54,625 (£35,400).
12.I.93
This tapestry depicts
Apollo and Daphne in a
scene from Ovid's
Metamorphoses, where the
nymph is transposed into a
laurel tree to escape the
pursuit of Apollo. The
tapestry is attributed to
the Brussels workshop of
Daniel Abbeloos, who is
first recorded in 1663.
(LEFT)

APPLIED ARTS

DEMETRE H. CHIPARUS
A bronze and ivory figural group
*c.*1925, height 52.1cm (20½in) New York $151,000 (£104,100). 19.III.93
Together with Frederick Preiss, Demetre Chiparus inspired a fashion in small, decorative, female figures
which he clothed in exotic costumes inspired by the Ballets Russes, the Ziegfeld Follies or by the chorus
lines of the Casino de Paris. As with this piece, he executed the skin in ivory and the clothing in bronze.
The figures of Chiparus tend to be more extravagant and fanciful than those of Preiss. (ABOVE)

CLEMENT MASSIER
**A symbolist
lustre-glazed
earthenware charger**
*c.*1898, diameter 49cm (19¼in)
London £10,925 ($16,700).
4.VI.93
Clement Massier, who is
thought to have been
born around 1845, and
died in 1917, was the son
of a Vallauris potter and
produced an imaginative
body of work with
crystalline and iridescent
glazes at his studio in
Golfe-Juan in the South
of France. The work of
certain symbolist painters
is called to mind by the
inchoate and blurred
outlines of the figure
emerging from the depths
of this charger. (RIGHT)

JOSEF HOFFMANN
**Part of a
twenty-three piece
porcelain tea-service**
*c.*1929,
the teapot height 17cm (6¾ in)
London £7,920 ($12,300).
30.X.92
Josef Hoffmann
(1870-1956), architect
and designer, was the
central figure in Austrian
avant-garde design from
around 1900 through to
the 1920s. He was
prolific and worked in a
seemingly contradictory
variety of styles, from
unadorned geometric
forms associated with the
emergent Modern
Movement to decorative,
whimsical motifs of
which this service is a fine
and charming example.
(BELOW)

A Tiffany Studios
favrile glass and
bronze mosaic
spider web lamp
1899-1918, IMPRESSED *TIFFANY
STUDIOS NEW YORK*,
height 71.1cm (28in)
New York $770,000
(£503,200). 7.XI.92
Property of the Kirkpatrick
Foundation, Oklahoma.

Louis Comfort Tiffany
(1848-1933) has become
a household name on
both sides of the
Atlantic, largely as a
result of the highly
distinctive and
innovative leaded
bronze and glass lamps
he conceived at the
beginning of this century
in America. This is a
fine example of his
work in this style.
(RIGHT)

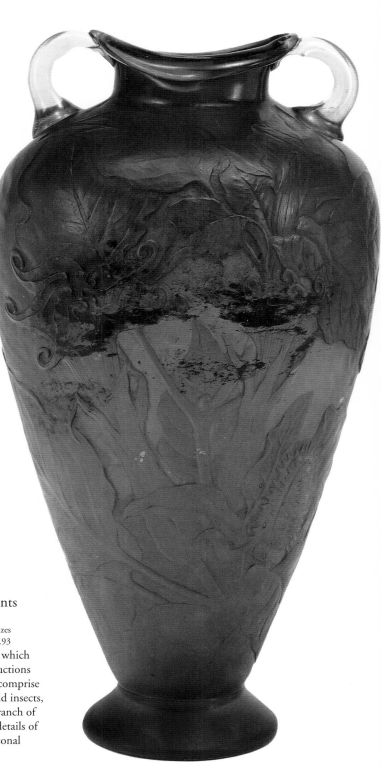

EMILE GALLÉ
A glass vase with trumpet flowers and butterflies
*c.*1900, height 34cm (13½in)
Monaco FF277,500 (£33,500:$50,900).
4.IV.93
Gallé was not only an artist and craftsman of extraordinary ability but he was also blessed with a strong business acumen. This enabled him to build up a large and flourishing factory in Nancy where he imposed production-line methods in order to keep abreast of the ever-increasing demand for his glassware.
(RIGHT)

EMILE GALLÉ
'Les Sept Princesses' cameo glass vase
1900, height 23cm (9in)
London £28,175 ($43,100).
4.VI.93
Emile Gallé (1846-1904) inspired a whole generation of artists and craftsmen in his home town of Nancy which soon established for itself a reputation to rival Paris as a centre for the applied arts. This important piece, which was included in the Paris exhibition of 1900, is engraved with the title 'Les Sept Princesses' and with the words 'Simplicité', 'Humilité', 'Patience', 'Fidelité', 'Douceur', 'Veracité', and 'Charité'. (ABOVE)

EMILE GALLÉ
One of a collection of documents and manuscripts
*c.*1880-1904, TWO HUNDRED PAGES, various sizes
Monaco FF166,500 (£20,100:$30,500). 4.IV.93
The dossier of notes and drawings from which this piece comes consists largely of instructions from Gallé to his associate Nicolas. They comprise annotated ink sketches, studies of plants and insects, illustrations in gouache (including the 'branch of magnolia' design for a vase shown here), details of specific projects and a quantity of personal memoranda. (ABOVE)

HECTOR GUIMARD
A mahogany gilt-bronze and glass two-tier tea table
SIGNED, height 86.4cm (34in)
New York $187,000
(£121,400). 19.XI.92
The work of the architect Hector Guimard (1867-1942) encompassed not only the design of his buildings but also the design of the artifacts to be used within them, thus creating a complete and comprehensive environment. Some of his most original furniture is that made between 1895 and 1903. This two-tier tea table is, according to current research, a unique design. (RIGHT)

ALBERT CHEURET
Figural chandelier
*c.*1925, height 38.1cm (15in)
New York $39,100 (£26,600).
19.III.93
Sculptural figures were a
popular feature of Art
Deco design and
appeared frequently on
a variety of objects. This
striking chandelier by
Albert Cheuret is cast as
an exotic bird in flight,
its wings and tail
composed of sections of
shaped alabaster, the rest
modelled in patinated
bronze. (LEFT)

EDGAR BRANDT
A wrought iron oval
table with veined
marble top
*c.*1925,
height 73cm (29in)
Monaco FF577,200
(£69,700:$105,900). 4.IV.93
Wrought iron enjoyed
a revival during the
Art Deco period.
Edgar Brandt (1880-
1960), who made his
name in the 1920s and
triumphed with his
extensive contribution
to the 1925 Paris
Exposition, was one of
the medium's most
skilled exponents.
(LEFT)

CERAMICS AND GLASS

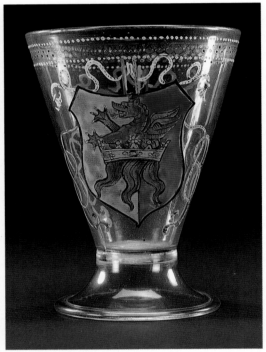

A Venetian enamelled armorial goblet

*c.*1500, height 13.2cm (5¼in) London £15,400 ($26,300). 6.X.92
Glass-making originated in Egypt, Syria or Iraq before
2000BC and was introduced to Europe after the
foundation of the Roman Empire in 27BC. The earliest
significant European industry was established in
Venice, initially on the Rialto although it was later
moved to Murano when it was thought that sparks
from the chimneys might set fire to the city. (ABOVE)

An English Adam and Eve Royalist goblet

DATED *1716*, height 20.8cm (8¼in)
London £22,000 ($41,800). 15.IX.92
This goblet is engraved with a scene depicting the Fall
of Man. A similar glass, dated 1714, was sold at
Sotheby's London in 1977. The two goblets are
thought to be the earliest dated examples in English
glass of the pedestal stem. The date and the Royalist
inscription, 'God Save King George', referring to
George I, make this an extremely rare piece. (LEFT)

A William de Morgan lustred pottery 'Sunset and Moonlight' charger

LATE FULHAM PERIOD, PROBABLY *c*.1900,
diameter 46.5cm (18¼in)
London £17,250 ($26,200). 25.V.93

William de Morgan established his firm of potters in Chelsea in 1872. In 1880 he transferred it to Merton Abbey in Surrey and in 1888 it finally came to rest in the Sands End Works, Fulham, where this piece was made. De Morgan's emphasis had always been on lustreware, together with pottery in the Persian and Dutch styles, and he considered the development of his 'Sunset and Moonlight' triple glazes to be the crowning glory of his career. (BELOW)

A Ruskin Pottery vase and stand

c.1915-25, total height 44cm (17⅜in)
London £12,000 ($18,500). 20.IV.93
From the Adam Ferneyhough Collection.

In 1898 Edward Taylor founded a small pottery which became known as the Birmingham Tile Pottery Company. Its specialization was in unusual glass effects applied to diverse forms of pottery. By 1903 it was enjoying an international reputation for its distinctive mottled and coloured glazes. (LEFT)

A Southwark delftware polychrome drug jar

DATED *1656*, height 36cm (14¼in)
London £49,500 ($85,600). 7.X.92
From the John Philip Kassebaum Collection.

Decorated pharmaceutical containers were a feature of English seventeenth-century apothecaries' shops and were often embellished with the arms of the Worshipful Society of Apothecaries. Here, the arms appear on a shield supported by two unicorns. (BELOW)

A Maiolica dish

FROM THE WORKSHOP OF GIORGIO ANDREOLI, SIGNED AND DATED *1531*, GUBBIO,
diameter 23.5cm (9¼in) New York $145,500 (£94,400). 24.V.93

This Maiolica dish is decorated in the *istoriato* style, which derived its
imagery from religion, mythology and history. It is centred with a
portrait of Fulvia, the wife of Mark Antony. (ABOVE LEFT)

A Maiolica documentary dish

DATED *1540*, URBINO, diameter 27.5cm (10⅞in) London £28,600 ($48,900). 6.X.92

This dish is by the 'Della Rovere' painter, so called because he was
responsible for five known *istoriato* dishes painted with a coat of arms
wrongly thought to be those of the Della Rovere family. (ABOVE RIGHT)

One of a pair of Maiolica albarelli, or drug jars

*c.*1510-20, SIENA, height 23.8cm (9⅜in)
New York $65,750 (£42,700) for the pair. 24.V.93

Tin-glazing is one of the few ceramic processes
not to have evolved through the Far East. The
technique spread to Italy from Spain in the late
eleventh century and flourished there until the
sixteenth century, when the centre of production
had shifted to Holland and Britain. (LEFT)

A Le Nove porcelain écuelle, cover and stand

*c.*1765, diameter of stand 21.6cm (8½in)
New York $27,500 (£17,400). 27.X.92

This set of écuelle, cover and stand is moulded
with rococo scrollwork and bowknotted floral
sprays. The painted decoration depicts scenes
with figures in a rural river landscape, figures
watching a parade and figures by classical
buildings. (RIGHT AND ABOVE RIGHT)

A Meissen porcelain pagoda figure
*c.*1725, height 20.8cm (8¼in)
Zürich SF143,000 (£65,600:$99,700). 24.XI.92
The second director of the Meissen factory,
Johann Gregor Höroldt, was responsible for
introducing the Chinese-style decoration by
which the period is instantly recognizable. This
rare figure was probably modelled by George
Fritzsche, who joined the factory in 1711. The
only other known example dating from the
same early period of Meissen production is now
in the Zwinger Museum, Dresden. (LEFT)

A Meissen porcelain 'Augustus Rex' bottle vase
1725-30, height 22cm (8⅝in) London £47,700 ($73,400). 2.III.93
The description 'Augustus Rex', sometimes applied to Meissen pieces
marked with an *AR* monogram, refers to Augustus II, King of Poland,
who became Elector of Saxony in 1694 and founded the Meissen
factory in 1710. After the taste for *chinoiserie* of the early Meissen
years, a new style was developed in the mid-1720s based on the so-
called 'oriental flowers', or *indianische Blumen*. (ABOVE)

A Meissen porcelain plate
1741-45, FROM THE EMPRESS ELIZABETH OF RUSSIA SERVICE, diameter 24.1cm (9½in)
New York $20,700 (£13,400). 22.V.93
This plate comes from a service ordered by the Empress Elizabeth of
Russia upon ascending the throne in 1741, and bears the Hermitage
inventory number. Some of the pieces from the service have *indianische Blumen* ('oriental flowers') as the central decoration (as here),
some have *Holzschnittblumen* ('flowers painted after prints'). (ABOVE)

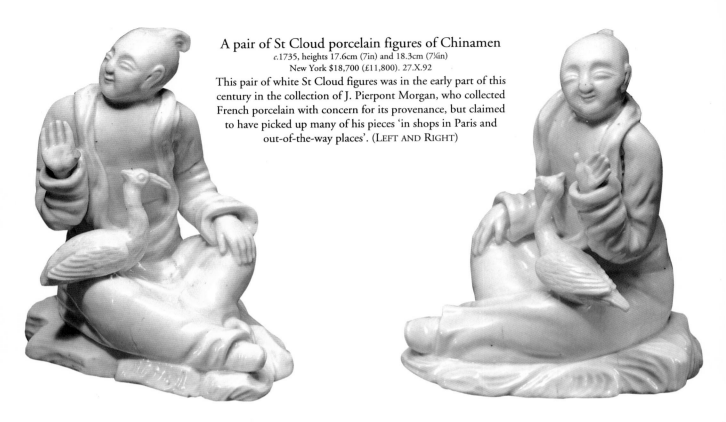

A pair of St Cloud porcelain figures of Chinamen
*c.*1735, heights 17.6cm (7in) and 18.3cm (7¼in)
New York $18,700 (£11,800). 27.X.92
This pair of white St Cloud figures was in the early part of this
century in the collection of J. Pierpont Morgan, who collected
French porcelain with concern for its provenance, but claimed
to have picked up many of his pieces 'in shops in Paris and
out-of-the-way places'. (LEFT AND RIGHT)

**A Vincennes
porcelain oval dish**
*c.*1753, width 43.5cm (17in)
London £29,900 ($47,200).
15.VI.93
Apart from the excellence
of the porcelain it
produced, the Vincennes
factory is celebrated for
being the parent of the
great Royal Sèvres
factory. The Vincennes
works moved to new
premises at Sèvres in
1756, and in 1759 it was
bought by Louis XV. At
around the time of the
move, lavish tableware
was much in vogue and
this dish is part of the
famed 'Louis XV Service',
supplied to the king
over three successive
Decembers from 1753
to 1755. (LEFT)

A Marseilles faïence turkey tureen and cover
*c.*1770, height 38.5cm (15⅛in)
London £42,750 ($61,900). 2.III.93

This rare and splendid piece was made in the Savy factory in Marseilles in around 1770, and is incised with the factory's mark of a double X. The bird has been given fine blue-black plumage and a blue-mottled red crop. It stands on a mound base with tree stumps applied with acorns. (BELOW)

A Berlin porcelain topographical vase
1832-37, height 76cm (30½in)
Zürich SF96,800 (£44,400:$67,400). 25.XI.92

This large, gilt-metal-mounted vase is painted with a continuous view of Potsdam. The Berlin factory was established in 1752 and its wares came to be much in demand when Meissen, the other great German porcelain-producing factory, was suffering the effects of the Seven Years War. In 1763, when the war ended, Frederick the Great bought the factory and under his ownership it achieved a monopoly in porcelain sales throughout the entire state of Prussia. (BELOW)

A pair of Paris porcelain gold-ground vases
*c.*1820, DARTE FRERES, height 36.5cm (14⅜in)
New York $19,550 (£12,600). 22.V.93

The stencilled marks on the base of this pair of gold-ground vases indicate that it was produced by the Darte brothers. Each of the vases displays a rectangular panel painted with a cluster of flowers on a russet and white marble ledge against a shaded brown ground. (BELOW LEFT)

PRECIOUS OBJECTS *by John Block*

During the 1992–93 season no area attracted as diverse, international and glamorous a following as Sotheby's Precious Objects sales. Items as varied as jewels, watches, clocks, silver, and objects of vertu attracted buyers from North America, South America, Europe, Asia, Africa and Australasia. Sales held in New York, Geneva, London, Monaco and Hong Kong offered the opportunity for collectors, dealers and institutions to acquire beautiful and well-crafted pieces wrapped in a sense of history, allure and mystery. The greater public had not seen many of these objects for decades or even centuries before they arrived in Sotheby's exhibition rooms.

The Marlene Dietrich ruby bracelet reflected the glamour, glitter and gutsiness of its original owner. The bold loop of Burmese rubies surrounded by babuette and pavé-set diamonds was an instant hit during the international pre-sale tour of the New York October sale. That the bracelet was worn by Dietrich in Alfred Hitchcock's 1950 film Stagefright, was Dietrich's signature piece of jewellery, and had not been seen for over thirty years, were all instrumental factors in the sale price of $990,000.

No name is more synonymous with the elegance of magnificent diamonds and jewellery than that of Harry Winston. Among the works in the Collection of the late Mrs Harry Winston, sold in New York in October 1992, was a magnificent pair of diamond chandelier pendant earclips, created for her in 1961 by her husband. This was the only pair of chandelier earclips made to this design, after an eighteenth-century girandole motif. The dazzling combination of pear-shape, round and marquise-shape diamonds surmounting a pair of rare elongated pear-shape diamond drops weighing over 15 carats each, had the intended effect on bidders and the earclips sold for $1,430,000.

The European season of Precious Objects also began auspiciously with the November sale in Geneva of the Thurn und Taxis Collection of silver, snuff boxes and jewels amassed by the Thurn und Taxis family over the past two centuries. King Frederick II of Prussia (Frederick the Great) was not only a

The J. P. Morgan Jr. 'Model A' Cartier Mystery Clock
SIGNED, 1913, PARIS, height 12.7cm (5in)
New York $310,500 (£201,600). 20.IV.93. (LEFT)

Diamond bracelet
BY HARRY WINSTON, 1959, length 19cm (7½in)
New York $473,000 (£290,100). 20.X.92
From the Collection of the late Mrs Harry Winston. (ABOVE)

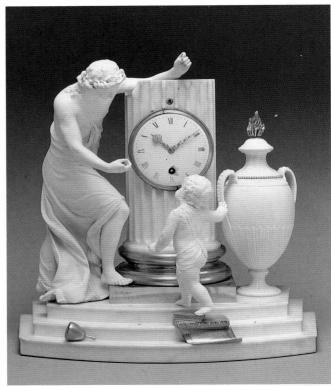

A George II silver
soup tureen,
cover and stand
BY JOHN EDWARDS, 1740,
AND PARKER & WAKELIN,
1768, LONDON,
length of stand 47.7cm (18¾in)
London £41,100 ($61,600).
10.VI.93
From the Harcourt Collection.
(ABOVE)

Marble and Derby
biscuit porcelain
mantel timepiece
BY BENJAMIN VULLIAMY,
1787, LONDON,
overall height 42cm (16½in)
London £35,200 ($61,200).
2.X.92. (ABOVE)

statesman, ruler and soldier, but also a major patron of the arts. Under his reign, workshops flourished creating intricate objects of vertu including a spectacular snuff box sold in November. Made in around 1770 after a design by Jean Guillaume George Kruger of Berlin, the box is encrusted with diamonds, rubies, emeralds and moulded pâte de verre. *The quality, rarity and provenance of the snuff box helped it to achieve the price of SF2,530,000.*

As with jewels and objects of vertu, the rarity of form and the importance of the artisan of a piece of silver is of great significance. One of the most unusual items sold during this season was an American silver two-handled, late seventeenth-century bowl by Cornelius Vander Burgh, New York. Not only is a piece of American seventeenth-century silver extremely rare, but also Cornelius Vander Burgh (b.1652) is considered New York's first native silversmith. The bowl brought $233,500 in New York in January 1993.

The sale of the Harcourt Collection in London included a George III silver soup tureen and cover with liner and stand for which the 1st Earl Harcourt was charged £81 16s 2d. This season the tureen achieved £20,700.

In Geneva in May a magnificent example of Napoleonic silver was sold for SF641,500. The silver-gilt soup tureen on stand by Jean-Baptiste Claude

Odiot dates from 1809–19, Paris. It is of a neoclassical architectural form, with winged female handles and decorated with figures of lions, vines and Silenian masks. When Odiot's portrait was painted by Robert Lefevre in 1822, the model of this tureen was one of three pieces placed beside the sitter.

The markets for both wristwatches and pocket watches continued to attract a wide variety of purchasers from around the world. The first stainless steel single-button chronograph to be offered at auction was sold in February in New York. Made in 1927 by Patek Philippe, the watch achieved $101,500. In London the highlight of the year was a miniature clockwatch from the Harcourt Collection. Apparently the only extant example from the seventeenth-century Hipp workshops in Kempton, the clockwatch was reputedly a gift from Queen Elizabeth of Bohemia. It sold for £133,500. Among pocket watches sold in New York was a double-dialled perpetual-calendar minute-repeating watch by Louis Audemars. Probably made for the Paris exhibitions of the late-nineteenth century, it was offered by the family of the original owner and made $255,500.

Many high-powered collectors throughout history have been fascinated by the mechanisms and beauty of clocks. Such a man was J. P. Morgan Jnr, who for Christmas 1913 ordered a clock from Cartier. Made by Maurice Couet, it was the first of the Cartier 'Mystery Clocks'. Called a 'Model A', it has a rectangular case of rock crystal with rose-cut diamond hands and is on a nephrite base. When sold in New York in April it fetched $310,500.

The economic climate has had an effect on the prices of English clocks by Tompion, Graham and Knibb and some levelling has taken place this season. Rarities such as the white marble and biscuit model by Vulliamy, which sold for £35,200, remain in demand.

The Precious Object market remained strong this season, seeming to defy recession in many countries. Sales attracted bidders from all over the world, with collectors from Asia being particularly prominent. Whether collecting these objects as works of art or amassing them as portable wealth, the buyers brought to the auction rooms an excitement that will carry over into the 1993–94 season.

A Russian gold, enamel and jewelled Imperial presentation snuff box
*c.*1900, ST PETERSBURG, length 8.9cm (3½in)
New York $56,100 (£35,000). 8.XII.92. (ABOVE)

Silver-gilt soup tureen, cover and stand
BY JEAN-BAPTISTE CLAUDE ODIOT, 1809-19, PARIS, overall height 39.4cm (15½in)
Geneva SF641,500 (£282,500:$436,300). 24.V.93 (BELOW)

JEWELLERY

A pearl and diamond tiara
1853, GABRIEL LEMONNIER,
SILVER AND GOLD MOUNT
Geneva SF935,000
(£428,800:$636,000). 17.XI.92
From the Thurn und Taxis Collection.
The pearls in this tiara came
from a parure assembled in
1810 for Napoleon's second
Empress, the Archduchess
Marie Louise. The tiara is set
with 212 pearls, weighing 2,520
grains, and 1,998 brilliants, and
was part of an order submitted
by Napoleon III to the leading
contemporary Parisian jewellers.
In 1887 the French Republican
government decided to sell the
crown jewels, and this tiara was
bought by Julius Jacobi who in
turn sold it to Prince Albert von
Thurn und Taxis. (LEFT)

A diamond brooch
LAST QUARTER OF THE EIGHTEENTH
CENTURY Geneva SF341,000
(£151,500:$231,900). 17.XI.92
From the Thurn und Taxis Collection.
This piece is set in the form of
the middle and upper sections
of the neck badge of the
Austrian Order of the Golden
Fleece and, according to the
Thurn und Taxis family
archives, was made for Fürst
Carl Anselm (1733-1805) who
became a Knight of that order
in 1775. The Thurn und Taxis
family can be traced back to the
fifteenth century. It reached
its great flowering in the
eighteenth and nineteenth
centuries, producing a host of
Hapsburg rulers. (LEFT)

A ruby and
diamond bracelet
LATE 1930S, FRENCH
New York $990,000
(£626,500). 19.X.92
From the Collection of
Marlene Dietrich.
This spectacular piece
belonged to Marlene
Dietrich and was worn
by the legendary film
star for her appearance
in Alfred Hitchcock's
Stage Fright. Dietrich's
screen persona was
largely developed by her
association with the
Austrian-American dir-
ector Josef von Stern-
berg, who persuaded her
to move from Berlin to
Hollywood in 1930. She
became his muse and he
directed her in many of
her most famous films,
including *The Blue
Angel, Shanghai Express*
and *Blond Venus*.
Dietrich died in Paris
in 1992. (LEFT)

A pair of Harry
Winston chandelier
pendent earrings
1961, DIAMOND,
MOUNTED IN PLATINUM
New York $1,430,000
(£905,000). 20.X.92
From the collection of the late
Mrs Harry Winston
These earrings are made
up from 28 pear-shaped,
marquise-shaped and
round diamonds weigh-
ing approximately 48.75
carats, supporting two
pear-shaped diamonds
weighing approximately
15.9 and 15.5 carats.
They were made for his
wife by Harry Winston,
who is widely considered
to be one of the major
innovators of twentieth-
century jewellery design.
(RIGHT)

A diamond bracelet
MOUNTED IN PLATINUM,
length 17.8cm (7in)
New York $363,000
(£232,600). 9.XII.92
This bracelet is
composed of seven
emerald-cut diamonds
weighing approximately
17.5 carats, thirty-five
pear-shaped diamonds
weighing approximately
37 carats, twenty-eight
marquise-shaped
diamonds weighing
approximately 19 carats,
and seven round
diamonds weighing
approximately 3 carats.
The bracelet was
reputedly bought from
Harry Winston in the
1950s. (LEFT)

A Harry Winston diamond ring
SIGNED, MOUNTED IN PLATINUM
New York $1,157,500
(£751,600). 19.IV.93
This emerald-cut diamond, weighing 51.33 carats, is flanked by two modified triangular-shaped diamonds and is mounted in platinum. (FAR LEFT)

A fancy blue diamond
MOUNTED AS A RING WITH DIAMOND SHOULDERS
Geneva SF5,283,500
(£2,348,200:$3,594,200). 26.V.93
Diamonds come in a variety of colours, blue being among the rarest and most desirable. This large example weighs 11.47 carats. (LEFT)

An emerald-cut diamond
Geneva SF5,393,500
(£2,397,100:$3,669,000). 26.V.93
This magnificent gem, which weighs 53.88 carats, is the second largest D-colour, internally flawless, emerald-cut diamond to have been sold at auction. (FAR LEFT)

A pear-shaped diamond
New York $4,732,500
(£3,134,100). 19.IV.93
Weighing 66.29 carats, this is the third largest D-colour, internally flawless, pear-shaped diamond to have been sold at auction. The largest, weighing 101.84 carats, was sold by Sotheby's in Geneva in November 1990. (LEFT)

A cultured pearl and diamond necklace

Length 43cm (17in)
New York $2,310,000 (£1,462,000). 19.X.92
Never before has a necklace made up of cultured pearls of this quality and size been
offered at auction. The pearls range from 16.0mm to 20.1mm, and the price the
necklace achieved was a world record. (ABOVE)

An emerald ring
Geneva SF1,488,500
(£661,500:$1,012,500).
26.V.93
The octagonal step-cut
stone of this very
important ring weighs
18.575 carats. The
emerald is Colombian in
origin and its
extraordinary colour,
brilliance and purity
make it an exceptional
example. (LEFT)

A ruby ring
BURMESE, THE STONE MOUNTED
BETWEEN LUNETTE-SHAPED
DIAMOND SHOULDERS
Geneva SF4,403,500
(£1,957,100:$2,995,500).
26.V.93
The exceptional colour
and quality of this ruby,
combined with its size,
make it one of the rarest
examples of a fine
Burmese ruby to come
on the market in recent
years. The oval-shaped
stone weighs 16.517
carats. (LEFT)

A sapphire and diamond ring
MOUNTED BY BULGARI
St Moritz SF828,500
(£368,200:$563,600). 19.II.93
The superb, octagonal,
step-cut sapphire in this
magnificent ring weighs
46.343 carats and,
according to the Gübelin
certificate which
accompanies the piece, is
Sri Lankan in origin.
(LEFT)

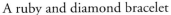

A ruby and diamond bracelet

*c.*1950, MOUNTED IN PLATINUM Geneva SF311,500 (£138,400:$211,900). 26.V.93

This bracelet is made from thirteen cushion-shaped rubies framed by radiating clusters of baguette and circular-cut diamonds. (TOP)

A ruby and diamond brooch

*c.*1950 Geneva SF124,500 (£55,300:$84,600). 26.V.93

This brooch is decorated with a cluster of twenty cushion-shaped rubies bordered by alternating segments of baguette and circular-cut diamonds. (ABOVE LEFT)

A pair of Chaumet ruby and diamond earrings

*c.*1950 Geneva SF43,700 (£19,400:$29,700). 26.V.93

These earrings are signed *Chaumet London*. Each is set with with a cluster of seven cushion-shaped rubies. (ABOVE RIGHT)

A 'Tutti Frutti' Cartier brooch

*c.*1930, SIGNED, EMERALD, COLOURED STONE AND DIAMOND

Geneva SF176,000 (£78,200:$119,700). 18.XI.92

The carved emeralds frequently used as centrepieces in jewels such as this were automatically associated with India despite the fact that the best stones were Colombian in origin, having made their way east with gem traders in the wake of the Spanish Conquistadores. (TOP)

A 'Tutti Frutti' Cartier bracelet

*c.*1930, EMERALD, ONYX AND DIAMOND

Geneva SF264,000 (£117,300:$179,500). 18.XI.92

In 1911, Jacques Cartier, the head of the firm's London branch, made the first of several journeys to India, marking the start of a long and fruitful professional relationship with the East which resulted in many purchases of rare jewels in Delhi, Culcutta and Bombay. (ABOVE)

A René Boivin gold, diamond and ruby necklace
*c.*1960
New York $148,500 (£93,600). 19.X.92
From the Estate of Barbara Cushing Paley
This unusual piece comes from the estate of Barbara Cushing Paley, the youngest of the famous Cushing sisters, who were famed for their intelligence and beauty. 'Babe' was for some time fashion editor of *Vogue* in America and herself became a fashion icon, playing a dominant role in high society until her death in 1978. (ABOVE)

A Paul Brandt Art Deco brooch
*c.*1930, SIGNED, PLATINUM, DIAMOND AND ONYX
New York $43,125 (£28,750). 19.IV.93
Paul Brandt received his training in Paris with Chaplain and Allard. Although his initial designs were in the Art Nouveau style, he is perhaps best remembered for his pure Art Deco jewellery. Brandt's creations often comprise planes of diamonds against a white-metal ground, usually contrasted by geometric segments of onyx, rock crystal or lapis. (ABOVE)

An agate, gold and enamel pendant
SECOND HALF OF NINETEENTH CENTURY
London £19,800 ($31,000). 4.XII.92

This pendant was probably designed by the German goldsmith Reinhold Vasters (1827-1909). Vasters formed an enduring association with the dealer and collector Frédéric Spitzer, who inspired many of Vasters' antiquarian productions and influenced his work in the Renaissance style, of which this pendant is an important example. (ABOVE LEFT)

An agate and diamond cameo pendant
EARLY EIGHTEENTH CENTURY
London £7,820 ($11,700). 1.VII.93

Cameo-cutting was first practised in Imperial Rome. Cameos were cut out of hardstones such as onyx and agate, using the natural colours in the stones to form designs. The eighteenth and early nineteenth centuries saw a revival in the popularity of this skill, and cameos of many kinds, particularly portraits, came to be widely worn. (ABOVE)

A gold, pearl, enamel and diamond brooch
*c.*1890 London £5,060 ($7,200). 18.III.93

Gold was relatively plentiful during the late nineteenth century and designs based on natural forms were popular. In England, the Boer War prevented the supply of South African diamonds and coloured stones and enamels were widely used as substitutes. (FAR LEFT)

An enamel and diamond brooch
*c.*1890 London £1,955 ($2,800). 18.III.93

This charming brooch is designed as a spray of pansies, the petals decorated with opaque purple and lilac enamel and the centres set with cushion-shaped stones. (LEFT)

RUSSIAN WORKS OF ART, MINIATURES & VERTU

SCHOOL OF DYONYSII
An icon depicting the Anastasis, or the 'Harrowing of Hell'
THIRD QUARTER OF THE FIFTEENTH CENTURY, 51.5 x 41.5cm (20½ x 16½in)
London £64,000 ($95,600). 17.VI.92
The iconography of the Anastasis dates from the early Christian period. The Evangelists do not write of this mysterious event, but the image follows closely the description in the Apocryphal Gospel of Nicodemus. Christ, the new Adam, is depicted trampling the broken gates of Hell; He holds the cross which gave Him victory over death and raises Adam and Eve from their tomb. (ABOVE)

A pair of silver ten-light candelabra
FABERGÉ c.1890, MOSCOW, height 68.6cm (27in)
New York $220,000 (£141,900). 8.XII.92
Carl Fabergé, with other craftsmen of the period, was much influenced by the style of the rococo and in particular by the lavish designs of Juste-Aurèle Meissonnier, in whose manner these massive candelabra are made. Manufactured under the Russian Imperial warrant, which Fabergé acquired in 1885, they remain with their original oak case. (ABOVE)

JACQUES-ANTOINE ARLAUD
**Prince James Francis
Edward Stuart**
SIGNED AND DATED *1703*, ON VELLUM,
oval 8.7cm (3½in)
London £26,450 ($37,800). 11.III.93
In 1688 Jacques-Antoine
Arlaud became miniature
painter to Philippe, Duc
d'Orléans. His skills attracted
members of the exiled Stuart
family gathered at St Germain,
resulting in this fine portrait of
the Old Pretender. (RIGHT)

**A Portuguese gold and
jewelled crown**
MID-EIGHTEENTH CENTURY,
height 21cm (8¼in)
New York $140,000 (£92,100). 8.VI.93
From the Richard Manney Collection.
This crown would have adorned a statue of the Madonna. It
is set with diamonds, rubies
and emeralds and is very close
in style to a gilt ciborium (an
ecclesiastical vessel) preserved
in the Museu Nacional de Arte
Antiga in Lisbon. (BELOW)

A desk timepiece
FABERGÉ, WORKMASTER M. PERCHIN,
ST PETERSBURG, 1899-1903,
SILVER-GILT AND ENAMEL,
height 14.6cm (5⅜in)
Geneva SF132,000 (£59,700:$90,700).
17.XI.92
At the height of Carl Fabergé's
success in the 1890s his
St Petersburg company had
branches in Moscow, Odessa,
Kiev and London, with more
than 500 craftsmen in his
employ to help produce the
exquisite objects so favoured by
his wealthy patrons. (BELOW)

A snuff box made for Frederick II, King of Prussia

*c.*1770, JEWELLED GOLD AND
HARDSTONE, BERLIN,
width 10cm (3⅞in)
Geneva SF2,530,000
(£1,150,000:$1,805,500). 17. XI.92
From the Thurn und Taxis Collection.

This magnificent snuff box
encrusted with diamonds, rubies,
emeralds and moulded *pâte de verre*
was made for Frederick II, King of
Prussia, after a design by Jean
Guillaume George Krüger. It is said
that Frederick the Great inherited a
passion for snuff boxes from his
mother, whose boudoir was found
on her death to contain more than
300 examples. A metal snuff box
saved Frederick's life during the
Battle of Kunersdorf in 1759, when
a Russian bullet was deflected by a
box in his pocket. (LEFT)

A Dresden snuff box

BY J. C. NEUBER, *c.*1780, GOLD AND HARDSTONE,
width 9cm (3½in)
London £166,500 ($249,700). 10.VI.93

Johann Christian Neuber (1736-1808), who
made this piece, was one of the most creative
and talented masters patronized by the
Saxon court, although by the late 1780s his
large workshop had started to suffer from
financial problems and, after retiring in
1805, Neuber died a pauper. (RIGHT)

CLOCKS AND WATCHES

A French quarter-striking calendar mantel clock
*c.*1840, ORMOLU, height 71cm (28in)
New York $26,450 (£18,900). 28.VI.93 From the Joseph M. Meraux Collection.
Ormolu decoration was extremely popular in France for nearly three centuries and was used to embellish a variety of objects, from furniture and porcelain to frames and clocks. The movement of the clock shown here is contained in a sphere faced with the signs of the zodiac and is supported by a winged lion, a griffin, a bull and a winged centaur for the four Evangelists. (ABOVE)

A French conical pendulum display clock
SIGNED, *c.*1865, SILVERED-BRONZE AND WHITE ONYX,
height 298.5cm (117½in) New York $134,500 (£89,600). 28.VI.93
From the Joseph M. Meraux Collection.
This rare clock comes from the collection of Joseph M. Meraux, who, by the time he died in 1992, had accumulated the largest, and arguably the finest, collection of nineteenth-century clocks in the world. (ABOVE)

An English chiming bracket clock and bracket

ELLICOTT, SIGNED, *c*.1770,
MAHOGANY AND BRASS,
height of clock 47cm (18½in)
London £17,600 ($27,600).
17.XII.92

This fine clock reputedly belonged to William Wales (1734-98), Astronomer to Captain Cook. It was made for John Ellicott by the firm of A. & J. Thwaites and bears its stamp and number *375*, indicating that it was probably made around 1768. It is unusual to find a clock retaining its original bracket, making this a rare example of its type. (LEFT)

A spiral spring skeleton timepiece

WILLIAM SMITH, SIGNED,
c.1850, height 40.5cm (16in)
London £11,220 ($17,600).
17.XII.92

William Smith set up as a clockmaker in Mussel-burgh, Scotland, in 1847. Early in his career he invented a form of rubber spring which was used to drive his clocks and for which he was awarded a silver medal by the Royal Scottish Society of Arts. This rare clock was kept by Smith and came by direct descent to the consignor. (LEFT)

A French world time and annual calendar terrestrial globe clock

ANDRÉ MATHY, SIGNED, *c*.1880, SILVERED-BRONZE, GILT-BRASS AND
ENAMEL, height 193cm (76in) New York $74,000 (£49,300).
28.VI.93 From the Joseph M. Meraux Collection.

The movement of this French globe clock is enclosed in a glazed rectangular case flanked with silvered-bronze figures representing the seasons. (ABOVE)

An English hunting-cased minute-repeating *grande sonnerie* clockwatch with chronograph

MARCKS & CO, SIGNED, *c.*1895, BOMBAY OR POONA,
diameter 5.5cm (2⅛in)
Geneva SF290,400 (£129,000:$197,500). 19.XI.92

The British Raj generated a market for high-quality timepieces in the sub-continent. This fine and rare example is in gold, enamel, diamond, ruby and split-pearl. (ABOVE)

An English gold and enamel verge miniature clockwatch

ATTRIBUTED TO ANDREAS HIPP OF KEMPTON, FIRST
QUARTER OF THE SEVENTEENTH CENTURY,
overall length 2.5cm (1in) London £133,500 ($200,200).
10.VI.93 From the Harcourt Collection.

This clockwatch was reputedly a gift from Queen Elizabeth of Bohemia (the 'Winter Queen') to Frederick Harcourt, and appears to be the only example of its type. (ABOVE)

An English hunting-cased minute-repeating *grande sonnerie* clockwatch with moon phases

MARCKS & CO. SIGNED, *c.*1900, BOMBAY OR POONA,
diameter 6cm (2⅜in)
Geneva SF411,400 (£182,800:$279,800). 19.XI.92

This Marcks & Co. clockwatch reflects a type of enamel design of an earlier Moghul period that can be found on a number of watches made for the Indian market. (ABOVE)

A Swiss minute-repeating perpetual calendar watch

PATEK PHILIPPE, SIGNED, *c.*1980, GENEVA,
diameter 5.4cm (2⅛in)
Geneva SF86,000 (£38,200:$58,800). 27.V.93

This fine gold watch by the Patek Philippe Company incorporates the perpetual calendar function with phases of the moon and the Equation of Time. (ABOVE)

An English verge clockwatch with astronomical dial

T. CHAMBERLIN, SIGNED, *c.*1630, diameter 5.1cm (2in)
London £34,500 ($51,700). 10.VI.93
From the Harcourt Collection.

This gilt metal clockwatch was reputedly given to the diarist John Evelyn by Charles II, whose grand-daughter Elizabeth was married to Sir Simon Harcourt. (ABOVE)

A Swiss skeletonized double-dialled minute-repeating perpetual calendar moon-phase watch

LOUIS AUDEMARS, SIGNED, *c.*1885, diameter 5.5cm (2⅛in)
New York $255,500 (£375,500). 25.VI.93

The glazed dials revealing the movement suggest that this late nineteenth-century Louis Audemars watch was probably made for exhibition purposes. (ABOVE)

A Swiss self-winding sweep seconds wristwatch

ROLEX OYSTER PERPETUAL, SIGNED, *c.*1949, diameter 3.2cm (1¼in)
Geneva SF69,000 (£30,600:$47,200). 27.V.93

This watch was reputedly made for Jawaharlal Nehru, and presented by him to Sherpa Tenzing, who, with Sir Edmund Hilary, was the first to conquer Mount Everest. (ABOVE)

A Swiss gold and platinum rectangular wristwatch

PATEK PHILIPPE, SIGNED, *c.*1938, length 3.5cm (1⅜in)
Geneva SF96,800 (£43,000:$65,800). 19.XI.92

This Patek Philippe rectangular wristwatch is typical of the wristwatches of the 1920s and 30s that have, in recent years, become so avidly collected. (ABOVE)

A Swiss gold cushion single-button chronograph wristwatch with register

PATEK PHILIPPE, *c.*1925, diameter 3.4cm (1⅜in)
New York $167,500 (£113,100). 25.VI.93

The first chronographs to be produced by the famous Patek Philippe Company were developed by Victorin Piguet in the latter part of the 1920s. This is a rare and early example in gold. (ABOVE)

A Swiss stainless-steel single-button chronograph with register and pulsemeter

PATEK PHILIPPE, *c.*1927, diameter 3.5cm (1⅜in)
New York $101,500 (£70,000). 11.II.93

Like the previous single-button chronograph, this is an early example, but also appears to be the first of its type in stainless-steel to have been offered at auction. (ABOVE)

A French gold 'cloche' wristwatch

CARTIER, SIGNED, *c.*1922, length 3.3cm (1¼in)
New York $60,500 (£38,200). 26.X.92

It is the bell-shaped face of this gold wristwatch that gives it its name. The 'cloche' style was developed in 1921, and is considered rare by collectors. (ABOVE)

A French gold calendar wristwatch with moon phases

CARTIER, SIGNED *c.*1940, length 4cm (1⅝in)
New York $99,000 (£62,600). 26.X.92

This elegant calendar wristwatch appears to be the third known example of a gold, rectangular moon-phase wristwatch made for Cartier. (ABOVE)

SILVER

A French basin and ewer
JEAN BELLON, 1768-69, MONTPELLIER,
height of ewer 27cm (10⅝in)
Monaco FF954,600 (£113,200:$175,500). 5.XII.92
From the Jourdan-Barry Collection.

Basins and ewers were popular items of
toiletware in seventeenth-century France,
although less common in the eighteenth
century when the emphasis was more on
elaborate tableware and candlesticks. The
ewer shown here is decorated in typical
rococo style with a scene depicting the
Triumph of Venus and bears the arms of
the Campan family, important magistrates
from Montpellier. (RIGHT)

A set of thirty-six French candlesticks
JEAN-JACQUES KIRSTEIN, 1781, STRASBOURG,
heights 24.5cm (9⅝in)
Geneva SF726,000 (£322,600:$493,800). 17.XI.92
From the Thurn und Taxis Collection.

This magnificent set of baluster
candlesticks bears the arms of Fürst Carl
Anselm von Thurn und Taxis (1733-
1805) and is recorded as having been
received from Strasbourg on 27 January
1782. The Musée des Arts Décoratifs in
Strasbourg possesses a pair of identical
design but without nozzles. (BELOW)

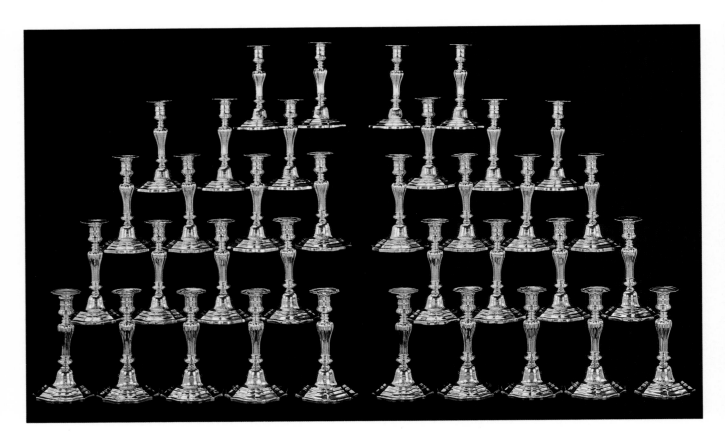

A German mother-of-pearl ewer with silver-gilt mounts

DIETERICH THOR MOYE, c.1640, HAMBURG, height 34cm (13⅜in)
Geneva SF366,500 (£161,400:$249,300). 24.V.93

The shape of this ewer derives from vessels produced in Persia and later during the Moghul Empire, whilst the mother-of-pearl decoration is of a type that found particular favour in Europe from the sixteenth century onwards. (RIGHT)

A Belgian silver-mounted Japanese porcelain coffeepot

MALINES, 1794, height 38.7cm (15⅛in)
New York $74,000 (£47,400). 23.IV.93

As the market for tea, coffee and chocolate expanded and prices fell during the eighteenth century, all three acquired great commercial and social importance.

This coffeepot is made of a combination of early eighteenth-century Japanese Imari porcelain mounted with Malines silver. (BELOW)

Four George II silver-gilt salvers

DAVID WILLAUME II, 1743, LONDON, diameters 34, 28.2 and 37.4cm (13¾, 11⅛ and 14¾in) New York $307,450 (£195,800). 28.X.92

These four salvers were made for George Booth, 2nd Earl of Warrington (1675-1758), a renowned collector of English silver. He started accumulating plate after his father's death, when he inherited the family seat, Dunham Massey in Cheshire, as well as debts amounting to some £50,000. He worked conscientiously to discharge this huge sum but ultimately had to resort to marrying the daughter of a wealthy London merchant. (ABOVE)

One of a pair of French wine coolers

ROBERT-JOSEPH AUGUSTE, 1766-67, PARIS, height 23.5cm (9¼in) London £254,500 ($381,700) for the pair. 10.VI.93
From the Harcourt Collection.

These wine coolers appear to be one of the earliest examples of a design which Auguste continued to use, with minor variations, for more than a decade. He enjoyed an international reputation and supplied silver to various European courts, including a service made between 1776 and 1785 for George III as Elector of Hanover. (LEFT)

A George II waiter
PETER ARCHAMBO, 1728, LONDON, width 15.2cm (6in)
New York $55,200 (£35,300). 23.IV.93
This waiter is decorated with a border of latticework interspersed with cartouches in what is known as the 'Hogarthian' manner. In 1727 the famous Huguenot silversmith Paul de Lamerie supplied a salver to Sir Robert Walpole which he had had engraved by the artist William Hogarth. The design was well received and came to be frequently imitated, with minor variations, by many English engravers. The original Walpole Salver is now in the Victoria and Albert Museum, London. (ABOVE)

A George II cake basket
JOHN PERO, 1735, LONDON, length 32.5cm (12¾in)
London £139,000 ($208,500). 10.VI.93
Although few items have been recorded with his mark, John Pero was clearly one of the most skilful of London's early eighteenth-century silversmiths. This fine, unusual piece with panels of trelliswork and foliage bears the arms of Pàlffy von Erdöd of Hungary.
(RIGHT)

A pair of William and Mary 'ox-eye' drinking cups
MAKER'S MARK IA, 1691, LONDON, heights 10.5cm (4in) London £68,200 ($104,300). 26.XI.92
This unusual type of cup was made almost exclusively for the colleges of Oxford University, although there is one particularly large example in the collection of the Mercers' Company, London. The arms displayed on this pair are those of Queen's College, Oxford. (ABOVE)

An American two-handled bowl

CORNELIUS VANDER BURGH, c.1690, NEW YORK, overall width 31cm (12¼in) New York $233,500 (£153,600). 28.I.93

The earliest New York silversmiths were originally Dutch and the forms of the objects they created tended to be those of their native country. Cornelius Vander Burgh was born in New York, in 1652, and is considered to be the city's first native silversmith. (RIGHT)

A set of four American table candlesticks

SAMUEL TINGLEY, c.1765, NEW YORK, heights 25.4cm (10in) New York $200,500 (£136,300). 23.VI.93

From the Collection of Gloria and Richard Manney.

The construction of this rare set of four candlesticks differs from that of their English prototypes in the use of a cruciform nut at the junction of the base and stem, the English equivalent usually being joined with solder only. (BELOW)

An American two-handled punchbowl: The Bennett Indian Yacht Trophy

TIFFANY & CO, 1894, NEW YORK, height 48.3cm (19in)
New York $167,500 (£113,900). 23.VI.93
From the Collection of John and Katsy Mecom.

This monumental trophy was made by Tiffany's as the prize for the James Gordon Bennett Cup yacht race, held off Nice in March 1895. The sports-loving millionaire Bennett was the only son of the founder of the *New York Herald,* which he inherited on his father's death. (RIGHT)

An American mirrored centrepiece

JOHN W. FORBES, *c.*1820-25, NEW YORK, length 161cm, (63½in)
New York $266,500 (£181,200). 23.VI.93

This centrepiece is one of only three examples extant in early American silver and is known as the De Witt Clinton plateau, after the family through which it descended. A second, almost identical, centrepiece by the same maker is in the White House collection, Washington. (BELOW)

Lou Gehrig says... Lou Gehrig says... Lou Gehrig says... Lou Gehrig says...

BOB BOKEN HAL TROSKY FRED OSTERMUELLER NAPOLEON

Lou Gehrig says... Lou Gehrig says... Lou Gehrig says... Lou Gehrig says...

(RED) ROLFE MYRIL HOAG JIM DeSHONG HOMER PEEL LINUS FREY

Lou Gehrig says... Lou Gehrig says... Lou Gehrig says... "Chuck" Klein says... "Chuck" Klein

LLOYD JOHNSON HAZEN (KI-KI) CUYLER DOLPH CAMILLI PAUL DERRINGER

"Chuck" Klein says... "Chuck" Klein says... "Chuck" Klein says... "Chuck" Klein says... "Chuck"

COMOROSKY BILL HALLAHAN MARTY McMANUS GEORGE DARROW

COLLECTORS' CATEGORIES *by Hilary Kay*

Often decorative, sometimes technically sophisticated, generally of wide appeal to connoisseurs and amateurs alike, the fields included within the Collectors' Categories offer something for everyone. The 1991-92 season saw several world record prices in these categories and interest was so strong that it belied the economic recession that influenced other areas of the art market. The 1992–93 season saw a continuation of this trend.

Since 1989 Sotheby's has worked closely with the Walt Disney Company. This year we held an auction on their behalf of artwork from Beauty and the Beast. *Located for the first time in Los Angeles, the sale was a tremendous success, with 100 per cent sold, realizing $1,141,650.*

The film theme continued with the sale of the Stanley Caidin Collection of Hollywood movie posters, offered by Sotheby's New York in September. The result showed that, in this as yet immature market, the marketability of a poster is affected by the type of film, the fame of those appearing in it, and finally the poster's visual impact. All three factors were present in The Blue Angel, *which made $27,500. The highest price was achieved by a poster for the controversial film* Birth of a Nation *($49,500).*

Sotheby's 1992 sale of Rock 'n' Roll Memorabilia in London was the most successful of its kind by any auction house in Europe, totalling £602,085. It featured a collection of Beatles' memorabilia from the estate of the late Mal Evans, who had been closely involved with the group from 1963 to 1970. The two highest prices achieved were £48,400 for John Lennon's autograph lyrics for A Day in the Life *and £45,100 for Paul McCartney's autograph lyrics for* She's Leaving Home. *In the Collectors' Carousel auction in New York in June, the highlight was Dizzy Gillespie's trumpet which sold for $50,600.*

**1934 Goudey
Uncut Sheet
with no. 106 Lajoie
(detail)**
Sheet of 25 baseball cards,
29.8 x 36.3cm (11¾ x 14¼in)
New York $74,000 (£49,300).
13.III.93 (Left)

**1946 Morris 8hp
Post Office
Telephone Van**
Falmouth £3,680 ($5,660).
3.V.93
From the Lamanva Collection
of Military, Commercial and
Action Vehicles. (Below)

Following the outstanding success of New York's inaugural sale of Sports Memorabilia in 1991, the subject has become a fixture in the auction almanac there. This season's sale included the last jersey worn by the baseball legend Mickey Mantle, which sold for $66,000.

In London, the buoyancy of the Collectables market continued this year with record prices achieved for a number of outstanding toys, dolls, automata and mechanical musical instruments. Two extremely rare 'H' pressed bisque dolls were sold in November, realizing £34,100 and £46,200, and a tinplate toy of a Russian carousel by the German company Märklin made a new world record for a European toy when it was bought for £62,000.

Auctions of instruments of science and technology held in London included a magnificent nineteenth-century microscope by Powell and Lealand which sold for £22,000, a world record price for such an instrument, while a Hahn-type mechanical equinoctial dial realized a remarkable £45,100.

Musical Instruments had some notable successes this season, with the added surprise of a saleroom duel over a violin bow by the French archetier Dominique Peccatte. Modestly estimated at £1,200 due to its various faults, it sold for £34,100. Stringed instruments by nineteenth-century Turin makers are now keenly sought after. For example, two violins by Giuseppe Rocca realized £99,000 and £78,500.

Analyses of trends in Arms and Armour revealed a transference of market strength towards continental Europe for pieces of non-British origin. In order to capitalize on this, arms and armour were sold in Zürich as well as London and New York. Highlights from Zürich included a French flintlock fowling-piece by Antoine Berthault of Paris, which was sold by private treaty to the Royal Armouries in London for SF201,960. In New York pieces such as a shanfron from 1550 and a burgonet from the 1540s were strongly in demand, realizing $36,800 and $41,400 respectively.

The Sporting Guns department held a series of highly successful sales this season with buoyant bidding in all categories. The demand is strong for high quality English guns, such as the set of three Boss & Co. 12-bore sidelock ejector guns which achieved £71,500.

A highlight this season for War Medals and Decorations was the record price set for a group of gallantry medals. This was the £132,000 paid for the VC, DSO and bar, and MC and bar awarded to Major 'Mick' Mannock, the most decorated and highest scoring British fighter pilot of the First World War.

A French flintlock fowling-piece
BY ANTOINE BERTHAULT, c.1670-80, PARIS, length 117.8cm (46½in) Zürich SF201,960 (£89,700:$137,300). 6.XI.92 From the Collection of Field Marshal Sir Francis Festing. (BELOW)

A German wheel-lock sporting rifle
BY MARTIN KAMERR, DATED 1658, AUGSBURG, barrel length 79.4cm (31¼in) New York $123,500 (£80,100). 24.V.93 (LEFT)

Celluloid from
Beauty and the Beast
WALT DISNEY, 1991,
29.2 x 68.5cm (11½ x 27in)
Los Angeles $18,700 (£12,300).
17.X.92 (ABOVE)

The postage stamp market was strong but selective this season, with buyers paying record prices for items and collections fresh to the market. An auction devoted to the Italian States saw a veritable invasion of Italian dealers and collectors and resulted in a 100 per cent sale, the highest price being £66,000 for the 'Borgotaro' cover. In another sale a collection from India was secured for £33,000 by a newcomer bidding over the telephone from his private jet.

The season has seen a considerable growth in coin sales with increased liaison between our London and New York departments. The sale of the 'Uruguayan Treasure of the River Plate', catalogued in London and offered in New York in March, was the largest single auction for years of gold coins, ingots and artifacts recovered from a shipwreck. The final aggregate total of $3,192,000 exceeded the sale's top estimate, with just 0.6 per cent unsold.

The Veteran, Vintage and Classic Car department saw the market poised for recovery after a period of depression. A private collection of Ferraris and Maseratis reached an international market in Zürich, with an ex-Edsel Ford GT40 sports/competition car realizing SF470,350. In Britain an ERA single-seater racing car, one of only twenty models produced, sold for £243,500.

The Wine department's tradition of selling wines from the cellars of top classified Bordeaux growths included a collection of the great classified St Julien, Château Gruaud Larose. Part of the private reserves from Château Pichon Longueville was also sold. Spanning vintages from 1908 to 1981 this section of the auction was a great success with every lot finding a buyer.

This season was another marked success for most of the Collectors' departments and, with an anticipated improvement in the world economy over the coming months, Sotheby's looks forward to further achievements within the Collectors' Categories next season.

John Lennon's
handwritten lyrics
for *A Day in the Life*
1967, BLACK FELT-TIP AND
BLUE BALLPOINT PENS,
27 x 19.5cm (10½ x 7¾in)
London £48,400 ($75,500).
27.VIII.92 (ABOVE)

POSTAGE STAMPS

New Zealand
1906 Christchurch
1d. claret
IN HORIZONTAL
INTERPANNEAU PAIR
London £10,450 ($19,850).
10.IX.92

Produced for the 1906
Christchurch Exhibition,
this pair was printed in
claret rather than the
vermilion which was
considered a more
suitable colour for the
issued stamp. Most
recorded examples of the
'unissued' claret shade
were either sold at the
Exhibition Post Office
or included in Post
Office presentation
books. (BELOW RIGHT)

New Zealand
1915-29 6d.
carmine
'IMPERFORATE THREE SIDES'
HORIZONTAL, MARGINAL BLOCK
OF THIRTY-SIX STAMPS (DETAIL)
London £5,175 ($7,610).
26.III.93

In *The Postage Stamps
of New Zealand* it is
recorded that four sheets
containing this variety
were issued in January
1928 at the Chief Post
Office in Wellington.
Thus, of the forty-eight
possible examples of this
variety in existence, one
quarter are encompassed
in this block, making it
probably the most
important piece of the
George V recess-printed
series. (RIGHT)

Great Britain
1910 2d. Tyrian Plum
London £4,370 ($6,420). 26.III.93

Very few examples of the Tyrian Plum survived the
destruction of the stock of sheets occasioned by the
death of Edward VII on 6 May 1910. None was
officially issued and this single specimen only recently
came to light when a general collector saw the stamp
fall out of an envelope he had just thrown on his
sitting-room fire. (LEFT)

Sweden
1918 55ö light blue and 80ö black
INCLUDED IN A PRESENTATION BOOK FROM THE SWEDISH DIRECTOR
GENERAL OF POSTS London £3,740 ($7,110). 10.IX.92

The issue of 50ö and 80ö adhesives had been
announced on 27 June 1918, but by 2 July it had been
decided not to proceed with it. Värnamo Post Office
had been sent a small supply, which was soon
withdrawn, and some examples later appeared in
Post Office presentation books. (LEFT)

Italy (Parma)
1859 Provisional Government 5c. verde giallo
THE BORGOTARO COVER
London £66,000 ($102,100). 4.XI.92

The stamps on this famous 1860 Borgotaro to Piacenza cover, with its unique horizontal strip of four of the 1859 Provisional Government 5c. verde giallo, were in use only between 9 June 1859 and 18 March 1860. The cover, from the collection of Maurice Burrus, is illustrated in colour in the Sassone handbook catalogue and is generally considered to be one of the most desirable items of Italian philately. (LEFT)

India
FROM A COLLECTION IN THREE OLD SCOTT SPRINGBACK ALBUMS
London £33,000 ($62,700). 10.IX.92

This selection of stamps from an exceptional collection was offered for sale intact, in three albums. Comprehensive, specialized ranges from 1817 to 1933 were included with essays, proofs, specimens, postal history and issued stamps, the last featuring one of India's rarest stamps, which appeared in 1926 with the head of George VI omitted. (ABOVE)

COINS AND MEDALS

Cob type 4 escudos
FROM THE URUGUAYAN TREASURE OF THE
RIVER PLATE, LIMA, 1750
New York $19,800 (£13,600). 24.III.93
'Cob money' is a generic term
for hand-made Spanish-
American coins, usually of crude
style. This coin is remarkable in
that one side is struck from a die
intended for the smaller
2 escudos coin.(RIGHT)

Silver medal of Doge Marcantonio Memmo of Venice
BY GUILLAUME DUPRÉ, SIGNED AND DATED 1612
London £15,950 ($23,610). 12.VII.93
A superbly-finished original cast, this medal was executed at a
time when the French medallist and sculptor Dupré was
employed in Italy. (LEFT)

The wooden model for a medal portraying
an unknown man
BY FRIEDRICH HAGENAUER, c.1520
London £15,840 ($23,440). 12.VII.93
An original model sculpted by the medallist Hagenauer and believed
to be one of his earliest works. (BELOW)

Bronze medal of
Georg Volckhamer of
Nuremberg, aged 24
BY HANS SCHWARZ, 1521
London £13,200 ($19,540). 12.VII.93
Active for only a few years around
1520, Schwarz stands out from
his German Renaissance
contemporaries for his vigorous,
individual style. This example is
only the second recorded
specimen of the medal, the other
being in Berlin where an original
drawing also survives. (LEFT)

Gold coins, ingots and artifacts from
the Uruguayan Treasure of the River Plate
SPANISH-AMERICAN, 1741–51
New York sale total $3,123,945 (£2,155,445). 24.III.93
Recovered in 1992 from the River Plate near Montevideo, the 'Uruguayan Treasure'
is believed to represent the contraband cargo of a Spanish-registered Portuguese vessel
wrecked by a violent storm in 1752. The river's notorious mud has preserved most of
the material in remarkably good condition. (ABOVE)

United States Gold Double-Eagle
'EXTREMELY HIGH RELIEF' TYPE,
1907 New York $143,000
(£89,400). 9.XII.92
Research into the surface
and edge details of this
recently-discovered coin
suggest that it is a proto-
type for the celebrated
double-eagle, or $20 piece,
designed by Augustus
Saint-Gaudens. It is a
unique variety. (ABOVE)

Australian Silver Threepence, or 'joey'
OF GEORGE VI, 1937
London £18,700 ($31,600). 8.X.92
Probably the only
Australian threepence dated
1937 in private hands, this
well-used example was
recovered from loose
change in Tasmania in
1966. (LEFT)

United States Gold Stella
FLOWING HAIR TYPE, 1879
New York $40,700 (£26,600).
10.VI.93
The concept of the Stella
was an unsuccessful
attempt by the United
States to issue a coin
valued at 4 dollars which
would be consistent with
the standard then in use
in Europe. (LEFT)

MUSICAL INSTRUMENTS

Violin by Giovanni Francesco Pressenda
1833, TURIN, length of back 35.6cm (14in)
London £74,800 ($114,400). 5.XI.92
Pressenda, Rocca's master (see right), was an inheritor of the
Cremonese tradition of violin making, and had studied under the
great Lorenzo Storioni. This instrument was offered at auction
completely unaltered, bearing its original contemporary fittings.
(ABOVE)

Violin after Stradivari by Giuseppe Rocca
1852, TURIN, length of back 35.6cm (14in)
London £99,000 ($151,470). 5.XI.92
The model for this instrument, as for many of Rocca's violins, was
'The Messiah' Stradivari of 1716, which Rocca would have had access
to by virtue of his acquaintance with the collector Tarisio. This
instrument was offered at auction unaltered since its production.
(ABOVE)

Chamber organ by Hugh Russell
*c.*1790, LONDON,
height 246.5cm (101in)
London £13,750 ($21,040).
26.XI.92

This chamber organ was made shortly after Russell's partnership with John England dissolved in around 1784, although a plaque above the keyboard reads *Hugh Russell London 1780*. The mahogany case contains gilded display pipes with very fine floral painted decoration.
(RIGHT)

Violin by Romeo Antoniazzi
1907, CREMONA,
length of back 35.7cm (14⅟₁₆in)
London £20,700 ($30,845).
1.VII.93

The market for modern violins of quality, such as this Italian example from 1907, has been seeing particular growth of late, and the names of the makers of the first years of the twentieth century may soon be as widely-known as their earlier forerunners.
(FAR RIGHT)

Concert guitar by Francisco Simplico
1927, BARCELONA,
length 48.5cm (19⅛in)
London £9,350 ($14,300).
26.XI.92

Made to order for Maria Angelica Pedreira de Cerqueira, a pupil of Oswaldo Soares, this instrument was used by her in notable concerts in the Instituto Nacional de Musica in Rio de Janeiro (9 April 1929) and the Theatro Polythema in Salvador (20 September 1932). (RIGHT)

ARMS AND ARMOUR

An ivory powder flask
NUREMBERG OR VIENNA, LATE SIXTEENTH/EARLY SEVENTEENTH
CENTURY, 15.6cm (6⅛in)
New York $46,000 (£29,800). 24.V.93
Powder for charging a firearm was carried in a flask
suspended from the belt. This fine example, which is
engraved in the manner of Paul Flindt and retains an
early suspension cord of bullion thread, would have
been purely decorative, as flasks for use on the
battlefield had to be made of more durable
materials than ivory. (ABOVE)

A Swiss suit of half armour
c.1600 Zürich SF39,550 (£17,900:$27,600). 6.XI.92
During the sixteenth century major advances were made in the development of
firearms. This had important implications for armour design, and mobility started to
become a greater priority than direct bodily protection. (ABOVE)

A French over-and-under single-trigger carbine
DATED 1836 Zürich SF90,400 (£41,000:$63,200). 6.XI.92
This rare carbine was made for the Duc d'Orléans by Le Page and is decorated on the
butt with the Duc's monogram. It is unfired and in pristine condition throughout,
revealing that it was only ever intended for ceremonial and display purposes. (BELOW)

SPORTING GUNS

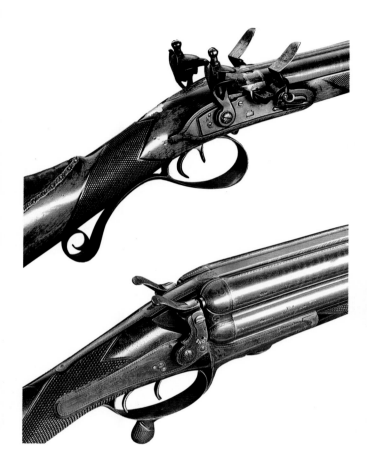

A matched set of three 12-bore single-trigger sidelock
ejector over-and-under guns by Boss & Co.
Gleneagles £71,500 ($141,600). 31.VIII.92
Boss & Co. was founded in 1812 by Thomas Boss, and the first
premises were at 73 St James's Street, London. During the 1890s the
firm was run by John Robertson, whose reputation was already
well-established as the inventor of a reliable single-trigger mechanism.
Gun numbers 7261 and 7262 in this example of Boss craftsmanship
were built as a pair in 1926, whilst number 7256 was ordered in 1927
to match the others and complete a set of three. (BELOW)

A 20-bore double-barrelled flintlock gun with
side-by-side twist barrels by Ezekiel Baker
INSCRIBED *Gunmaker to His Royal Highness The Prince of Wales*
London £14,000 ($21,800). 15.IV.93
At the end of the eighteenth century the Prince of Wales (the future
George IV) showed great interest in the work of Ezekiel Baker, one of
London's leading gunmakers, from whom he purchased several guns.
This example was given by the Prince to a close friend in 1806. (TOP)

A 16-bore/.577 four-barrelled 1884 patent
Hammer 'Cape' Rifle by Charles Lancaster
London £15,000 ($23,400). 15.IV.93
This rifle was built in 1883 and retained by the maker, presumably in
order to demonstrate his particular skills to prospective customers.
The rifle's four barrels make this a particularly rare piece. (ABOVE)

WAR MEDALS AND DECORATIONS

Russian Order of St Catherine
UNMARKED, *c.*1890
Geneva SF55,000 (£24,200:$37,400). 19.XI.92
The order of Saint Catherine was founded in 1714 by
Peter the Great in honour of his wife, Catherine
Alekseyevna. It came in two classes and was awarded
only to women of the highest nobility. (ABOVE)

The First World War V.C., D.S.O. and two bars, M.C. and bar
awarded to Major E. 'Mick' Mannock of the Royal Air Force
Billingshurst £132,000 ($232,300). 19.IX.92
Edward 'Mick' Mannock was the highest scoring and most decorated British pilot of
the First World War. He was finally shot down over France in 1918, and while it was
assumed at the time that his body was consumed by the flames that engulfed his
aircraft, it was later discovered that he had been buried by an unknown German
soldier, who returned his identity discs, notebook and other personal effects to the
British authorities at the end of the War. (ABOVE)

WINE

A selection of classic Champagne,
Burgundy and Bordeaux
Left to right:
A jeroboam of Louis Roederer Cristal Brut 1985
£374 ($583)
A bottle of Romanée Conti 1964
£418 ($652)
A double magnum of Château Lafite 1970
£297 ($463)
All London 21.IV.93
(ABOVE)

An historic collection of Krug Collection Champagnes
direct from the Krug cellars in Reims
Left to right:
A magnum of Krug Collection 1964
£396 ($594)
A magnum of Krug Collection 1947
£616 ($924)
A magnum of Krug Collection 1938
£660 ($990)
A magnum of Krug Collection 1953
£605 ($907)
A bottle of Krug Collection 1929
£396 ($594)
A magnum of Krug Collection 1973
£352 ($528)
All London 9.VI.93 (ABOVE)

VETERAN, VINTAGE AND CLASSIC CARS

1914 Hispano-Suiza 8/10hp four-seater open tourer
Hendon £33,350 ($51,300). 22.V.93

The name Hispano-Suiza usually summons up images of the six- and twelve-cylinder luxury cars which provided competition for Rolls-Royce and other bespoke makers. However, the company did manufacture a number of smaller models prior to the First World War. (RIGHT)

1934 ERA R1A single-seater racing car
Hendon £243,500 ($353,000). 20.II.93

The setting up of English Racing Automobiles in 1933 heralded the start of a new chapter in British motor racing history. The company aimed to produce a car that was sufficiently versatile for road or circuit racing, sprints and hill climbs. The first car to carry the ERA name was R1A, shown here. (RIGHT)

1926 Rolls-Royce 20hp three-quarter drophead coupé
Hendon £36,300 ($71,800). 5.IX.92

Introduced in 1922, the 'Twenty' was the first entirely new Rolls-Royce model since the 40/50hp Silver Ghost of 1906. This model was for some time displayed at the Science Museum, London. (RIGHT)

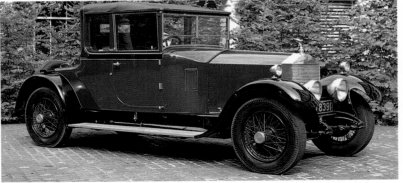

1958 BMW 507 V8 sports two-seater
Zürich SF244,300 (£108,600: $166,200). 8.III.93

The Bayerische Motoren-Werke began by building aircraft engines in 1916. Car production started in the 1930s. In 1955 Count Albrecht Goertz was recruited to style a sports car for the US market. The result was the 507. (RIGHT)

1929 Bentley 4½ litre Vanden Plas Tourer
Hendon £112,750 ($223,200). 5.IX.92

The 4½ litre Bentley was introduced in 1927. One of the most popular of body styles was the fabric-bodied Vanden Plas Tourer. This particular example was supplied new to Major E. G. Thompson and passed shortly afterwards to John C. Sword. (RIGHT)

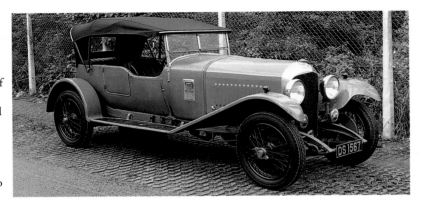

COLLECTORS' SALES

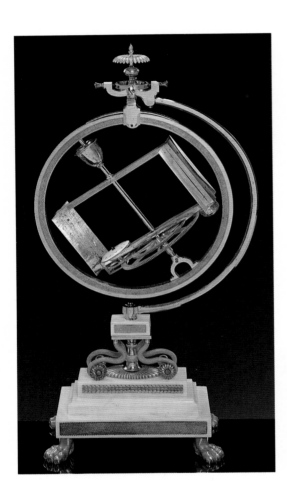

A French *chrono-photographe* cine-matographic camera
*c.*1899, GAUMONT DEMENY
London £7,475 ($11,500).
2.VI.93
In 1896 Léon Gaumont, one of the pioneers of synchronized sound and image, asked Georges Demeny to redesign the projector he had patent-ed in 1893 to accom-modate perforated film. The result was the *chronophotographe* cinematographic camera: a major breakthrough in film projection technology. (LEFT)

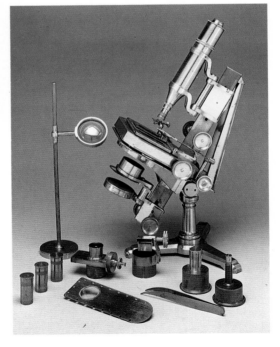

An English brass compound monocular microscope
POWELL AND LEALAND,
SIGNED AND DATED *1842*
London £22,000 ($38,000).
1.X.92
This massive microscope is signed *Powell and Lealand,* who are recorded as having worked from 24 Clarendon Street, London, between 1842 and 1846. (LEFT)

A Hahn-type gilt and silvered-brass mechanical equinoctial dial
*c.*1805, PROBABLY SWEDISH
London £45,100 ($70,800). 1.X.92
The equinoctial dial was used to check the accuracy of clock and watch movements. This gilt and silvered-brass example is signed *F. J. Sauter,* who in 1808 is recorded as being a clockmaker working in Stockholm.
(ABOVE)

A German 'Russian' carousel

MARKLIN, *c.*1904, height 52.5 cm (20⅝in)
London £62,000 ($94,200). 10.II.93

This extraordinarily elaborate toy is made from hand-painted tinplate and incorporates a cylinder musical accompaniment. It was manufactured by the German firm of Marklin, one of the foremost producers of tinplate toys at the beginning of the century. A very similar toy is shown in the 1904 Marklin Hauptkatalog as item 1123.
(ABOVE)

A French musical automaton

ROULLET ET DECAMPS, *c.*1910, height 104cm (41in)
London £67,500 ($101,200). 18.V.93

The mask-seller depicted by this rare papier-mâché automaton holds four articulated masks in his left hand and an inactive mask in his right. A sixth mask, which sticks out its tongue, appears on the sole of the clown's right foot, revealed as he lifts his leg. In addition, he lifts a mask to his face while the masks in his left hand raise their eyebrows and moustaches, stick out their tongues, look upwards or move their eyes from side to side. A devil mask, suspended over the figure's standing foot, also sticks out his tongue and closes his eyes. (LEFT)

A French bisque H-pressed doll
*c.*1880, height 46cm (18in)
London £34,100 ($52,100). 10.XI.92
A French bisque H-pressed doll
*c.*1880, height 38cm (15in)
London £46,200 ($70,600). 10.XI.92
Doll manufacture was established in Europe as an
industry at the beginning of the nineteenth century.
Early examples tended to be made of carved or turned
wood, but later on in the century ceramics were used,
as with these French bisque examples dating from
around 1880. (ABOVE AND ABOVE RIGHT)

An American cast-iron pull-along toy
*c.*1885, length 26.7cm (10½in)
New York $6,900 (£4,600). 23.VI.93
Although the American Civil War curtailed the supply of metal for non-military use,
demand was stimulated when firms returned to peacetime production. Throughout
the nineteenth century American toys were modelled closely on European imports
but from 1860 onwards the toy industry began to make a bid for overseas markets.
This 'swan chariot' dates from a little after that period.
(ABOVE)

Dizzy Gillespie's trumpet
MANUFACTURED BY KING MUSICAL INSTRUMENTS
New York $50,600 (£33,700). 23.VI.93
This trumpet was consigned with a letter of authenticity from the legendary jazz
musician. Gillespie's bent trumpet was one of his hallmarks. It began as a mistake
(he dropped one of his instruments) but when he heard the sound the 'mistake'
produced, he decided to stick with it. The keys are finished in mother-of-pearl
and the rim of the horn is inscribed *Dizzy*. (BELOW)

Judy Garland's dress from *The Wizard of Oz*
New York $48,400 (£30,800). 18.XII.92
What must be one of the most famous films of all
time, MGM's 1939 *The Wizard of Oz* broke all box
office records on its release and still remains extremely
popular. This blue and white gingham pinafore is
undoubtedly one of the trademarks of that film, and
bears Garland's name on a label. (ABOVE)

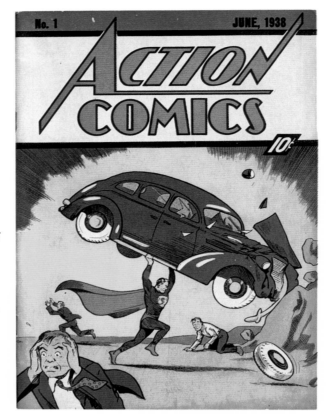

Action Comics No. 1
comic book
JUNE 1938, PUBLISHED BY D. C. COMICS
New York $82,500 (£53,900). 30.IX.92
This completely unrestored copy of
Action Comics' number one issue
features the first appearance of
Jerry Siegel and Joe Schuster's
legendary Superman, the latter
arguably the most imitated cartoon
creation of all time. Historically,
this makes it the most important
comic book ever printed and its
appearance on the commercial
market can be considered a rare
event by any collecting standard.
(RIGHT)

CARL BARKS
Hands Off My Playthings
OIL ON MASONITE, 39.4 x 49.5cm
(15½ x 19½in)
New York $112,500 (£75,000). 26.VI.93
This was the 106th painting
completed by Carl Barks
illustrating one of Walt Disney's
most famous cartoon characters.
Here Uncle Scrooge is shown
entering his money store and
catching Donald Duck and his
nephews playing with the treasure.
(BELOW)

The Birth of a Nation poster
1916, EPOCH, 104 x 68.6cm (41 x 27in)
New York $49,500 (£31,700). 12.IX.92
From the Stanley Caidin Collection.

D. W. Griffith's 1915 work *The Birth of a Nation* is a significant landmark in the history of world cinema, and can be considered the first example of the 'epic' film, engendering a long-lasting cinematic tradition. Set in South Carolina immediately after the American Civil War, the story centres on the problems of the dispossessed white population which spawned the Ku Klux Klan. (RIGHT)

Celluloid from Snow White and the Seven Dwarfs
1937, WALT DISNEY, 33 x 40.6cm (13 x 16in)
New York $34,100 (£21,700). 19.XII.92

Snow White and the Seven Dwarfs, which was premiered in 1937, was not only Walt Disney's first feature-length cartoon but also the first to be produced in the United States. In 1938 it won a special Academy Award for pioneering animation and significant screen innovation. Half a century later it remains firmly established as a classic. (BELOW)

COLLECTIONS OF THE SEASON *by Ronald Varney*

ANDERS ZORN
Portrait of Maud Cassel, Aged Seven
SIGNED AND DATED *87*, WATERCOLOUR, 99 x 59cm (39 x 23¼in)
London £99,000 ($150,400). 25.XI.92
From the Estate of the Rt Hon the Earl Mountbatten of Burma. (LEFT)

I n June and July of 1984, Sotheby's London conducted a three-part sale of paintings and works of art from the collections of the late Lord Clark of Saltwood, whose grand career in the world of arts and letters might be summarized by two particular achievements: being appointed Director of the National Gallery at the age of twenty-nine and, in later life, writing and fronting a hugely popular television series for the BBC entitled *Civilisation.*

It was perhaps no surprise that the collections he assembled over the course of his eighty years were refined and wide-ranging. Visitors to the Bond Street exhibitions in that summer of 1984 viewed civilization through the prism of Lord Clark's extraordinary possessions: there were Japanese prints and European ceramics, French nineteenth-century paintings and drawings, antiquities, Old Master paintings and drawings, Chinese vases and censers, Impressionist and Modern sculpture, and pieces of tribal art. A large group of Medieval and Renaissance miniatures, which had previously been assembled into a red morocco album by the renowned Scottish antiquary James Dennistoun, and which Clark bought around 1930, formed the core of the collection. Among the many British paintings and drawings was one of J. M. W. Turner's last great sea pictures, *Seascape: Folkstone*, which sold for £7,370,000, breaking the world record for a painting. Interestingly, it had been Clark himself who had discovered the last cache of neglected Turners in the vaults of the National Gallery in 1939, 'some 20 rolls of canvas, thick with dirt, which I took to be old tarpaulins'.

As if trying to comprehend his own lifelong passion for art, Clark once wrote, 'Why do men and women collect? As well ask why they fall in love: the reasons are as irrational, the motives as mixed, the original impulse as often discoloured or betrayed. The collector's instinct, if animals and children are any guide, has two roots; the desire to pick up anything bright and shining and the desire to complete a series.'

In reviewing the collections offered at Sotheby's during the 1992-3 season, one would have to say that the collecting instinct – whether one agrees with Lord Clark's analysis or not – is to be found at work in a most amazing diversity of collecting fields. Some of the more intriguing areas represented at Sotheby's this past season were: Melanesian art (the Peter Hallinan Collection), Hollywood posters (the Stanley Caidin Collection), postage stamps of the Italian states, Japanese prints of the Kabuki theatre (the Kühne Collection), Ruskin pottery (the Adam Ferneyhough Collection), military vehicles (the Lamanva Collection), tea caddies, Scandinavian furniture (the Bronson Pinchot Collection), metalware (the Robert M. Holland-Martin Collection) and lustreware.

To give one a sense of the importance of many of the less-heralded collections offered during the season, there was the Cavanagh Collection, sold in London in May and comprising major works on the theatre in Western Europe, Russia, Asia and the United States. It included many books, pamphlets, prints, drawings and paintings, all evoking the colour and character of the dramatic arts through the ages. Biographies and memoirs of such theatre luminaries as Garrick, Sheridan and Kean were complemented by mezzotint portraits of early English actors and actresses, stirring histories of such major theatres as La Scala in Milan, and many volumes of late eighteenth-century plates portraying costumes from the world of Parisian theatre. This treasure trove, formed over a period of fifty years, was the best collection of its kind ever to appear at auction.

Many of the collections offered at Sotheby's during the season were similarly rare and distinctive. In reviewing the highlights, one hears Lord Clark's voice as he describes the finest

JAMES MILLER
Selections from a sketchbook of drawings of London and the Upper Thames
WATERCOLOUR OVER PENCIL, each opening 20 x 32cm (7¾ x 12½in) London £24,200 ($37,000). 19.XI.92 From the collection of the late Dudley Snelgrove. (LEFT)

collectors as those who 'look at their possessions with the feelings of an artist and relive, to some extent, the sensuous and imaginative experiences which lie behind each work.'

In the centre of Verona, with its palaces of 'glowing orange and pale warm red', as Ruskin described them, lies the Palazzo Barocco, which dates back to the medieval age. The present owners of the Palazzo Barocco had, over many years, furnished it with paintings, furniture and works of art from the surrounding area of the Veneto. In late October 1992 at the Hotel Due Torri in Verona, Sotheby's offered the contents of the palazzo, as well as furniture and decorations from two villas of a noble Lombard family. The sale offered some magnificent early-eighteenth century furniture from the series of rooms that form the *piano nobile* of the Palazzo Barocco, as well as four chairs richly carved in the manner of Andrea Brustolon, one of the finest Venetian craftsmen of the period.

Two exceptional collections of twentieth-century decorative arts were offered in New York in the autumn, beginning in October with the John and Katsy Mecom Collection of European and American Art Nouveau, with its prodigious quantity of fine Tiffany glass; and the twentieth-century design collection of Barry Friedman, a New York dealer. This latter collection, which included sleek Modernist works by such designers as Marcel Breuer, René Crevel, Gerrit Rietveld and Carlo Bugatti, yielded two new auction records: $101,750 for a René Crevel Art Deco wool carpet, and $187,000 for a Hector Guimard mahogany, gilt-bronze and glass two-tier tea table, the latter a beautifully sinuous piece.

'People! Drama! Romance! What more could you want?' While these words were once used by Harry Winston to describe his own career, they might equally apply to two prominent jewellery collections offered early in the season – one of which was the collection of the late Mrs Harry Winston. Amongst the major innovators in twentieth-century jewellery design, Harry Winston included among his clients some of the most powerful and famous people in the world. One of the most dazzling of these was the Duchess of Windsor, who purchased a number of major

The Kid
First National Attraction,
1921, one-sheet,
104 x 68.6cm (41 x 27in)
New York $27,500 (£14,200).
12.IX.92
From the Stanley Caidin
Collection of Hollywood
Movie Posters. (Left)

pieces from Harry Winston which were eventually offered in the historic 1987 sale of her collection at Sotheby's in Geneva. Over one hundred pieces were included in the 1992 sale of Mrs Winston's collection, and nearly half of these had been made especially for her by her husband. This exciting auction filled the New York saleroom, and the feverish bidding in some cases drove prices to two or three times their estimate. The star lot, a spectacular pair of diamond chandelier pendant-earrings by Harry Winston, made in 1961, brought $1,430,000. The sale total of $5.1 million was well above expectations, showing once more how a famed collection can seize the public's attention.

This was again the case on the evening of 17 November 1992 at the Hôtel des Bergues in Geneva when silver, jewellery and objects of vertu from the Thurn und Taxis Collections were auctioned. The princely family of Thurn und Taxis has played a central role in the history of Europe since the days of the Holy Roman Empire, and the sale of property from their vast

THOMAS MORAN
Castle Butte, Green River, Wyoming
SIGNED AND DATED *1900*,
WATERCOLOUR ON PAPER,
50.2 x 39.4cm (19¾ x 15½in)
New York $264,000
(£169,200). 3.XII.92
From the Transco Energy
Company collection of
American watercolours.
(ABOVE)

collections stirred the world's media into a cyclone of print, radio and television coverage. Certainly, there was a grand, sweeping story to relate behind the collections: the founding of the family fortune by Franz von Taxis (1459-1517) who established the first postal service between Brussels and Vienna; the rapid spread of this postal system, and the family's influence, throughout Europe; the establishment in 1748 of the family's principal residence in Regensburg, northern Bavaria; the move in 1812 to the nearby monastery of St Emmeram, a sprawling complex of medieval buildings; and the death of Prince Johannes, 11th Prince of Thurn und Taxis, in 1990, leading to the auction of selected items

from the family collections. These comprised around 150 lots of jewellery dating from the eighteenth to the twentieth century, highlighted by the magnificent pearl and diamond tiara commissioned by Napoleon III on the occasion of his marriage to Princess Eugénie in 1853. There were also about fifty exquisite snuff boxes, many from the finest eighteenth-century Paris goldsmiths, and an extensive collection of breathtaking table silver, mainly from Augsburg.

The auction in Geneva, in a packed saleroom that evoked the glamour and drama of the Windsor sale, yielded a total of SF19.6 million, with nearly every lot sold. The highest price in the sale, SF2,530,000, was paid for a jewelled gold and hardstone snuff box made for Frederick the Great of Prussia in 1770, breaking the previous world auction record set at Sotheby's Geneva in 1989 by a snuff box of Catherine the Great. The 'Eugénie Tiara' was acquired by Le Société des Amis du Louvre and will be exhibited with other French crown jewels at that museum.

The radiance of the Thurn und Taxis sale seemed to cast itself over a host of other auctions that took place in the late autumn and early winter, lending an air of hopeful expectation. This was quickly borne out with the sale of paintings from the collection of designer Mollie Parnis Livingston in New York in November, when for the first time in two years the $10 million level was exceeded in the Impressionist and Modern market. The painting that earned this distinction was Henri Matisse's 1946 oil, *L'Asie*, which came to Sotheby's York Avenue saleroom from the Museum of Modern Art in New York, where it was displayed in the landmark Matisse retrospective exhibition. The Kimbell Art Foundation in Texas paid $11 million for the painting, which was returned to the Museum of Modern Art for the duration of the exhibition. The Mollie Parnis Livingston Collection also included a number of important paintings by Vuillard and Picasso, as well as furniture and decorations from her Park Avenue apartment.

The Wright Ludington Collection also offered a Matisse from the Museum of Modern Art show, *La Plage Rouge*, painted in 1905, as well as works by Bonnard and Vuillard. Wright

Bureau mécanique
By Jean-Henri Riesener and
Jacques-Laurent Cosson,
Rosewood, burr walnut
and marquetry,
height 75cm (29½in)
Monaco FF4,440,000
(£505,000:$792,800). 4.XII.92
From the Estate of Mme
Hélène Beaumont. (Above)

Ludington was an avid supporter of the Santa Barbara Museum of Art, which he had helped found. During his lifetime he donated more than 300 works of art to the institution, from Near Eastern bronzes and Roman ceramics to seminal works by such Modernists as Charles Sheeler, Marsden Hartley and Joseph Stella. Born to a family that traced its roots to the *Mayflower*, Ludington had begun collecting during the early 1920s with an inheritance from his mother, buying works by such emerging artists as Derain, Picasso and Braque. He bought *La Plage Rouge* for $3,000 from the Pierre Matisse Gallery in the 1940s, while an army lieutenant. At its sale on 10 November 1992 it fetched $1,375,000.

Other paintings highlights in the autumn included the sale of the Royal S. Marks Collection in New York, which comprised nineteen works by the Latin American artist Joaquin Torres-Garcia, all of which sold for a total of $1.9 million, and the sale of the Transco Energy Company Collection of American watercolours, also in New York, which offered exceptional works by Maurice Prendergast, Thomas Moran, Andrew Wyeth and Edward Hopper.

Also offered in London over the course of the season was the collection of the late Earl Mountbatten of Burma, former Viceroy of India. The collection included paintings, works of art, furniture, antiquities, silver and other items taken from the private apartments at Broadlands in

Hampshire, where Lord Mountbatten lived from 1939 until his death in 1979. Among the superb paintings was the charming *Portrait of Maud Cassel, Aged Seven* by Anders Zorn and *An Iron Forge* by Joseph Wright of Derby, which had been bought direct from the artist by Henry, 2nd Viscount Palmerston, one of the former owners of the Broadlands estate who had assembled part of the collection. This masterpiece was sold privately to the Tate Gallery in London.

Two exquisite collections were offered back-to-back in Monaco in early December, both of which conjured up images of lavish living in the great houses of France. Hélène Beaumont was one of the *grandes dames* of the Côte d'Azur, a philanthropist who owned, and generously entertained in, one of the most beautiful villas of the Cap d'Antibes. In the great French furniture sales of the 1920s, notably the Anthony de Rothschild Collection sale at Aston Clinton, Buckinghamshire in 1923, Mme Beaumont acquired the finest pieces of French eighteenth-century furniture for her villa. Many of these pieces were offered for sale in Monaco. The highlights were a Louis XVI *bureau plat* by Weisweiler, which achieved FF8,436,000, a small Louis XV porcelain-mounted marquetry table attributed to RVLC (Roger Vandercruse Lacroix), which sold for FF6,438,000, and a very rare Louis XVI *bureau mécanique* by Riesener and Cosson, which made FF4,440,000. This stunning collection, the finest of its kind to appear during the season, totalled over FF30 million, with French buyers playing a particularly active part.

The next day at the Sporting d'Hiver in Monaco saw the auction of the Jourdan-Barry Collection of silver. Comprising 250 pieces of seventeenth- and eighteenth-century silver, including some extremely rare pieces which survived the melting of plate under Louis XIV and Louis XV and during the Revolution, the Jourdan-Barry Collection was the most important of its kind to appear at auction in over two decades. The collection was formed over several generations of the Jourdan-Barry family, and a sense of connoisseurship seems to have been passed from one generation to the next. On being asked his reasons for selling the collection, Pierre Jourdan-Barry, who began collecting in 1960, replied, 'Collecting, for me, is a journey of seeking and discovery, a solitary journey because the collector is alone in his madness.... I think I have completed my long adventure in the field of French silver. I have decided to separate myself from my treasured objects with the hope that their new owners will feel the same excitement in acquiring and delight in owning them as I did.'

The autumn season drew to a triumphant close with the sale in New York of the Norbert Schimmel Collection of antiquities. One of this century's pioneering collectors of ancient art, Schimmel spent over fifty years assembling a comprehensive group of ancient Near Eastern, Egyptian, Greek, Etruscan and Roman works of art in bronze, marble, gold, faïence, terracotta and other materials. In 1989 Schimmel gave 103 works to the Metropolitan Museum of Art in New York, and in 1990 further donations were made to the Israel Museum in Jerusalem and to the Arthur M. Sackler Museum at Harvard. The 128 pieces offered at Sotheby's represented the remainder of Schimmel's famed collection. Prices in general greatly exceeded expectations, as shown by the top lot, a blue faïence inlay head of a king or god, late-eighteenth/early-nineteenth Dynasty, which sold for $484,000, three times its high estimate. The stunning sale total, $4,221,250, was as much a reflection of the quality of the individual pieces as it was a tribute to a great

An Achaemenid mirror
BRONZE, c. FIRST HALF OF THE 5TH CENTURY BC, diameter 21.6cm (8½in) New York $159,500 (£101,500). 10.XII.92 From the collection of Norbert Schimmel. (LEFT)

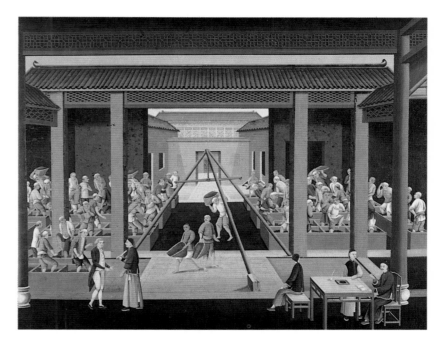

collector who exemplified the concept of old-world connoisseurship.

Archibald Thorburn (1860-1935) is widely regarded as Britain's greatest wildlife artist, and a sale in March 1993 in London offered 119 works by the artist from the Thorburn Museum at Liskeard in Cornwall. As Simon Taylor, the expert in charge of the sale, explained, Thorburn has always had a devout group of buyers because of the exquisite clarity and rendering of movement in his paintings: 'There is an almost

CHINESE SCHOOL
One of the stages in the processing of tea, from one of two albums of gouaches
CHINA, c. 1790, large folio London £166,500 ($249,700). 2.IV.93 From the collection of Rudolf von Gutmann. (ABOVE)

PIERRE-AUGUSTE
RENOIR
Buste de jeune fille
SIGNED, OIL ON CANVAS,
34.5 x 29cm (13⅝ x 11⅜in)
London £705,500
($1,072,300). 22.VI.93
From the Collection of Mme
d'Alayer, née Marie-Louise
Durand-Ruel. (ABOVE)

classical sense of space and peace in even his most dramatic compositions. His Highlands are wild and remote.... His England is a land of small fields and dense oak woods, of hedge-rows dotted with wild flowers, of deep snow in winter and glowing days in summer.' The lyrical appeal of Thorburn's art proved irresistible at the March auction, where, amid a packed saleroom, every single lot was sold and the total soared above the high estimate. The top lot, Thorburn's 1913 watercolour *Swerving from the Guns – Red Grouse*, made £111,500, a world auction record for the artist. The enormous success of this sale ensured the survival of the Thorburn Museum.

One of the most striking and beautiful catalogues of the season was produced in London for the sale there in April of the collection of

books, drawings and prints formed by Rudolf von Gutmann (1880-1966). The von Gutmann family owned the largest ironworks in Austro-Hungary, and Rudolf's considerable means allowed him to pursue his interest in art with studies at the Albertina in Vienna, whose directors advised on his collection. While prints were his special passion, he furnished his family houses with tapestries, porcelain, silver, glass, bronzes and paintings. In May 1938, however, von Gutmann fled Austria for Czechoslovakia, abandoning his collections, and then emigrated to British Columbia, where he died in 1966.

The Austrian Bundesdenkmalamt catalogued his collections, some of which were stored in the Hallein salt mines near Salzburg and partially recovered after the War. The print collection, which had been designated for Hitler's proposed museum at Linz, was removed to Dresden and is now in the process of being recovered. The sale of more than 100 lots from this remarkable collection was highlighted by a group of some 200 watercolour drawings of the Vatican and the various insignia of the Pontificate which had first been assembled by the early eighteenth-century architect John Talman. The collection also contained such exotica as two albums of Chinese gouache paintings depicting, among other subjects, the cultivation and production of silk and the processing of tea, and an important group of mid-eighteenth-century French watercolour designs for ballet costumes. As the catalogue to this sale observed, Rudolf von Gutmann was 'survived by collections of remarkable breadth and depth as befits one of the last of a now vanished breed of wealthy polymath.'

The season drew to a close with the sale of a number of distinguished collections in a delightfully diverse range of collecting fields, with several achieving outstanding results. For example, the Field Marshal Sir Francis Festing Collection of Japanese Swords, which was offered in London, totalled £754,300, well above the high estimate, setting a world record of £265,500 for a sword, with a piece by Yamaura Masayuki. In New York, the Otto Kallir Collection of Aviation History, the most extensive and comprehensive collection of its kind to be sold in decades, achieved

$1,014,000, with 99 per cent of the lots sold; and the Joseph M. Meraux Collection of rare and unusual clocks, an immense assemblage of largely nineteenth-century clocks taken from the New Orleans home of a lifelong enthusiast in this field, was wildly successful, setting several records and achieving $2,738,672, with an astonishing 100 per cent of the 500 lots sold.

One of the joys of perusing a single-owner catalogue lies in reading the preface. In the brief space of a page or two, these passages often provide a wealth of biographical information on the collector, how the collection was formed, its highlights and historical resonances and the like. One of the most memorable such essays this season appeared in the catalogue for the sale in late June in London of Impressionist paintings, drawings and sculpture from the Collection of Madame d'Alayer, née Marie Durand-Ruel. Of course the name Durand-Ruel needs no introduction in the Impressionist field, and yet the story of how Paul Durand-Ruel indomitably promoted the careers of these great painters, often against daunting rejection, seemed to be a wonderful way of introducing this sale of works from the estate of his daughter. The collection included several portraits by Renoir and works by Monet, Cassatt, Boudin, Sisley and Corot, and achieved an outstanding total of £4,710,000, with every one of the twenty-two works sold. Two Renoir portraits brought around £700,000 each, and a work by Monet, *Femme à l'Ombrelle*, achieved £353,500, a record for a drawing by the artist. Offered on the same evening as the Durand-Ruel sale was an unusual group of early twentieth-century paintings from a Californian private collection, which featured a group of fifteen works by the Czech artist Frantisek Kupka (1871-1957), an early pioneer of abstraction. This was the first time that such a significant group of the artist's work had been offered at auction, and all the works sold extremely well.

In summing up the 1992-3 season, one would have to agree once more with the venerable Lord Clark: 'When all is said, the world owes private collectors an enormous debt. Without them many of the greatest works of art would have been lost or destroyed.'

FRANTISEK KUPKA
Notre Dame
SIGNED, OIL ON CANVAS, 73 x 60cm (28¾ x 25⅜in)
London £238,000 ($361,700). 23.VI.93 (ABOVE)

SLEEPERS AWAKE *by Philip Mould*

So astonishing was the discovery on 26 November 1923 that nothing since has been able to rival its impact. The account by the discoverer himself has become one of the most famous pieces of narrative journalism ever written, setting the tone for many subsequent attempts to sensationalize a great find:

'The decisive moment had arrived. With trembling hands I made a tiny break in the upper left-hand corner ... At first I could see nothing, the hot air escaping from the chamber causing the candle flames to flicker.... Lord Carnarvon, unable to stand the suspense any longer, inquired anxiously, "Can you see anything?" it was all I could do to get out the words, "Yes, wonderful things."'

And so it was, in Howard Carter's words, that the tomb of Tutankhamun was discovered. Art dealers are asked constantly whether it is still possible to find wonderful things. Surely, it is said, people know too much. It was quite one thing for the archaeologist Carter to find the tomb of Tutankhamun, but that was in 1923. How, with the massive international art trade, the huge increase in education, countless books, articles and the boundless greed of the late-twentieth century, does anyone have the remotest chance of discovering anything?

The answer is that this is exactly why discoveries are now so much more possible. The whole point about a 'find' is that it must first be 'lost'. For it to be treated as a loss, it has to be appreciated or valued; and for that to happen, it has to have been established in some way. This is precisely what happens every time an art-historical book, article or thesis is written: a new subject, or category is summoned. One reason why Tutankhamun had so much impact was that

Howard Carter and Lord Carnarvon opening the tomb of Tutankhamun in November 1923. (BELOW)

Howard Carter and Lord Carnarvon taking the effigy bust of Tutankhamun from the tomb. (BELOW RIGHT)

Howard Carter, a plausible scholar, was able to establish the antiquarian significance of his find to the world at large. A hundred-and-fifty years earlier, an undisturbed tomb from the Valley of the Kings may well have been viewed as little more than a hoard of sumptuous booty for a lucky grand tourist.

American folk art is a case in point. Much of it used to be regarded rather patronisingly as charming but lightweight: the stuff of craftsmen rather than artists in the Renaissance sense. But all that has had to change now that scholarship has taken hold. Many pieces by the better practitioners have achieved the status of hallowed artifacts, with enough attendant literature and expertise to allow the sort of drama played out recently at Sotheby's offices in New York.

It began in the autumn of 1992 when a Los Angeles seller got in touch with the American Folk Art department about a painting of an unknown lady by the mid-nineteenth-century primitive American portrait painter Erastus Salisbury Field. He had purchased it from a sale in Paris. Field is a highly regarded and greatly sought-after American folk artist, and on seeing this new example the department eagerly set about trying to identify the female sitter. In the background was a harbour scene, painted with painstaking attention to detail; emphasis on background detail to this degree is unusual and had, therefore, to be a crucial clue as to her identity. With the available recent literature the department was soon able to establish another example by Field using a distinctive port scene – a portrait of Louisa Galland Cook hanging in the Shelbourne Museum in Vermont. The hunt closed in when documentation revealed that Field had undertaken a series of paintings of all the members of the Galland family in 1838. The last time the set was remembered as being complete was in 1912 when the family moved house, but it was not exactly a happy memory. Someone had accidently placed them on rubbish barrels with the result that they were picked up and carted off into the unknown. Despite this catastrophe, by 1992 all but two had been found, and by a process of deduction they worked out that this, the unknown lady, had to be Louisa's long-lost

sister, Clarissa. With the arrival of Clarissa, all but one of the set were accounted for.

The best was yet to come. Precisely eight weeks later the department received a telephone call, this time from a client in New England who wished to sell a portrait of an unknown boy with an added ingredient – an elaborate harbour scene in the background. From the other side of the continent, Field's lost portrait of Clarissa's son, William, had surfaced to join that of his mother. Having fully proved his identity they were then reunited by the department for the sale of Fine Americana in January 1993, the fruits of modern art history and synchronicity.

Art history has developed at such a pace in recent years that it can sometimes outstrip the object of its own scholarship. In the late 1980s, Cambridge art historian J. M. Massing embarked on a detailed study of a painting that no longer appeared to exist: *The Calumny of Apelles* by the sixteenth-century Italian master Garofalo. Fascinated by the unusually extensive contemporary records of the picture, and the numerous references to it in the nineteenth century, Massing decided, in the absence of the work itself, to rebuild the image from these sources. His findings were published in *Du text á l'image. La Calomnie d'Apelles et son iconographie* in 1990.

One morning, shortly before Christmas two years later, one of the specialists in Old Master paintings at Sotheby's London opened his post to find a photograph of a large allegorical work in the style of Garofalo. It had been sent to him for comment by an American architect and collector of Old Masters. The department instantly set about researching it, and when looking into the artist and his known works inevitably came across Massing's publication. There was a flurry of excitement as it became clear that the picture Massing was describing was the one of which he was holding a photograph in his hand. As if by sorcery, Massing's exhaustive description and concentration on this one work seemed to have summoned it, spirit-like, from the unknown. A letter with a photograph was swiftly despatched to Cambridge, putting Massing quite unexpectedly in the position of coming face to face with the real life object of his hypothesis. Fortunately,

ERASTUS SALISBURY
FIELD
**Portrait of William
Lauriston Cook**
OIL ON CANVAS,
77.5 x 60.3cm (30½ x 23¾in).
(ABOVE)

ERASTUS SALISBURY
FIELD
**Portrait of Clarissa
Gallond Cook**
OIL ON CANVAS,
87 x 71.8cm (34¼ x 28¼in).
(ABOVE RIGHT)

it closely matched his expectations, providing a conclusion few scholars would dare to seek. Only rarely does circumstance corroborate academic research so neatly. Many historians would be in danger of high embarrassment should concrete evidence appear after their speculations had been published.

A painting I always think of as exemplifying the potency of academic knowledge, and one that still makes my mouth dry with feelings of missed opportunity, can be seen in a recent rehang amongst the artist's contemporaries in the seventeenth-century rooms of the National Portrait Gallery, London. It is a portrait of Charles II as a boy by van Dyck, and shows the Prince as an eight-year-old standing with a look of solemn good behaviour in a suit of armour, holding a pistol in one hand and leaning on a plumed helmet with the other. Had you been wandering through the salerooms of one of London's major auction houses just before Christmas in 1983, you may not have given it a second look. Van

Dyck had in fact painted a number of versions of this picture, and his studio and followers produced many replicas. Estimated at £400-600 and extremely dirty, it was described as one of these copies, and consequently appeared as an early lot in a routine end-of-season British picture sale – the sort of object that might have been bought by an interior designer as up-market decoration for the drawing room of some country house hotel. There was one man however, sitting not that far away in an office in Trafalgar Square, who would view it quite differently.

Dr Malcolm Rogers, Deputy Director of the National Portrait Gallery, and now one of the country's leading experts on seventeenth-century British portrait painting, inspected the sale during his lunch break. He spotted the familiar van Dyck image from across the room, and although he assumed it to be yet another late replica, decided it was worth a careful look. He was instantly alerted by some writing in the bottom right-hand corner. Both the words of the

BENVENUTO TISI,
CALLED GAROFALO
**The Calumny of
Apelles**
OIL ON CANVAS,
79 x 109cm (31 x 43in).
(ABOVE LEFT)

inscription, conspicuous despite the dirt 'Charles Prince of Wales, about 1640 ... p.s. Ant: Vandike,' and the style of the lettering, a sort of primitive gothic, pointed unequivocally to its provenance as having belonged to Philip, Lord Wharton. All the pictures from this particular collection had the same style of inscription, and work that Rogers had carried out on seventeenth-century collectors told him that this was from very select company indeed. In all, the statesman 4th Baron Wharton (1613-96) owned thirty-two portraits by van Dyck, including fourteen life-size full-lengths; as the artist's patron he was quantitatively second only to the Royal family. Rogers knew that the quality of the collection was notable, and the best of them, including this composition, had been sold to Sir Robert Walpole at Houghton Hall in Norfolk, where it was noted by the eighteenth-century art commentator George Vertue: 'Charles Prince of Wales in armour at length 1640 ... all by V. Dyk.' Others from the series can now be seen in the Hermitage, St Petersburg, having been sold to Catherine the Great later that century.

This was an illustrious stable indeed. Where it had been since, Rogers didn't know, but that was unimportant. At this stage, by this piece of academic detection he could, circumstantially at least and on the basis of early provenance, prove its likely authenticity. Certainty would not come until after cleaning. Rogers then discussed it with his colleagues and they all agreed it was a risk worth taking. Indeed, it was rare to have so much factual corroboration to hand at so early a stage in a discovery. On the morning of the sale the trustees of the Gallery purchased it for £1,965.

The picture was taken to the Gallery's restorers who then carefully removed the discoloured top layer of varnish. As Rogers expected, under the discoloured varnish had been hidden a marvellously well-preserved original, by the master himself, with some background additions by assistants. His knowledge had saved the Gallery about £500,000, and provided a further

SIR ANTHONY VAN DYCK
Charles II when Prince of Wales
OIL ON CANVAS,
150.5 x 130.7cm (58⅜ x 51⅛in).
Now in the collection of the National
Portrait Gallery, London. (RIGHT)

example of how academia can ignite opportunity. By researching the content of a collection, a fairly novel approach compared to the more traditional method of simply listing collections through whose hands a work has passed, Rogers was in an almost unique position. 'It had always', he explained, 'been traditional to take vertical connections with provenance. Horizontal connections, however, have become increasingly interesting and it was this approach which helped establish the picture.' Were it not for his knowledge of the voracious collecting habits of the seventeenth-century Lord Wharton, it is likely that the picture would still be unrecognized today, even in a cleaned state.

Ironically, scholarship can also create extraordinary opportunities when flawed, especially for the fresh and unprejudiced eye. Shortly before Christmas 1992 the specialist flower-painting dealer Peter Mitchell, together with David Scrase, Keeper of the Fitzwilliam Museum's art gallery in Cambridge, could be found scrabbling through the racks in the Museum's basement. They were making an initial selection for a major show at Mitchell's Bond Street art gallery of still life paintings from the Fitzwilliam. The Museum's celebrated collection of works in this area is probably the most significant in the world. At the end of one rack, furthest from the light, Scrase drew Mitchell's attention to a picture which at first was very difficult to see. He could just make out the dim form of a bouquet of flowers, but it was inaccessibly stacked and surrounded by an enormous, highly ornate Victorian plaster frame. The reason for its exile to the basement was evident from the Museum's catalogue of the collection made in 1960. As number 1487, the work was dismissively described by the cataloguers as a 'copy after Jan Davidsz de Heem' and had remained in the darkness ever since. The 'experts' had gone on to state that the original composition from which this copy derived was unknown, but must date from the 1660s. Instantly intrigued, Mitchell angled himself to get a closer look. The effect then became physical. 'I felt that tingle. Despite the dirty surface and the dim light the quality seemed to be staggering.' Mitchell got Scrase to agree to cleaning the

picture for the exhibition. It turned into a revelation – a large and monumental work, a masterpiece by de Heem himself, which despite its manifest quality and extremely clear signature had had to suffer ignominious obscurity: a work that, as described by the catalogue, would have made £25,000 on a good day in a minor Old Master sale was transformed into a £2 million masterpiece. It was a startling discovery for 1993 and a reminder that the most dramatic discoveries are not, as is often believed, from the attics of old ladies, but are there before our eyes, just waiting for their names to be called.

JAN DAVIDSZ DE HEEM
Flowers in a Vase
SIGNED, OIL ON PANEL,
93.5 x 70.2cm (36⅝ x 27½in)
From the collection of the
Fitzwilliam Museum,
Cambridge. (ABOVE)

STOPPING THE CLOCK *by Edward Bulmer*

APPROACHES TO ARCHITECTURAL RESTORATION

Uppark House, Sussex, on fire on the night of 30 August 1989. (LEFT)

Containers holding the charred contents of Uppark House, Sussex, awaiting cataloguing prior to restoration. (ABOVE)

In some respects it is a sad coincidence that three of the country's most important heritage organizations have had to tackle major restoration projects concurrently. In the case of the Historic Royal Palaces Agency and the National Trust disastrous fires instigated conservation and restoration schemes on an unprecedented scale, at Hampton Court and Uppark respectively, while English Heritage, through the generosity of the owner, Mrs Williams, and the National Heritage Memorial Fund, were able to assume guardianship of Brodsworth Hall in happier circumstances. How each organization has approached and carried out their task of restoration and conservation makes a fascinating and instructive comparison in the context of the current debate on the subject.

Inevitably there were lessons to be learnt in the aftermath of the Hampton Court fire in 1986 – lessons that were put into practice at Uppark

nearly three and a half years later – yet an impressive salvage and conservation programme was in place as soon as the fire was extinguished. Palace staff and English Heritage advisors, among others, organized the archaeological recovery of objects and fragments from the sodden debris, the location of everything found was recorded and the objects then stored for conservation. So thorough was this operation that not one of the thousands of crystal beads that had made up the fine chandelier in the King's Audience Chamber was lost. Much redeemable architectural detail was salvaged along with a great proportion of Grinling Gibbons' fine carvings, though all were blackened and water-logged.

The National Trust carried out a similar operation after the more serious fire at Uppark in Sussex, storing the debris in a garrison of black bins all carefully mapped. The first priority, in both cases, was to erect a temporary roof over the building, thus preventing further damage from exposure to the elements.

In taking over responsibility for the decaying Brodsworth Hall in Yorkshire, English Heritage's first action was to make a complete survey of the house, including rectified photography. All the moveable objects were then catalogued and their conservation needs assessed, before being removed to allow structural repairs to be carried out. A large warehouse was found in which to store the house's contents, and a programme of short-term remedial work was put into action to eradicate pests which were attacking the textiles, involving fumigation and a freezing technique pioneered by experts at London's Victoria and Albert Museum. Tragic though it is, damage by fire does present certain opportunities; both in archaeological terms, in disseminating the building's history, and in practical terms, in allowing the invisible incorporation of modern technology and safety precautions in the rebuilding.

At Hampton Court, a great deal was learnt about the building methods used by Christopher Wren in his construction of the State Apartments for William III between 1689 and 1700. New information augmented an already comprehensive picture of the building provided by very detailed contemporary accounts. Hampton Court ceased to be used for courtly purposes in the reign of George III, and it was first opened to the public by Queen Victoria in 1838. Since then, the King's Apartments had gradually become a series of damask-hung picture galleries. Given the success of the salvage operation it was, in principle, feasible to restore the rooms to their appearance at any stage between 1700 and 1986. The Historic Royal Palaces Agency, in close consultation with English Heritage, decided that, although many of the Williamite furnishings were long gone, the situation represented an opportunity to restore the appearance of the King's Apartments as they were in 1700. This would involve little structural alteration and would be the most informative way of presenting the rooms to the public.

The walls had largely escaped the effects of the fire so that new structural work was limited mainly to the floors and ceilings. The floors

throughout the Apartments have been replaced with random-width pine boards, nailed and left untreated. Sea-shells were re-used underneath the boards, reinstating Wren's original solution for sound-proofing. The ceilings were similarly restored (in line with the same guiding principle) using the original method of lath and plaster. The only significant casualty of the wall decoration had been the loss of a whole 'drop' of Grinling Gibbons' carving, and damage to others. Here was a problem that might have been thought insuperable given the outstanding quality of Gibbons' work. To the surprise of many, the project organizers established a 'Gibbons workshop' in the Palace, where three master carvers and three others worked closely together, using working methods likely to have been employed by Gibbons' own workshop.

All the rooms were refurnished according to the late seventeenth- and early eighteenth-century

The Cartoon Gallery, Hampton Court Palace, shortly after the fire on 31 March 1986. (TOP)

A master carver at work in the workshop set up at Hampton Court. (ABOVE)

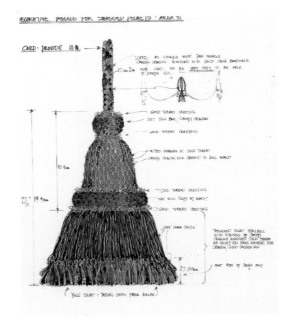

One of the designs for pelmet tassels made by the textile restoration department at Hampton Court. (RIGHT)

The Presence Chamber in the King's Apartments at Hampton Court after restoration, showing the repaired throne canopy. (BELOW)

inventories, which was possible only through a degree of reproduction. Conservation policy prevented the exact Williamite disposition of tapestries, as some would have been cut down and others obscured behind pictures. This problem has been solved by the use of bordered mohair hangings, some coloured to be evocative of tapestry tonalities. The discovery of a series of painted copies of the Raphael Cartoons in the Ashmolean Museum in Oxford, and their subsequent loan for use in the Cartoon Gallery at Hampton Court, has enabled Hampton Court's own tapestry copies of the Cartoons to be hung elsewhere in the King's Apartments. These tapestry copies were fortunately being restored at the time of the fire, and escaped damage.

The contemporary inventories indicated that there would be certain gaps that could not be filled by the Royal Collection; sconces, pier tables, torchères and curtains amongst other things. Those objects that it was felt were crucial to the understanding of the Williamite furnishing have been reproduced from appropriate models and empirical evidence. All materials and fringes have been recreated using the original constituents and levels of richness, rather than using modern, less costly, substitutes.

All surviving textiles have been carefully conserved by Hampton Court's renowned conservation studio, which had to build a special washing facility to cope with the large scale of items such as tapestries. A great quantity of molten lead had fused with the silver thread fringe of the original throne canopy that had hung in the Presence Chamber and had to be painstakingly removed. The lessons and techniques learnt have greatly endowed what is now a national resource. A computerized environmental control system has been introduced, and the previous heating system upgraded: it is now concealed under a boarded drugget, thus obviating the need for obtrusive radiators and pipe-work.

At Uppark, the National Trust, like the Historic Royal Palaces Agency, decided to use only traditional materials worked in the traditional way. This has meant finding the skills required to recarve ornamental details, to carry out freehand stucco-work, and to throw chimney

pots by hand, as well as making use of many other skills already established in conservation and restoration workshops. The National Trust's aim at Uppark is to restore the house to its appearance on 29 August 1989, the day before the fire. This, in effect, means restoring the impression of interiors unaltered since the late eighteenth century save by the passage of time. Though the wooden cornices and window frames were largely destroyed, the exterior brickwork was left all but unmarked as the fire was able to rise straight through the roof. This greatly facilitated the restoration of the previous external appearance of the house.

While the first floor contents at Uppark were entirely lost, many of the pieces from the ground floor were saved and, for the most part, remain as they appeared the day before the fire. The challenge that the Trust has taken up is that of re-incorporating as much salvaged fabric as possible, adding in new work and treating the whole so as to disguise the effects of the fire. As at Hampton Court, much of the wall detailing escaped the ravages of the fire, although subsequent storm damage took a further toll. Thus there is in most cases enough surviving material to act as an accurate guide for the finishing of the new work. New

flock papers and silks present particular problems of re-integration, unlike painted surfaces which are easily toned down by applying glazes.

The conserved contents will therefore be returned to rooms that they would recognise and feel comfortable in, particularly as the National Trust has taken the opportunity to build in sophisticated environmental control systems which should ensure optimum conditions for their future preservation. All modern necessities such as security systems are incorporated as invisibly as possible, and where new introductions are necessary, the aim is to disguise them by giving them some form of decorative articulation (as at Hampton Court).

At Brodsworth, English Heritage inherited one of the most intact Victorian ensembles in the country, but also a house in need of much structural repair work to ensure its future. Few are unaffected by the charm of faded grandeur and forgotten rooms redolent of a way of life that has passed. But it is surely short-sighted to want a decaying house not to be touched, for that is to deny future generations the chance of seeing it at all. Decay is always progressive.

Brodsworth Hall engenders just such feelings, and one cannot help thinking that they are what

The Dining Room at Uppark, Sussex, before the fire. (ABOVE LEFT)

The Dining Room at Uppark, Sussex, shortly after the fire in August 1989. (ABOVE)

Brodsworth Hall, Yorkshire, undergoing external restoration in 1992. (ABOVE)

underpin the seemingly dispassionate approach taken by English Heritage to its treatment of the house. Its policy, described as the first (and possibly the last) step, is to retain the appearance of the house as found in 1990, while carrying out all structural work necessary to render it safe and secure for the future. Decay having been arrested, the painted surfaces in the State Rooms have been surface-cleaned only. (The effect of this treatment in an area of England that has suffered high industrial pollution is dramatically apparent.) No attempt has been made to remove discoloured varnish from decorative painting, or indeed from the oil paintings, and retouching of losses has been confined to a discernible toning layer, similar in effect to the Italian picture restoration principle of hatched retouching.

The approach rules out 'improvements' save those necessitated by public safety, and so the existing heating systems will be retained, although the introduction of a security system is obligatory. The only visual changes to the interior of the house are to be in the introduction of a number of reproduced carpets, as the originals were so worn that the public would have destroyed them in the first visitor season. On the first floor the decorative state of the rooms had fared much less well and many rooms have large areas of damaged or lost wallpaper. The appearance of these rooms will be unchanged; in

fact they will be actively 'frozen in time'. Even peeling wallpaper has been 'set' in place as a hairdresser would 'set' someone's curls. Where new materials have had to be used, primarily on the exterior, English Heritage is not attempting to harmonize their appearance with the existing materials, the philosophy being to introduce minimal but honest and visible repair.

It is edifying that the Historic Royal Palaces Agency, the National Trust and English Heritage should all define particular dates at which to 'stop the clock' for the presentation of their properties to the public. Only the Historic Royal Palaces Agency chose a pre-photography period to recreate, and therefore chose the path most likely to produce problems that would require informed speculation or compromise for their solution. Even before the fire at Hampton Court there had been considerable debate as to whether it was ethical to sweep away subsequent decoration in returning to the supposed appearance of William III's Apartments. The fire obviously shifted the goalposts and a motive of public education won the day. One wonders, however, had the fire not taken place, whether the superb and elaborate model that has been made to demonstrate William's courtly use of the Apartments would not have sufficed.

A visitor's experience of any historic building is always made up of what is seen as well as what is learnt. At Hampton Court it is impossible not to speculate on whether the juxtaposition of the new dry-scrubbed pine floorboards with the unaltered dark finish of the oak panelling would have existed in 1700. Equally, the effect of the impressive electroplate silver sconces is diminished by the angle at which they hang, owing to their careful suspension to avoid puncturing the tapestries and the imbalance caused by the electrical apparatus on their backs. These are, of course, subjective matters and however objective the concept such anomalies can never be entirely avoided. English Heritage has encountered the same situation at Brodsworth where, even though the approach is one of extreme self-effacement, some decisions have had to be taken that indicate modern involvement. The National Trust steers a course somewhere in between, acknowledging

One of the bedrooms at Brodsworth Hall, Yorkshire, before restoration. English Heritage plans to alter the look of such interiors as little as possible. (LEFT)

its role as one of a succession of patrons in the evolution of a historic building, rather than attempting to impose suspended animation.

It is arguable that much of what we preserve today arose out of the rebuilding and remodelling of something that was destroyed; much of the work of Robert and James Adam is a case in point. In pursuing a policy of invisible interference one necessarily rules out the possibility of continuing the process of patronage that has produced so much of what we preserve. On the other hand, as Ruskin and Morris perceived a hundred years ago, restoration can be as destructive as neglect or accidental damage. What restoration projects on the scale of those at Hampton Court and Uppark have demonstrated is that they are very much creative processes, regenerating dormant crafts and encouraging the reproduction of first class artistic and architectural work. Perhaps the natural extension of this is to believe firmly that we have the artistic ability

to reproduce large-scale decorative work, instead of relying on technology and artifice, as was the case in the recreation of the Gentileschi ceiling at the Queen's House in Greenwich, where a photographic method of reproduction was used.

With work currently in progress at Windsor Castle after the devastating fire in November 1992, differing attitudes to restoration are now more in the news than ever. If one had to choose a universal policy for the future there is no doubt that the approaches of the three major heritage organizations outlined above would offer vital ingredients. English Heritage's approach, when viewed as a first step, is difficult to fault. If one is to allow for a next step, the meticulous regard for quality and authenticity of the Historic Royal Palaces Agency would need to be added, along with the National Trust's ability to accept that some decisions can be successfully taken only by assuming the mantle of a present-day patron with an unswerving sense of preservation.

VICTORIAN CROSSCURRENTS *by Lynn Stowell Pearson*

LEWIS CARROLL
**Julia and Ethel
Arnold in Straw
Boaters**
*c.*1872, ALBUMEN PRINT,
16.1 x 13.2cm (6⅜ x 5⅛in)
London £5,980 ($9,020).
7.V.93. (RIGHT)

Collecting has been variously described as an illness, an addiction, a passion, a romance and an intellectual endeavour. Norbert Schimmel, a renowned collector of ancient art, once explained: 'The passion to chase an object, the pleasure in discovery and the exciting acquisition are the most rewarding stimuli for any possessed collector.' Today it seems as if anything is collectable – this current season at Sotheby's has seen vigorous bidding in such diverse fields as animation art, comic books, teddy bears, baseball memorabilia and even conjuring apparatus. Exploring these outer limits of the auction world can prove a highly entertaining and rewarding pastime; however, there are still many fascinating pockets within the more traditional markets capable of providing just as much interest and enjoyment. Nineteenth-century photographs and Victorian pictures are two such markets: both promise many areas for discovery and both offer excellent collecting opportunities. Yet surprisingly, neither of these now firmly established markets was an habitué of the auction rooms until the 1970s.

Photographs have been collected since the invention of photography. They had been handled primarily by antiquarian book dealers before coming to the attention of the auction-going public nearly twenty years ago. Among those who attended those first auctions of photographs were Sam Wagstaff, Curator of Modern Art at the Detroit Institute of Arts, and Howard Gilman, head of the Gilman Paper Company in Manhattan. These two visionary collectors went on to form two of the most important private collections of photographs in the world. That compiled by the late Sam Wagstaff spanned both the nineteenth and twentieth centuries, and was eventually sold in 1984 to the J. Paul Getty Museum. In 1993 Howard Gilman's encyclopaedic collection received wide-ranging attention through an exhibition at the Metropolitan Museum of Art, *The Waking Dream, Photography's First Century.*

Philippe Garner, Director of Sotheby's Photographs Department in London, credits Sam Wagstaff with opening everyone's eyes to what photography could be. Sotheby's London held its first photographs auction in 1971. Garner, who presided over that sale, quotes a client who recalled those early days when collecting photographs was like picking up seashells along the seashore. A year before that sale, Sotheby's New York had held what is considered to be the breakthrough auction in this field: the sale of the collection of Sidney Strober. By 1975 sales of photographs had become an annual Sotheby's event.

Collecting nineteenth-century photographs in the 1990s is done in the context of a much more established market than was the case twenty years ago, and Philippe Garner feels that 'We are now confident in recognizing rarity when we see it.' It is still, though, an area ripe for exploration by the intrepid collector. 'There are so many less-explored byways, a collector can still make exciting discoveries', says Garner. Beth Gates-Warren, Director of Sotheby's New York's Photographs Department, believes that if the market for nineteenth-century photographs is ever to be more widely known and appreciated by the general public, now is the time.

Daguerreotypes – unique images fixed on a metal plate – form an area that, according to Denise Bethel of Sotheby's New York's Photographs Department, is 'probably the most undervalued segment of the nineteenth-century photography market in the US'. Excellent examples, she says, can still be found for under $1,000. In April 1993 Sotheby's New York sold Robert Vance's daguerreotype of *James King of William*, made in about 1855, for $9,200. The high price represents the historical importance of this portrait of one of San Francisco's crusading newspapermen during the Gold Rush.

Two photographers who epitomize the very essence of the Victorian era have also recently been achieving strong prices at auction – Lewis Carroll and Julia Margaret Cameron. Best known as the author of *Alice's Adventures in Wonderland* and *Through the Looking Glass and What Alice Found There*, Lewis Carroll sketched for pleasure before taking up photography in 1856, a medium he pursued for the next twenty-five years. His photographs are primarily portraits of members of his family or close acquaintances, most notably the daughters of his circle of friends. Carroll's extraordinary staging of images of childhood is evident in *Julia and Ethel Arnold in Straw Boaters*, of around 1872, which sold at Sotheby's London in May 1993 for £5,980. Carroll is well known for having made strong demands of his sitters. Ethel Arnold has recalled 'It was no joke being photographed in those days, and for a nervous child, dressed up as a Heathen Chinese, a beggar child, or a fisher maiden, to keep still for forty-five seconds at a time was no mean ordeal.' But those who leap to criticize Carroll's methods and motives should bear in mind that Ethel Arnold

also remembers that 'He was indeed a bringer of delight in those dim, far-off days, and I look back to hours spent in his dear, much loved company as an oasis of brightness in a somewhat grey and melancholy childhood.' ('Reminiscences of Lewis Carroll', *The Atlantic Monthly*, Boston, 1929.)

An equally passionate photographer, but a portraitist with quite different aims, Julia Margaret Cameron strove to capture the souls of her subjects. In many cases she preferred soft focus, which it was felt helped achieve an ethereal effect. In her portrait of the astronomer Sir John Herschel, Cameron went to his house and 'had him wash his hair so that a brilliant halo would

JULIA MARGARET
CAMERON
Sir John Herschel
1867, ALBUMEN PRINT,
32.9 x 25.2cm (12⅞ x 9⅞in)
New York $25,300 (£16,400).
6.IV.93. (ABOVE)

ROBERT VANCE
James King of William
*c.*1855, QUARTER-PLATE
DAGUERREOTYPE
New York $9,200 (£6,090).
6.IV.93. (RIGHT)

(ATTRIBUTED TO)
EADWEARD MUYBRIDGE
**The Domes, from
the Merced River,
Yosemite Valley**
*c.*1872, ALBUMEN PRINT,
39.6 x 52cm (15½ x 20⅜in)
New York $20,900 (£12,200).
9.X.91. (BELOW)

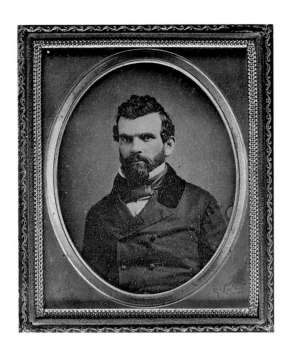

encircle his head' (*The Waking Dream, Photography's First Century*, The Metropolitan Museum of Art, New York, 1993). An albumen print of this photograph, dated 1867, sold at Sotheby's New York in April 1993 for a remarkable $25,300.

Collected not only for their historical importance as documents of a rapidly changing landscape, nineteenth-century photographs of the American West are also cherished as poignant and beautiful images. In October 1990 Sotheby's New York sold an album of cyanotype photographs of dam-building along the Mississippi River by H. Bosse for $66,000. Denise Bethel recalls that at the time no one had heard of Bosse and 'now prices have really taken off and people are calling about discoveries of Bosse photographs.' Mammoth-plate photographs, in the form of prints 15 x 20in, have an extraordinary capacity to capture the wide expanses of the western American landscape. One superb example from the 1870s by Eadweard Muybridge, *The Domes, from the Merced River, Yosemite Valley*, was sold at Sotheby's New York in October 1991 for $20,900.

Muybridge is best remembered for his sequential views of human and animal locomotion made with a high-speed camera in the late 1870s and 80s, which vividly demonstrated the inaccuracies of conventional representations of movement. Suddenly, and for the first time, it could clearly be seen just how a horse's legs moved when galloping, or exactly how a man's limbs were stretched when throwing a ball. This was revolutionary and invaluable information for many artists. Animal and history painters, particularly, immediately subscribed to these revelations, though, inevitably there were other artists who objected. Not what actually exists, they said, but only what can be seen to exist may legitimately become the subject of art.

The implications of photography on the art of painting were recognized from the very beginnings of photographic experimentation in the late 1830s. On the one hand it could supply artists with 'sketches' from nature of an accuracy never before known; on the other it was an open threat to artists whose sole function was to reproduce the appearance of the physical world. In a review of the 1859 Paris Salon, Baudelaire famously called photography 'the mortal enemy of art'. 'Since photography gives us every guarantee of exactitude that we could wish,' he continued, 'then photography and Art are the same thing .... If photography is allowed to stand in for Art in some of its functions it will soon supplant or corrupt it completely .... It must return to its real task, which is to be the servant of the sciences and of the arts, but a very humble servant.'

Sir George Clausen and Sir Lawrence Alma-Tadema were two nineteenth-century painters who employed photography as a trusted and valuable servant, albeit in two distinct ways. Clausen studied photographs of peasants to help portray workers in the field, whereas Alma-Tadema used photographs of archaeological excavations and classical antiquities to help bring to life everyday details of ancient Rome. The extent of Alma-Tadema's use of photography in his preliminary studies can be gauged by the extraordinary collection of 164 volumes of photographs once owned by the artist that is now in the collection of Birmingham University.

The work of George Clausen came to the attention of many in 1980 with a well-attended monographic exhibition at the Royal Academy in London. Clausen is now as popular as ever among collectors, although Simon Taylor, Director of Sotheby's London's Victorian Pictures Department, believes that Clausen's watercolours are still under-priced. In his recent book *Beyond Impressionism, The Naturalistic Impulse* (New York, 1992), Dr Gabriel Weisberg describes how Clausen purchased one of the new portable cameras in the early 1880s, which allowed him to take pictures of field labourers without posing them. In November 1982 Sotheby's London sold Clausen's *Winter Work*, 1883-4, for £34,100. Now in the collection of the Tate Gallery in London, it depicts workers gathering sugar beets. One of the main figures, a peasant woman, was inspired by a photograph now in the collection of The Royal Photographic Society, Bath. Clausen's pictures from the 1880s are thought to be his most accomplished and are the most sought after. In November 1990 a record auction price for the artist was achieved by Sotheby's London with the

SIR GEORGE CLAUSEN
The Shepherd Boy,
SIGNED AND DATED *1883*,
OIL ON CANVAS,
92 x 62cm (36¼ x 24½in)
London, £78,500 ($118,500).
30.VI.93. (LEFT)

sale of *A School Girl*, painted in 1889, for £137,500. This season, the continued market interest in such works was confirmed by the £78,500 achieved at Sotheby's by another work from the 1880s, *The Shepherd Boy*.

Sir Lawrence Alma-Tadema became one of the most popular artists during the Victorian era, yet he was all but forgotten by the time of his death in 1912. During the first half of the twentieth century the work of nineteenth-century history painters and academic artists tended to be dismissed by art historians and collectors, and no one seems to have suffered quite as much as Alma-Tadema. Vern Swanson notes in his monograph on the artist in 1977 that if Alma-Tadema was referred to at all it was as 'the worst painter of the Victorian era.' One reviewer of the unpopular Royal Academy's retrospective of the artist in 1913 wrote that his 'painted anecdotes ... are about worthy enough to adorn bonbon boxes!'

A reappraisal was inevitable, but it did not begin until the late 1950s. Robert Kashey,

SIR LAWRENCE
ALMA-TADEMA
The Baths of
Caracalla (Thermae
Antoniniane)
SIGNED, OIL ON CANVAS,
152.4 x 95.3cm (60 x 37½in)
New York $2,532,500
(£1,633,800). 26.V.93.
(ABOVE)

Kirk Askew and the ballet impresario Lincoln Kirstein with influencing a new generation of art dealers like himself. In 1962 the Robert Isaacson Gallery celebrated the fiftieth anniversary of Alma-Tadema's death with an exhibition of his work. At the same time a number of young American curators were starting to buy in this field, looking for quality works without spending a great deal of money. Frank Trapp, former Director of the Mead Art Museum of Amherst College, Massachusetts, remembers that 'We [museum curators and directors] operated with a small budget, so we had to be discerning – we sometimes bought against current fashion.'

Sotheby's played an important role in bringing Victorian art to a wider audience with the opening of Sotheby's Belgravia in 1971. This pioneering effort put a spotlight on an area of the market that until then had been largely disdained. It flourished for a decade, as many dealers in nineteenth-century art opened galleries in the same neighbourhood. Successful sales, like the auction of paintings by Alma-Tadema from the collection of Allen Funt, helped to bring the art of this period into the mainstream. Funt, the creator of the television programme *Candid Camera*, had bought his first Alma-Tadema in 1967, and continued collecting until 1973, when he learned that he had been the victim of a large-scale embezzlement. Forced to sell his collection of thirty-five Alma-Tademas, Funt offered them at Sotheby's Belgravia in 1973. The sale was an extraordinary success, achieving £177,000.

One of the pictures formerly in the Allen Funt collection, *The Baths of Caracalla*, was sold again in May 1993 at Sotheby's New York for the record price of $2,532,500. In this work Alma-Tadema endeavoured to recreate a scene from Imperial Rome. To achieve this end, he relied upon the latest archaeological evidence, using the diagrams, reconstructions and photographs of surviving parts of the building that had been published in Rodolfo Lanciani's *The Ruins and Excavations of Ancient Rome* (1897). He also called upon his own extensive collection of photographs of classical architecture. The picture took two years to complete and was exhibited at the Royal Academy, London, in 1899.

Director of the Shepherd Gallery in New York, claims that 'a very select group' of dealers and collectors living in New York were largely responsible for a renewed interest in artists like Alma-Tadema, Tissot and Gérôme. 'It was very much a New York thing', recalls Kashey, who credits Robert Isaacson, of the Robert Isaacson Gallery, as well as dealers and collectors like James Coats,

SIR LAWRENCE
ALMA-TADEMA
Caracalla and Geta
SIGNED, OIL ON CANVAS,
126 x 155cm (49½ x 61in)
London £1,431,500
($2,147,200). 8.VI.93. (LEFT)

In 1907 Alma-Tadema painted another monumental work based on a scene from the life of Caracalla entitled *Caracalla and Geta*. The artist explained some of his intentions in an extremely lengthy letter to Messrs Arthur Tooth and Sons, who had commissioned the picture. 'It is therefore no wonder that so great a lover of Roman civilization as myself should have been moved to try to paint his conception of the place as it must have looked when full of people, showing in what way the seats may possibly have been filled and the arena utilized .... I have from the very outset counted the number of spectators as I painted them in, and have now reached a number approximating 2,500. Allowing that the columns and garlands hide as many more, this would give a total of 5,000 figures for that seventh part of the Coliseum which is shown in the picture, and for the entire building 35,000, the number usually believed to have found accommodation in the auditorium.' This shows an almost bizarre level of commitment to historical accuracy, and may offer us some indication of the sort of care that Alma-Tadema took over his preliminary studies. Photography must have served him well. The picture was sold in London at Sotheby's on 8 June 1993, and made £1,431,500.

Since the early 1970s when photographs and Victorian pictures were first offered as separate collecting areas by Sotheby's, prices have risen dramatically. Nancy Harrison, of Sotheby's New York's Nineteenth-Century European Paintings Department, is sure that 'many new connoisseurs are discovering the rich rewards of collecting in these areas'. Harrison sees many opportunities for new collectors in the field of nineteenth-century paintings. 'With a variety of prices, it is still an area where a collector can trade up and the prices are not prohibitive. Masterworks by little known artists continue to be discovered.'

AMERICAN MUSEUMS AT SOTHEBY'S *by Michael Conforti*

The international art community has long been fascinated by the market activity of American museums. Since the earliest years of this century, when the *Burlington Magazine* began what soon became a European-wide protest against the export of artistic legacy to North America, the outcries have continued. While there is still political purpose to rhetoric aimed at maintaining European public awareness of the importance of enhancing national collections, real fear for the loss of cultural heritage has lessened in recent years. With the exception of the collecting activity of a dwindling number of American institutions capable of challenging Europe's larger national museums, current professional curiosity is directed more at sales *from* US museums than at purchases *for* them.

During the art boom of 1987-90 many American museums chose to rethink the nature of their collections in order to raise cash to continue buying exceptional works of art. Occasionally an institution's collecting mission was altered, as when the Kimbell Art Museum divested itself of its drawings in 1987, or when Washington's Corcoran Gallery sold its nineteenth-century European paintings in 1988 and 1989. At that time, sacrifices were also made in the depth of certain collections, as valuable works of less-than-first quality were cashed in to acquire singular masterpieces. This was the case when the Art Institute of Chicago acquired a $12 million Brancusi and New York's Museum of Modern Art bought the *Portrait of Joseph Roulin* by van Gogh. Many Europeans ask how existing collections can be compromised in this way, and question the alteration of an institution's collecting tradition to support current tastes.

The differences between American and European collecting philosophy are based less on law than on differing traditions regarding a museum's role in society. In simplified terms, American museums could be seen as educational institutions, programme-oriented and public service-directed, whereas the larger European museums, while providing educational services, are national cultural symbols housing state collections of art. Unlike the situation in Europe, the United States federal government does not restrict the export of cultural objects, feeling that the disposal of a work of art should be entirely the responsibility of its citizens and their institutions. In the early 1970s, the New York State Attorney General did become involved when deaccessioning at the Metropolitan Museum raised a public outcry, but in this instance his action was most effective in catalyzing museums and professional societies to develop deaccessioning guidelines. These ethical

JOSEPH WRIGHT
OF DERBY
An Iron Forge
SIGNED AND DATED *1772*,
OIL ON CANVAS,
119 x 132cm (47 x 52in)
Sold by private treaty
through Sotheby's London.
Now in the collection of the
Tate Gallery, London. (BELOW)

and procedural codes now represent the parameters of deaccessioning practice in the United States today, parameters founded on the fundamental rule that money raised from selling art cannot be used to support an institution's operating expenses, and, instead, must be applied to the enhancement of collections.

In Britain, as in much of the rest of Europe, deaccessioning regulations are few in number and are usually directed at sales from specific national institutions. London's National Gallery and the Tate, for example, are not allowed to sell. The British Museum Act (1963) and the National Heritage Act (1983) only restrict certain kinds of sales from specific museum collections. In fact, recent government action in England has focused on the cost of maintaining collections, encouraging institutions to be both more independent of government and more management-conscious in their collection policies. More restrictive than any legislation has been the 1988 Museums and Galleries Commission's professional *Guidelines for a Registration Scheme for Museums in the United Kingdom* (see *Museum Management and Curatorship*, vol. 10, no. 3, September 1991; vol. 11, no. 1, March 1992).

European institutions are discouraged from deaccessioning by both explicit and implicit codes of professionalism stemming from a different public attitude towards museum holdings than in America. Collections are widely perceived as national cultural patrimony, a belief enhanced by the fact that the large majority of museums are funded by governments and overseen by some form of government ministry. The notion of cultural patrimony has a positive ring amongst influentials throughout Europe, whether generated by idealism or national pride. There has been no significant deaccessioning in Britain since the 1960s when the country was outraged over the sale of pictures from Dulwich College.

When government is involved in museum practice in America, it is usually not the federal, but civic government that exerts influence. The operations of many of the country's largest institutions are governed by private boards of trustees, but their running costs are partially funded by city or county governments. Such

CASPAR DAVID FRIEDRICH **Waldinneres bei Mondschein, vorne Leute bei hellem Feuer (A Wood by Moonlight, with People by a Fire)** OIL ON CANVAS, 71 x 50cm (28 x 19⅝in) Sold by private treaty through Sotheby's New York. Now in the collection of the National Gallery, Charlottenburg Palace, Berlin. (LEFT)

funding, generally around 10 to 40 per cent, encourages museums to be more public-service directed, and more focused on a collection's current and future use than on its nature as the preserved testament of the aesthetic assumptions of the past. Given the educational mandate implicit in most US museum charters and the pragmatic, ahistoric tradition of the country as a whole, collections are often seen as institutional assets ready to serve a museum organization in a variety of ways. The strongest forces determining the direction of assets from deaccessioned art towards the enhancement of collections (rather than towards the support of a museum's operations) are the deaccessioning codes of America's two strongest professional art organizations, the American Association of Museums, and the Association of Art Museum Directors (see *Apollo*, vol. CXXX, no. 330, August 1989, pp. 77-86).

The differences between European and American museum collecting practices are as evident in accessioning as they are in deaccessioning practices. Two of the most splendid objects to be sold by Sotheby's this past year, Joseph Wright of

Derby's *An Iron Forge* and Caspar David Friedrich's *Waldinneres bei Mondschein*, were acquired by private treaty for national collections with little possibility for American competition. Such purchasing with funds from government-directed sources has no parallel in America. Museums in the United States also look longingly at a European system that can pre-empt a picture at auction, as the Prado did to acquire the Valencian School *The Life of St Ursula* before its proposed sale at Sotheby's Madrid in October 1992. Nor do American museums always have a completely free hand when a desirable work does come to the open market. The country's civically-responsive institutions are such that most boards of trustees would have found it difficult to support the particular nudity of Renoir's *Le Jeune Garçon au Chat*, sold at Sotheby's New York on 10 November 1992, despite the painterly appeal of such early works by the artist.

It is hard for US institutions to be consistently active in the auction market for other reasons as well. Unlike in Europe, American museum trustees are appointed with the assumption that the financial stability of these precariously funded institutions are their special responsibility. Thus board consideration tends to be required for every institutional decision. Distances from salerooms and the frequent necessity of a trustee's personal financial involvement contribute to making buying at auction difficult. Not surprisingly, when purchases were made by US institutions at auction in the past year, they were generally modestly-priced additions to collections recognized for the depth of their holdings, where a potential query over an addition would not present a significant barrier. One example is the purchase of Degas' crayon lithograph *Song of the Dog* at Sotheby's New York on 5 November 1993 by the Art Institute of Chicago, which added to its outstanding collection of works on paper.

The most significant purchases by American museums at auction in 1992-3 were made by two of the richest, most accessions-directed museums in the country, the Kimbell Art Museum in Fort Worth and the J. Paul Getty Museum in Malibu. Their ongoing collecting activity is supported by a little-mentioned American museum tradition,

but one that drives most of the country's deaccessioning as well as accessioning practices. For decades the educational directive of American museum charters has been supported by an associated goal of forming 'masterpiece' collections, intended to be representative of the highest artistic achievement of whatever cultures and historical periods are covered by the institution. Ultimately deriving from the 'national school' display tradition of late eighteenth-century European museums, as well as the focus on 'object specialness' promoted by Wilhelm von Bode around 1900, the American 'representative masterpiece' ideal was catalyzed by the idealism of the early decades of this century when an unqualified critical understanding of 'masterpiece' gave special favour to Impressionist and Modernist paintings. America's National Gallery of Art was formed in the late 1930s with no interest in collecting American art, but with a commitment to building a representative

VALENCIAN SCHOOL
**The Life of
St Ursula**
TEMPERA ON PANEL
WITH GOLD GROUND,
each 184 x 67cm (72 x 26¼in)
Sold by private treaty through
Sotheby's Madrid. Now in the
collection of the Prado
Museum, Madrid. (ABOVE)

ATTRIBUTED TO PIERRE
FRANCQUEVILLE, CALLED
FRANCAVILLA
The Fountain of
Neptune, one of
two pages from a
sketchbook
PEN AND BROWN INK OVER
TRACES OF BLACK CHALK,
13.8 x 10cm (5⅜ x 3⅞in)
London £23,000 ($34,700).
5.VII.93
Now in the collection of the
Victoria and Albert Museum,
London. (RIGHT)

collection of the finest European paintings possible. The Museum of Modern Art, formed in the 1930s, still adheres to 'representative masterpiece' goals within its special Modernist vision. Thus, a few years ago, paintings of considerable merit by artists better represented in the collection – including Picasso, Kandinsky and Monet – were exchanged for a work deemed superior to all, van Gogh's *Portrait of Joseph Roulin*.

The decreased availability of significant works of art over the last thirty years has not deterred institutions from continuing to interpret their educational mandate in a similar 'representative masterpiece' manner, using both deaccessioning and accessioning to achieve their goal. The philosophy has reached a particular refinement in the collection policies of the Kimbell and the Getty. The Kimbell, which reconsidered the breadth of its holdings a few years ago by selling drawings in order to concentrate on greater pictures, was successful in satisfying two areas of need this season, acquiring Matisse's *L'Asie* at Sotheby's New York on 10 November 1992 for $11 million, and the *Portrait of Jacob Obrecht*, an anonymous Flemish picture, at Sotheby's New York on 15 January 1993 for $2,422,000. While the Getty deaccessioned a less-than-first-rate Gauguin from its nineteenth-century paintings four years ago, the development of a larger nineteenth-century collection is still taken to be a vital need, as was made clear by its purchase of Goya's 1824 *Bullfight, Suerte de Varas* for £4,950,000 at Sotheby's London in November 1992.

In spite of different collecting philosophies, there are some similarities between European and American institutions towards deaccessioning. 'Collections management' is currently a buzz phrase on both sides of the Atlantic. Most institutions sell deteriorated material, although sales are little reported as smaller auction rooms are used and modest prices realized. The educational value of copies and fakes is considered questionable in many European and American institutions, as is the worth of maintaining duplicates. The definition of a duplicate can vary considerably. The guidelines laid out by the British Museum Act of 1963 allow for the sale of duplicates of identical prints and photographs, for example, but do not allow a museum to consider the equal representation of an artist, school or object type as duplication in a collection. This latter, broader interpretation recently allowed the Metropolitan Museum in New York to consider a Sano di Pietro a questionable holding, and the Brooklyn Museum to determine Rodin's *La Faunesse à Genous* to be superfluous.

'Collections management' is also the impetus for the sale of objects of distinctly lower quality, which might have been accepted as gifts when knowledge was less refined and accessions policies less restrictive. The refinement of collections in store prompted the Metropolitan Museum to sell a number of 'school' pictures this past year. The Nelson-Atkins Gallery in Kansas City and the Detroit Institute of Arts did the same, the latter also consigning a large group of modest American works. In a somewhat parallel fashion the Hirschhorn Museum sold three Rufino Tamayos at Sotheby's New York in November 1992. The money raised could then be applied to the acquisition of one greater work. Occasionally such sales from storage can produce soberingly positive results, as was the case when a double portrait attributed to van Dyck was sold by the Detroit Institute of Arts at Sotheby's New York on 15 January 1993, making an unexpectedly high $109,750. For the most part, however, sales motivated by 'collections management' transfer modest museum works into similarly modest amounts of cash.

There was less deaccessioning with a 'cash for new accessions' motivation in 1992-3 than during the market boom of 1987-90. At that time, when collectors were rushing to send their best items to auction, American museums stretched the deaccessioning guidelines to raise money for what many considered the last opportunity to buy. The Guggenheim Museum, for example, realized $47.3 million from the sale of three pictures – a Chagall, a Modigliani and a Kandinsky – at an auction on 17 May 1990 at Sotheby's New York. The cash realized this year through the sale at Sotheby's New York of three appealing works owned by the Museum of Contemporary Art in Chicago – a Klee, an Ernst and a George Segal – was allowed to be used to

support operating expenses, as the works had been donated for the benefit of the Museum, but were not accessioned into the collection. Since tax concessions in the United States on donations of art for sale, rather than collection use, have not been particularly attractive to contributors in most tax years, such gifts are hard to encourage. The principle is that museums can receive works of art as gifts that are not designated to go into permanent collections. When a gift comes with this non-collection purpose, it can be sold immediately, but the donor does not get the same tax write-off as he would if he were giving it to a permanent collection. It is treated as a gift of money and the tax deductability is less. Objects of insufficient quality for the permanent collection can come to the museum in this way (or objects which the museum would rather see immediately turned into cash).

The issue of deaccessioning from museum collections to support operating expenses will be an important one over the next decade in both Europe and America. In Britain, the lingering pressure from 1980s' Conservative public policy is combining with the non-traditional perspectives of a new generation of museologists to produce a reassessment of collections management policies. In these discussions, deaccessioning to benefit the running costs of museums is fully and openly part of the debate. This is becoming true in America as well (*Museums News*, vol. 71, no. 6, November-December 1992, pp. 54 ff). Increasingly, American museum directors are being encouraged by trustees to consider collections as a financial asset, and to act as any good manager would with a convertible good that could balance operational deficits. Under pressure from two of the most publicized 'needy cases' in the last two years – the potential closure of both the Everhart Museum in Scranton, Pennsylvania, and the New-York Historical Society – consideration is being given to modifications in the deaccessioning code of the Association of Art Museum Directors. Sales of art to benefit operations might be allowed if the museum's survival is in doubt, or if part of the collection is not considered central to an institution's declared mission.

GEORGE SEGAL
Girl washing her foot on a chair
PLASTER AND WOOD, overall 122 x 117 x 61cm (48 x 46 x 24in)
New York $187,000 (£122,200). 17.XI.92
Formerly in the collection of the Museum of Contemporary Art, Chicago. (RIGHT)

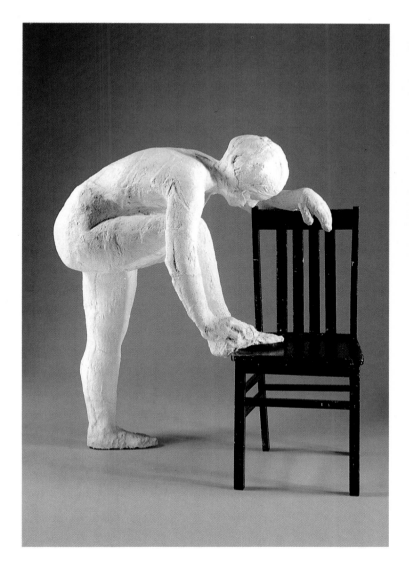

Such pressure will continue to mount as trustees and university administrators look for ways to keep their institutions alive and vital. The debate will not only involve the appropriateness of collections to a museum's mission, but also the cost and effectiveness of keeping collections in store. The discussion will extend to the question of how many museums a society can support, and how societies should deal with institutions that are no longer considered viable: those, perhaps, whose original purpose is no longer deemed relevant to today's needs. How would American trustees justify their role as a museum's fiscal agents if their institution were to feed on itself to survive? If a financially troubled museum sells a work to support operating funds, how would that affect the case for requesting further public or private support? In this largely extra-legal enterprise of collections-deaccessioning anything is possible, but any adjustments will continue to be subject to public scrutiny. Museums will constantly have to equate their needs with public expectation and trust, and any action taken will be subject to an ever-evolving code of professional conduct for ethical collection practices. It should prove to be a fascinating future.

PIERRE-AUGUSTE
RENOIR
**Le Jeune Garçon
au Chat**
SIGNED, OIL ON CANVAS,
123.8 x 66.7cm
(48¾ x 26¼in)
New York $797,500
(£528,100). 10.XI.92 (ABOVE)

FROM COVENT GARDEN TO MANHATTAN

THE HISTORY OF SOTHEBY'S PREMISES *by John Martin Robinson*

The understated cream stucco façade of Sotheby's in New Bond Street, with its gold-lettered name and the ancient Egyptian black-basalt head of the lion-goddess Sekhmet perched over the front entrance, is a well-known London landmark. It shares the quietly restrained self-confidence of many old-established English institutions such as Eton, the College of Arms and St James's Palace. The statement made by buildings of this type is one of discretion, scorning the need to make more of a show, and expressing a civility akin to that of an old suit made by the very best tailor.

The firm of Sotheby's is going to be 250 years old next year and has been at its present address since 1917. Before that time it was at 13 Wellington Street for a hundred years, following a brief sojourn at 145 The Strand, which proved to be too cramped for the needs of the business. When first founded by Samuel Baker in 1744, the firm was situated in York Street, Covent Garden, where it flourished for fifty years.

These earlier premises have long been demolished, though the appearance of Wellington Street is recorded in old sketches. No. 13 was on the west side of the north approach to Waterloo Bridge, facing the handsome Pennethorne façade of Somerset House. It was surprisingly similar to the present building in Bond Street, having, like it, developed out of a pair of early-Georgian houses. It was given distinction by Tuscan pilasters, a pair of flanking pediments, and moulded architraves to the first-floor windows. The central main entrance led into a small hall and stairway, which in turn led to the two top-lit salesrooms on the first floor, sandwiched between

Wellington Street in the nineteenth century, showing the firm's premises, the second building from the right.
(RIGHT)

Portrait of Samuel Baker, the firm's founder. (LEFT)

by public auction of cabinet pictures, drawings, engravings, antiquities and all works of art'. Auctions were held there until No. 13 was reconstructed, so that the interruption caused by the fire was kept to a minimum.

When first founded by Samuel Baker the firm auctioned a wide range of artifacts, yet for most of the nineteenth century Leigh & Sotheby (later Leigh, Sotheby & John Wilkinson) specialized in books and manuscripts. Wellington Street was well-suited for such a business, being close to many other book dealers in the Covent Garden area. With the increase in traffic over Waterloo Bridge, the grandiose proposals for widening The Strand, and the creation of Aldwych and Kingsway at the beginning of the twentieth century the area ceased to be a quiet, bookish backwater, and so the partners of Sotheby's decided to move to the West End. The present building in New Bond Street was acquired in 1917.

The new premises already had an interesting commercial and artistic pedigree, bearing out Lord Lytton's description of Bond Street in *The Siamese Twins* (1831) as a place 'Where each who wills may suit his wish. / Here choose a Guido – there his fish.' Nos. 34 and 35 have been in turn private houses, an inn, livery stables, the premises of royal parfumiers, commercial art galleries and art printers, milliners and wine merchants. New Bond Street forms part of the Conduit Mead Estate owned by the Corporation of the City of London, and was originally developed in the decade 1720-30. It was fashionable from the beginning. In 1749 the author Fielding had his hero Tom Jones describe it as 'a very good part of town' and that certainly remains true today. The street changed early on from residential to luxury commercial use, and handsome Georgian shop windows filled the ground floors, as recorded in a view of the street in the 1830s by Tallis.

Formerly, No. 34 was probably The Black Horse Inn. Certainly the building was known as 'The Black Horse' through several changes of use up until the mid-nineteenth century, although this name may have derived from its time as a livery stables. No. 35 was the shop of Rigge, Brockbank & Rigg, parfumiers to George IV,

an exhibition gallery at the front and the partners' room at the rear. An unexpected feature of the building (shared by Somerset House) was a deep double basement, made possible by the slope of Savoy Hill, which gave anybody staring absently into the front area a sharp shock of vertigo.

The Wellington Street premises were reconstructed following a terrible fire in June 1865 when the interior was gutted, and most of a collection of valuable books awaiting sale was destroyed. The fire was started in some wood shavings left by a careless workman in a yard leading to Savoy Court. J. Joseph Techner, a Parisian book-dealer whose consignment of 40,000 volumes was lost in the conflagration, wrote 'the flames ... roared up to reach every inch of the worm-eaten panelling on all sides of the antiquated premises. Within a few hours the fire had devoured everything!' *The Times* reported that, at its height, the fire could be seen 'from all the fire-engine houses in London'. Fortunately for Sotheby's, another gallery had been built ten years earlier at 21 North Wellington Street, 'as an addition to their house of business, for the more advantageous disposal

The Egyptian sculpture of the goddess Sekhmet, which presides above the front entrance of Sotheby's in New Bond Street. (RIGHT)

The entrance façade of Sotheby's New Bond Street offices, after the refurbishment programme completed in February 1993. (BELOW)

from 1804 to 1864. (The Tallis view shows their royal warrant displayed over the entrance.) No. 34 became a wine-merchant's shop in the 1860s when Fettoe & Sons moved in. Fettoes' were replaced in 1867 by Basil Woodd & Sons, also wine merchants. It was at that time that the two houses were combined, the present central entrance created, and large wine cellars excavated underneath. It was partly the existence of this voluminous storage space which decided Sotheby's on its choice of the building in 1917. A record of the occupation of Basil Woodd can still be seen in the form of the monogram 'B. W.' which is embossed on several of the iron piers in the basement of the building.

The first recorded artistic occupation of part of the site dates from 1861, when James Stewart, 'artist and photographer', made a brief appearance in the Post Office Directories. In 1870 Fairless & Beeforth, picture dealers, moved in and since then there has always been some artistic occupation of the building. Fairless & Beeforth came to grief over their attempt to monopolize the London sale of Gustave Doré's artistic output. In 1898 they were supplanted by the Lemercier Gallery and a succession of art publishers. Part of the premises was also occupied in the late-nineteenth century by a milliner.

It is this complex history of multi-occupation which is responsible for the fascinating, rambling – even confusing – interior, although the company has, in a series of architectural campaigns over a period of 70 years, improved the layout and imposed order on apparent chaos. When it moved in, in 1917, various alterations were made, including the construction of two new galleries in the centre of the premises and a remodelled entrance. This work was done to the design of J. G. S. Gibson (the architect of the former Middlesex Guildhall in Parliament Square and the old Debenham and Freebody store in Wigmore Street). It was at this time that the Sekhmet was moved from Wellington Street to her present position over the front door in Bond Street. This sculpture, which dates from around 1320BC, is the oldest privately-owned monument in London. It was sold in the nineteenth century as part of a

collection of Egyptian artifacts for £40, but the buyer never materialized and the goddess found a new home with Sotheby's.

Another phase of alterations was embarked upon in 1928 when the Bond Street premises were joined to the eighteenth-century houses in St George Street, on the other side of a triangular block abutting Conduit Street, most of which is now occupied by Sotheby's. The renowned firm of Mewes and Davis (architects of The Ritz on Piccadilly) were used for that work. A further small gallery at the rear of No. 35 was created in 1957, to the designs of Westmore Partners of Cheapside.

In the 1970s schemes were considered by Sotheby's for the comprehensive redevelopment of the whole complex to rationalize 'the labyrinthine and seemingly illogical geography of the premises'. A highly original design was conceived by Sir Denys Lasdun in 1975 for demolishing all the existing buildings and constructing a circular concrete rotunda in the centre of the site. This, however, was shelved on grounds of expense. Instead, a more conservationist approach has been adopted, which has woven together all the disparate elements to create a coherent and spacious interior, while retaining many fine old features which give the building its character. The first phase, in the 1980s, was the reconstruction to the designs of the Rolfe Judd Partnership of the St George Street houses to make new offices, while keeping several listed early eighteenth-century staircases and panelled rooms. The second phase, carried out during the last five years, was the addition of a new East Gallery to the main galleries on the

The main galleries at New Bond Street, after the recent programme of refurbishment.
(ABOVE)

The portico of the Palais am Festungsgraben, Sotheby's offices in Berlin.(TOP)

The entrance hall of the Palazzo Broggi, Sotheby's offices in Milan. (ABOVE)

first floor, thus creating one of the largest auction house gallery spaces in the world, and a dramatic remodelling of the ground floor. This included the restoration of the original Bond Street main entrance, and created a logical sequence of communications between the different parts of the building through the new axial Entrance Hall and the Colonnade Gallery. These connecting spaces, designed by Lionel Stirgess, were conceived in a classical manner with Tuscan columns reminiscent of the low colonnaded ground floors of English Palladian country houses such as Houghton, Wentworth Woodhouse and Nostell Priory. The restored and remodelled Entrance Hall was opened in 1993.

The worldwide expansion of Sotheby's under the chairmanship of Peter Wilson in the 1960s and 70s led to the acquisition of many overseas offices. In a number of European cities these comprise notable historic buildings such as the Palazzo Broggi in Milan, with its splendid marble-pillared hall, and the Palais am Festungsgraben on the Unter den Linden in Berlin. This imposing set piece was built in 1751-3 by the architect Christian Feldmann as a Baroque palace for the Chancellor Johann Gottfried Donner, who sold it on to the Finance Ministry in 1787. In 1863 the building was transformed by the addition of a neo-classical façade and an impressive marble ballroom. In 1945, having been badly damaged by Allied bombardment, it was taken over by the Soviet military authorities, who opened it in 1947 as the Soviet House of Culture. The dramatic events of the late 1980s gave Berlin a new lease of life, and Sotheby's set up its offices there in October 1990, moving into the Palais am Festungsgraben the following May.

The major headquarters of Sotheby's outside Britain is at 1334 York Avenue, on the corner of 72nd Street, in New York City. Sotheby's had achieved a powerful presence in New York with the acquisition of the Parke-Bernet Galleries in 1964, a move which was to prove the most important development in the firm's history since the eighteenth century. Parke-Bernet had started out as the American Art Association, whose first major auction of paintings was held in 1885 at premises on Madison Square at

East 23rd Street in New York. In 1937 Hiram Parke and Otto Bernet left the American Art Association to set up Parke-Bernet. By 1949 they had moved into 980 Madison Avenue, a building that was to remain the headquarters of the company until the 1980s, when what had become Sotheby Parke Bernet was moved to the former Kodak Building in York Avenue.

Originally constructed in around 1929 for the Laure Part Company, purveyors of Chester-field cigarettes, 1334 York Avenue became the Kodak Distribution Centre in the 1950s. The site was ideal for Sotheby's purposes as, filling a whole block between 71st and 72nd Street, it provided plenty of room for expansion and growth. Sotheby's took over the building in 1978, moving in over the next four years after an extensive programme of conversion to designs by the architects Lundquist and Stonehelm.

The conversion of the York Avenue site involved creating a block-long, four-storey building, with a façade of Canadian granite pierced by picture windows 22 feet high, through which passers-by could glimpse the activity inside. With 160,000 square feet of floor space, comprising auction rooms, exhibition galleries and offices, it is the largest custom-built auction house in the world. A full range of audio-visual devices, including large viewing screens in the salerooms and closed-circuit television, were installed to supplement the traditional saleroom procedures. The Governor of the State of New York and the Mayor of the city opened the new galleries in September 1980, and during the three Heirloom Discovery Days that followed, more than 10,000 people visited the building. It is now considered one of the landmarks of New York.

The unquestionably modern character of the Lundquist and Stonehelm conversion of the Kodak building in New York makes a startling contrast to the accretive Bond Street London headquarters with their strong English classical character. Such a contrast is entirely consistent with Sotheby's persona, as each can be seen to represent a different side of a concern which is both an eminently traditional and a vehemently modern international business.

1334 York Avenue, Sotheby's main offices in New York, opened in 1980. (TOP)

The main gallery at York Avenue. (ABOVE)

PRINCIPAL OFFICERS AND SPECIALISTS

Michael Ainslie
*President and Chief Executive
Officer, Sotheby's Holdings, Inc.*

Diana D. Brooks
*President and Chief Executive
Officer, Sotheby's Worldwide
Auction Operations*

The Rt Hon. The Earl of Gowrie
Chairman, Sotheby's Europe

John L. Marion
*Chairman, Sotheby's North and
South America*

Julian Thompson
Chairman, Sotheby's Asia

Roger Faxon
*Managing Director, Sotheby's
Europe*

Timothy Llewellyn
*Deputy Chairman, Sotheby's
Europe*

Simon de Pury
*Deputy Chairman, Sotheby's
Europe*

American Decorative Arts
Leslie B. Keno
New York (212) 606 7130
William W. Stahl, Jnr
New York (212) 606 7110
Wendell Garrett
New York (212) 606 7137

American Folk Art
Nancy Druckman
New York (212) 606 7225

American Indian Art
Ellen Napiura Taubman
New York (212) 606 7540

American Paintings
Peter B. Rathbone
New York (212) 606 7280

Animation and Comic Art
Dana Hawkes
New York (212) 606 7424
Stephen Maycock
London (071) 408 5206

Antiquities and Asian Art
Richard M. Keresey (antiquities)
New York (212) 606 7328
Carlton Rochell (Asian)
New York (212) 606 7328
Felicity Nicholson (antiquities)
London (071) 408 5111
Brendan Lynch (Asian)
London (071) 408 5112

Applied Arts from 1880
Barbara E. Deisroth
New York (212) 606 7170
Philippe Garner
London (071) 408 5138

Arms, Armour and Medals
David Erskine-Hill
London (071) 408 5315
Gordon Gardiner
Sussex (0403) 783933
Margaret Schwartz
New York (212) 606 7260

**Books and Autograph
Manuscripts**
Roy Davids
London (071) 408 5287
Stephen Roe (music)
London (071) 408 5300
David Park
London (071) 408 5292
David N. Redden
New York (212) 606 7386
Paul Needham
New York (212) 606 7385

British Paintings 1500-1850
David Moore-Gwyn
London (071) 408 5406
Henry Wemyss (watercolours)
London (071) 408 5409
James Miller
London (071) 408 5405

British Paintings from 1850
Simon Taylor (Victorian)
London (071) 408 5385
Susannah Pollen
(twentieth-century)
London (071) 408 5388

Ceramics
Peter Arney
London (071) 408 5134
Letitia Roberts
New York (212) 606 7180

Chinese Art
Carol Conover
New York (212) 606 7332
Jisui Gong (paintings)
New York (212) 606 7334
Julian Thompson
London (212) 408 5371
Colin Mackay
London (212) 408 5145
Mee Seen Loong
Hong Kong (852) 524 8121

Clocks and Watches
Tina Millar (watches)
London (071) 408 5328
Michael Turner (clocks)
London (071) 408 5329
Daryn Schnipper
New York (212) 606 7162

Coins
Tom Eden (ancient and Islamic)
London (071) 408 5315
James Morton (English and paper)
London (071) 408 5314

Paul Song
New York (212) 606 7391

Collectors' Department
Dana Hawkes
New York (212) 606 7424
Hilary Kay
London (071) 408 5205

Contemporary Art
Lucy Mitchell-Innes
New York (212) 606 7255
Anthony Grant
New York (212) 606 7254
Tobias Meyer
London (071) 408 5400

European Works of Art
Elizabeth Wilson
London (071) 408 5321
Margaret Schwartz
New York (212) 606 7250

Furniture
Graham Child (English)
London (071) 408 5347
Jonathan Bourne (Continental)
London (071) 408 5349
Larry J. Sirolli (English)
New York (212) 606 7577
William W. Stahl
New York (212) 606 7110
Phillips Hathaway (Continental)
New York (212) 606 7213
Alexandre Pradère
Paris 33 (1) 42 66 40 60

Garden Statuary
James Rylands
Sussex (0403) 783933
Elaine Whitmire
New York (212) 606 7285

Glass
Simon Cottle
London (071) 408 5135

Lauren K. Tarshis
New York (212) 606 7180

Impressionist and Modern Paintings
David J. Nash
New York (212) 606 7351
Alexander Apsis
New York (212) 606 7360
Marc E. Rosen (drawings)
New York (212) 606 7154
Simon de Pury
London (071) 408 5222
Michel Strauss
London (071) 408 5389
Melanie Clore
London (071) 408 5394
Asya Chorley (drawings)
London (071) 408 5393
John L. Tancock
Tokyo 81 (3) 3503 2944

Islamic Art and Carpets
Richard M. Keresey
(works of art)
New York (212) 606 7328
Mary Jo Otsea (carpets)
New York (212) 606 7996
Prof. John Carswell (works of art)
London (071) 408 5153
Jacqueline Bing (carpets)
London (071) 408 5152

Japanese Art
Neil Davey
London (071) 408 5141
Yasuko Kido (prints)
London (071) 408 2042
Suzanne Mitchell
New York (212) 606 7338

Jewellery
John D. Block
New York (212) 606 7392
David Bennett
Geneva 41 (22) 732 8585

Alexandra Rhodes
London (071) 408 5306

Judaica
David Breuer-Weil
Tel Aviv 972 (3) 22 38 22
Camilla Previté
London (071) 408 5334
Paul Needham (books)
New York (212) 606 7385
Kevin Tierney (silver)
New York (212) 606 7160

Latin American Paintings
August Uribe
New York (212) 606 7290

Musical Instruments
Graham Wells
London (071) 408 5341
Leah Ramirez
New York (212) 606 7190

Nineteenth-Century European Furniture and Works of Art
Christopher Payne
London (071) 408 5350
Elaine Whitmire
New York (212) 606 7285

Nineteenth-Century European Paintings
Michael Bing
London (071) 408 5380
Nancy Harrison
New York (212) 606 7140

Old Master Paintings and Drawings
Hugh Brigstocke
London (071) 408 5485
Elizabeth Llewellyn
(drawings)
London (071) 408 5416
George Wachter
New York (212) 606 7230

Scott Schaefer (drawings)
New York (212) 606 7222
Nancy Ward-Neilson
Milan 39 (2) 7600471
Etienne Breton
Paris 33 (1) 42 66 40 60

Oriental Manuscripts
Marcus Fraser
London (071) 408 5033

Photographs
Philippe Garner
London (071) 408 5138
Beth Gates-Warren
New York (212) 606 7240

Portrait Miniatures, Objects of Vertu, Icons and Russian Works of Art
Gerard Hill
New York (212) 606 7150
Haydn Williams
(miniatures and vertu)
London (071) 408 5326
Ivan Samarine (Russian)
London (071) 408 5325
Heinrich Graf von Spreti
Munich 49 (89) 291 31 51

Postage Stamps
Richard Ashton
London (071) 408 5224
Robert Scott
New York (212) 606 7288

Pre-Columbian Art
Stacy Goodman
New York (212) 606 7330
Fatma Turkkan-Wille
Zürich 41 (1) 422 3045

Prints
Nancy Bialler (Old Master)
New York (212) 606 7117
Mary Bartow (19th & 20th C.)
New York (212) 606 7117

Robert Monk (contemporary)
New York (212) 606 7113
Ian Mackenzie
London (071) 408 5210
Ruth M. Ziegler
Tokyo 81 (3) 3503 2944

Silver
Kevin L. Tierney
New York (212) 606 7160
Peter Waldron (English)
London (071) 408 5104
Harold Charteris (Continental)
London (071) 408 5106

Sporting Guns
Adrian Weller
Sussex (0403) 783933
Windi Phillips
Houston, TX (713) 780 1744

Tribal Art
Jean G. Fritts
New York (212) 606 7325
Jean-Baptiste Bacquart
London (071) 408 5115

Trusts and Estates
Warren P. Weitman
New York (212) 606 7198
Timothy Sammons
London (071) 408 5335

Veteran, Vintage and Classic Cars
Malcolm Barber
London (071) 408 5320
David Patridge
Rumney, NH (603) 786 2338

Western Manuscripts
Dr Christopher de Hamel FSA
London (071) 408 5330

Wine
Serena Sutcliffe MW
London (071) 408 5050

INDEX

ACKNOWLEDGMENTS

PROJECT EDITOR Sandy Mallet
ART EDITOR Ruth Prentice
ASSISTANT EDITOR Kate Sackville-West
PICTURE RESEARCH Bella Grazebrook

The publisher would like to thank Luke Rittner, Amanda Brookes, Ronald Varney, Lynn Stowell Pearson, David Lee, Peggy Vance, Antonia Demetriadi, Slaney Begley, Gail Jones and all the Sotheby's departments for their help with this book.

Prices given throughout this book include the buyer's premium applicable in the saleroom concerned. These prices are shown in the currency in which they were realized. The sterling and dollar equivalent figures, shown in brackets, are based upon the rates of exchange on the day of sale.

PHOTOGRAPHIC ACKNOWLEDGMENTS
The publisher would like to thank the following photographers and organizations for their kind permission to reproduce the photographs in this book:
17 The Tate Gallery, London © DACS 1993; 18 Courtesy of Belvoir Castle, Leicestershire/Bridgeman Art Library; 19 Reproduced by courtesy of the Trustees of The National Gallery, London; 21 The Tate Gallery, London; 22 The Shell Art Collection at the National Motor Museum, Beaulieu; 23 London Transport Museum; 26 The Ford Motor Company; 27 The Museum of American Folk Art; 28 Popperfoto; 29-31 Copyright © BBC; 32-3 Geoff Dunlop/Illuminations; 38 The 1993 Biennial Exhibition, Whitney Museum of American Art, New York; 42 Archiv für Kunst und Geschichte, Berlin; 43 Isabella Stewart Gardner Museum, Boston; 44 left By permission of the Governors of Dulwich Picture Gallery; 44 right The National Galleries of Scotland; 45 above Phil Starling/The National Gallery, London; 45 below Tim Stephens/The National Trust Photographic Library; 47 The Tate Gallery, London; 49 © The Munch Museum, Oslo, 1993/Bridgeman Art Library; 50 Stephen White/'The Ancient Art of Mexico' 1992,The Hayward Gallery, London; 51 'The Sixties: Art Scene in London' 1993, Barbican Art Gallery; 265 above, 270 © The Stanley and Frances Caidin Trust 1992; 276 Photo: Bryan Wharton/Sunday Times Magazine; 280 The National Portrait Gallery, London; 281 The Fitzwilliam Museum, University of Cambridge; 282 above Ian West/The National Trust Photographic Library; 282 below Patsy Fagan/The National Trust Photographic Library; 283 above Historic Royal Palaces; 283 below Crown copyright. Historic Royal Palaces, wood carver: David Esterly; 284 Crown copyright. Historic Royal Palaces; 285 left The National Trust Photographic Library; 285 right Tim Stephens/The National Trust Photographic Library; 286-7 English Heritage
Sotheby's Amsterdam: 63 above
Sotheby's Berlin: 304 above

Sotheby's Billingshurst: 20 left, 186 above right, 256 right
Sotheby's Geneva: 11, 221 above, 222, 225 above right and below left, 227, 228, 232 below right, 233 above, 236 above left and right, 236 below left, 237 above left and centre
Sotheby's Hong Kong: 34, 160 right, 161 right, 162 left, 165 above, 288
Sotheby's London: 1, 4-5, 6 above and below, 13, 20 right, 24, 41, 46 above, 48, 55-56, 61, 63 below, 64 above, 65, 67, 68-71, 72 above, 73-5, 76 below, 77-9, 80 left, 81, 82-3, 88-90, 92-4, 96 above, 100-3, 119-121, 124-131, 132 below, 133, 136 right, 138-9, 141-4, 146-7, 149, 151 above, 152-153, 155, 158-9, 163, 167 above right and below, 169 below, 170 above and below left, 171 below, 172, 180-1, 182 right, 183 right, 184-5, 186 above left and centre, 186 below, 190-2, 194 above, 196 below, 197, 199, 204 below, 207, 209 above left, 212-3, 214 above right, 215 below left, 216 below, 217, 220, 230, 231 left, 232 above, 233 below, 235 left, 236 above centre and below right , 245, 247 below, 248-250, 251 above and centre, 252-3, 257-9, 260-1, 262 above right and left, 268-9, 273-5, 279, 291, 293- 294, 297, 301-3
Sotheby's Madrid: 296-297 above
Sotheby's Melbourne: 148
Sotheby's Milan: 196 above left, 304 below
Sotheby's Monaco: 6 centre, 35-7, 60 above, 150, 193, 209 below left and right, 211 below, 272
Sotheby's New York: 2, 10, 12 above and below, 35-7, 46 below, 54, 57-9, 60 below, 62, 64 below, 66, 72 below, 76 above, 80 right, 84-7, 91, 95, 96 below, 97-99, 104-115, 118, 122 left, 123, 132 above, 134-136 left, 137, 145, 151 below, 154, 156-7, 160 left, 161 left, 162 right, 164, 165 below, 166, 167 above left, 168, 169 above, 170 below right, 171 above, 173-9, 182 left, 183 centre and left, 187-9, 194 below, 195, 196 above right, 198, 200-204 above, 205-6, 208, 210, 211 above, 214 above and below left, 214 centre and below right, 215 below right, 216 above, 218-9, 221 above, 223-4, 225 above left and below right, 226, 229, 231 right, 232 below left, 234, 235 right, 237 above right and below, 242-244, 246-7, 251 below, 254 above right, 262 below right, 263-5, 268, 270-1, 273 above, 278, 288-90, 292, 295, 299, 305
Sotheby's St Moritz: 227 below
Sotheby's Sydney: 117
Sotheby's Taipei: 39
Sotheby's Tel Aviv: 140
Sotheby's Tokyo: 122 right
Sotheby's Toronto: 116
Sotheby's Zürich: 215 above, 217 below right, 246, 254 above left and below